# Communist China
# and Arms Control

Written Under the Auspices of
the East Asian Research Center
and the
Center for International Affairs
Harvard University

 PRAEGER SPECIAL STUDIES IN
INTERNATIONAL POLITICS AND PUBLIC AFFAIRS

# Communist China and Arms Control

## MORTON H. HALPERIN
## DWIGHT H. PERKINS

FREDERICK A. PRAEGER, *Publishers*
New York • Washington • London

The purpose of the Praeger Special Studies is to make specialized research monographs in international economics and politics available to the academic, business, and government communities. For further information, write to the Special Projects Division, Frederick A. Praeger, Publishers, 111 Fourth Avenue, New York, N. Y. 10003.

This report was prepared under contract with the United States Arms Control and Disarmament Agency. The judgments are those of the authors and do not necessarily reflect the views of the United States Arms Control and Disarmament Agency or any other department or agency of the United States Government, or of Harvard University.

FREDERICK A. PRAEGER, PUBLISHERS
111 Fourth Avenue, New York 3, N.Y., U.S.A.
77-79 Charlotte Street, London W.1, England

Published in the United States of America in 1965
by Frederick A. Praeger, Inc., Publishers

Library of Congress Catalog Card Number: 65-26757

Printed in the United States of America

# CONTENTS

|  |  | Page |
|---|---|---|
| | Foreword | vii |
| | Introduction | ix |
| **Chapter** | | |
| I | China's Foreign Policy: Goals and Perceptions | I |
| II | Domestic Politics and Foreign Policy | 20 |
| III | The Economics of Foreign Policy | 28 |
| IV | Nuclear Strategy | 48 √ |
| V | Proliferation | 67 |
| VI | Conventional War | 75 |
| VII | Arms Control and War | 83 |
| VIII | Arms Control and Insurgency | 93 |
| IX | The Chinese Public Record on Arms Control | 98 √ |
| X | The Chinese Attitude Toward Arms Control | 132 √ |
| XI | Chinese Attitudes Toward International Agreements, Organizations, and Inspection | 141 |
| XII | Making China Arms Control Minded | 155 |
| XIII | The Impact of Arms Control on China | 168 |
| **Appendix** | | |
| A | Chinese Statement on Arms Control, November 22, 1964 | 173 |
| B | Participants in the China Arms Control Conferences | 179 |
| | Index | 183 |

# FOREWORD

Early in 1964 the United States Arms Control and Disarmament Agency arranged with Harvard University for the East Asian Research Center and the Center for International Affairs to undertake a study and sponsor a conference on Communist China and Arms Control.

Although this book was prepared as a report to the United States Arms Control and Disarmament Agency as part of the project on Communist China and Arms Control, it is not a group product but the work of two authors: Morton H. Halperin, Assistant Professor of Government at Harvard University and Research Associate at the Harvard University Center for International Affairs and Dwight H. Perkins, Assistant Professor of Economics and Associate of the East Asian Research Center at Harvard University. The text does reflect work done under the project, such as information and ideas developed in background papers, during conferences and discussions, through consultations with project members at Harvard, and from the comments and suggestions of the Conference participants and officials of the Arms Control and Disarmament Agency. The two authors, however, are responsible both for the form and for the contents of this work.

Because of the lack of specialists on the important subject of Chinese attitudes toward arms control and disarmament, we sought to bring together scholars and specialists on both arms control and Chinese affairs from across the country and from abroad during a ten-day Conference (July 9-19, 1964) at Airlie House in Warrenton, Virginia, in order that each group would make its contribution through intensive discussions and study of prepared papers. We were fortunate in having twenty regular participants at the Conference and a number of observers and guests, representing a wide variety of specialization and experience. In December a smaller group met for a weekend in Cambridge, Massachusetts, to review work done and to reconsider some of the problems taken up at the summer Conference. (For participants at these Conferences, see Appendix B.)

The project had the ambitious purpose of identifying and clarifying the factors affecting the formulation of the policies of Communist China toward arms control and disarmament issues and of assessing the implications of such policies, particularly for United States security and arms control objectives. As a guide to understanding Chinese objectives and their underlying motivations, we sought to take account of relevant political, ideological, economic, technological, military, and cultural factors, as well as predisposing historical and traditional influences which affect Chinese attitudes. It is clear that our resources of scholars and of information only permit us to make a beginning in a study of this dimension. Moreover, the absence of direct dialogues between Chinese Mainland and American scholars on many aspects of such a subject impedes judicious appraisals of the weight to be assigned to various motivations and other factors affecting Chinese policies. The element of unintended distortion must affect Chinese policy specialists as it does American specialists.

In view of the difficulties and problems of dealing with China and arms control, we were particularly fortunate in having Morton H. Halperin and Dwight H. Perkins serve as vice-chairmen of the project and prepare a report on this subject. Dwight Perkins is an economist trained in Chinese who also has an interest in policy problems. Morton Halperin is among the first of the arms control specialists to turn his attention to China.

Many people contributed to this project. The conference discussions were put in ordered and succinct summaries by two rapporteurs: Michael Gordon and Ellis Joffe, both graduate students at Harvard University. Most of the details of conference mangement and project organization were precisely and cheerfully handled by Miss M. Lois Driscoll, the administrative secretary of the project. Two liaison officers of the Arms Control and Disarmament Agency gave invaluable help. Robert E. Matteson helped to make the project a reality, and Colonel Kent K. Parrot followed the work of the project with understanding and provided many kinds of assistance. This study was intended to complement an earlier study by a group at Columbia University—the 1963 summer study on Soviet attitudes toward arms control and disarmament carried out under contract with ACDA. Hence, we benefited from the experiences of the Soviet study and particularly from the helpful participation of its chairman, Alexander Dallin, in our project. Professor Thomas C. Schelling was throughout a source of special counsel to those of us who were responsible for this project.

John M. H. Lindbeck, Chairman
Project on Communist China and
Arms Control
Harvard University

# INTRODUCTION

This study arose out of a concern for the effect of Communist China's increasingly active role in international affairs on the possibilities for arms control and disarmament arrangements around the world. Any understanding of China's position on specific arms control measures requires, of course, an analysis of Chinese attitudes and the strategic, political, and economic stake in arms control as viewed from Peking. Thus, though our immediate concern related to arms control, the study touches, at least briefly, on a number of aspects of Chinese policy.

We carried out this study, which was completed after China's second nuclear explosion, as part of a project undertaken jointly by the East Asian Research Center and the Center for International Affairs, Harvard University, under contract with the United States Arms Control and Disarmament Agency. The judgments are those of the authors and do not necessarily reflect the views of the United States Arms Control and Disarmament Agency or any other department or agency of the United States Government or of Harvard University.

We are indebted to those who participated in the ten-day Conference at Airlie House in Warrenton, Virginia, in July, 1964, and the two-day follow-up Conference in Cambridge, Massachusetts, in December. Individual participants collectively contributed so much to this enterprise that it is not possible to single them out here. Without their help this study would have been difficult, if not impossible, to write. Particular mention must be made, however, of the tireless efforts of John M. H. Lindbeck, chairman of the overall project and each of the Conferences. It was his continuing guidance and support that made this study possible.

Acknowledgments are also due to those who prepared papers for the project (our reliance on particular papers is indicated in the text) and to the Harvard-M.I.T. Faculty Seminar on Arms Control for devoting several of its sessions to discussion and criticism of our efforts.

While both the foreword and the above acknowledgments make clear our great indebtedness to many people, needless to say, we alone take responsibility for the final product.

Because arms control and disarmament policies are a part of a nation's foreign policy, we felt that no proper understanding of Chinese attitudes toward arms control was possible without first considering what Communist China is attempting to achieve in the international arena. Thus Chapter I is a study of China's overall foreign policy objectives as they relate broadly to arms control. But no country makes foreign policy decisions without regard to its own internal conditions. For many nations, domestic political considerations may outweigh international issues in importance in making foreign policy, whereas for others economic capacity and economic growth problems may dominate. The relation of these questions to arms control is the subject of Chapters II and III.

It is in the military sphere, however, where arms control and foreign policy broadly conceived are most closely related. Peking's nuclear and conventional strategies, discussed in Chapters IV and VI, respectively, determine what kinds of arms China needs or desires and hence what military equipment she is likely to be willing to do without. Intimately connected with questions of strategy are such key arms control issues as China's interest in inhibiting or encouraging proliferation of nuclear weapons (Chapter V), the role of war-limiting measures in Chinese strategy (Chapter VII), and arms control as a technique for dealing with insurgency (Chapter VIII).

With Communist China's foreign policy objectives and constraints and her military strategy clearly in mind as a basis for further analysis, the discussion is turned to a direct consideration of Peking's attitudes toward a variety of specific arms control and disarmament measures. First, Communist China's public record on issues relevant to arms control is reviewed at length (Chapter IX). The public record alone, however, is an inadequate guide to a country's true attitude toward foreign policy issues. Chapter X, therefore, explores, in the light of previously discussed foreign policy and military strategy considerations, what China's real attitudes toward arms control measures probably are and how they are likely to evolve over time.

Even if China and the United States or some other country were to find they had a mutual interest in a formal arms control agreement, the process of drawing up, verifying, and enforcing such an agreement would be a formidable one. Communist China's attitude toward international agreements, the United Nations and other international organizations, and inspection are of particular relevance to these problems and are discussed in Chapter XI.

One of the basic conclusions of this study is that Peking's current interest in arms control measures is extremely limited and that there are formidable barriers to any enhancement of this interest. If China's interest is to increase, part of the responsibility will lie with what American policy makers and others interested in arms control can do to educate Peking about the potential significance of arms control for China. This problem is the subject of Chapter XII. Even if no arms control agreements with China are possible, however, it does not follow that arms control is of no significance for China or for United States policy toward China.

American and Soviet actions in this area greatly affect China in many ways, and this needs to be kept in mind when decisions about arms control policy are made. The final chapter, therefore, deals with why and in what manner the United States must, apart from seeking agreements with China, pay more attention to the interaction between its arms control position and the foreign policy of Communist China.

Morton H. Halperin
Dwight H. Perkins

Cambridge, Massachusetts
June 1965

# I CHINA'S FOREIGN POLICY: GOALS AND PERCEPTIONS

The key contentions of this chapter are that the main foreign policy goals of the Chinese Communist leadership are highly stable and, therefore, will probably have potent and continuing influence in action. It is our further belief that, given the present state of outside knowledge of China's foreign policy behavior, a productive way to analyze these goals is in terms of two general objectives: China's national interest, narrowly conceived, and the achievement of Marxist-Leninist international goals. We will argue below that the ideological goal of a world Communist revolution is an important determinant of Chinese foreign policy, and probably will remain so, that pursuit of this objective is not synonymous with acquisition of national power, although the two frequently overlap, and that Mao Tse-tung and his associates probably give a higher priority to these ideological goals than their Soviet counterparts do. The evidence to be presented in support of this hypothesis is suggestive rather than definitive. Nevertheless, the effort to sort out the facts behind this interpretation must be made, because it is this hypothesis that underlies much of the reasoning in subsequent chapters on why it is likely to be difficult to reach arms control agreements with Peking, particularly those few agreements that might meet the requirements of national interest goals narrowly conceived (e.g., a non-proliferation agreement [ see Chapter V]).

Foreign policy goals, however, are not the only relevant or predictable determinants of China's foreign policy actions. Some of these relevant and predictable elements are found in the domestic economic and political resources of the regime. China's economic might, for example, is severely limited, and this in turn inhibits Peking's ability to exercise influence over other nations through aid and trade. Numerous other examples can be cited; they are the subject of the next two chapters.

No attempt, on the other hand, is made to go behind Chinese goals to ask what psychological and historical elements brought these particular objectives to the fore. An investigation of the nature and persistence of the notion that China is the center of the world or of any indications of paranoia or other psychological disturbances among the Chinese Politburo would be interesting, but not enough groundwork has been laid for us to go into them here.

It is not possible, however, to ignore the way in which Peking has pursued its goals. It is a second major hypothesis of this chapter that the Chinese Communist leadership pursues its objectives in a systematic and logical way, given its perception of the world around it. However, Marxist-Leninist ideology, among other reasons, makes that perception somewhat different from that of, say, a Western social scientist.

## THE NATIONAL INTEREST INTERPRETATION

The world in which China's foreign policy operates is primarily an Asian world, unlike the Soviet Union, whose major concern (for geographical reasons, as well as others) is Europe. With the exception of Djakarta and Kuala Lumpur, no Asian capital, from Tokyo to Kabul, is more than a few hundred miles outside of China's borders. Every Asian nation, including China, has had considerable experience with European colonialism. All of them (except China, Japan, and Thailand) have been European colonies for various periods of time. All except Japan are underdeveloped, predominantly rural societies. All have also begun to change. Economic growth, urbanization, and dissolution of old social patterns have been under way for several decades or more. Traditional ruling groups are in varying stages of dissolution. New leadership groups from the army, from the rising middle classes, and in some cases even from the peasants, are struggling for power and survival. Only in China, Japan, and, to a lesser extent, India are those presently in power resting on a stable base. While China did not create such trends, she has undoubtedly helped to accelerate them. The resulting situation is one with which any regime in China would have had to reckon and which any regime would have been tempted to exploit for its own ends.

Nor did the Communist regime, which attained control in China in 1949, create the world's two great superpowers, the United States and the Soviet Union, or the conflict of interests between them. The two opposed systems of alliances were well on their way to formation before October, 1949. Moreover, atomic and hydrogen bombs lent new meaning to this confrontation. China, as well as all other nations, regardless of geography or ideology, had to contend with this world of opposing blocs possessed of overwhelming destructive power.

The Chinese Communists were not completely free to choose the direction of their foreign policy, whatever the true underlying objectives of the leadership. The Communists came to power by a civil war in which their opponent, the Kuomintang (Chinese Nationalist Party), was supported by the United States. Although United States support was only half-hearted during the final years of the war, it had been substantial for many years before that. Events after 1945 convinced the Communists that the United States was still wholeheartedly behind the Kuomintang, however different the facts looked from an American perspective. Therefore, the Chinese Communists had every reason to believe that, of the two great powers, the United States was the more opposed to their interests. Ideological considerations greatly reinforced this view in a number of ways and may have been the major element in Mao Tse-tung's decision to "lean to one side." The point here is that a non-Communist regime, coming to power under similar circumstances, could have reached the same decision, just as have non-Communist regimes elsewhere in the world, such as Guinea during its initial years of existence, or Indonesia.

Whatever United States intentions toward the Communists' continued existence in China were, American policy was clearly directed at checking any further Communist expansion. Therefore, even setting aside Mao's ideological predilections, he had to reckon with American opposition any time he desired to extend Chinese power. This mutual hostility was crystallized by the Korean War, which began only a few months after the Communists had driven the last regular Kuomintang troops from the mainland of China. When President Truman sent American land forces into Korea and (more importantly from China's point of view) directed the Seventh Fleet to seal off Taiwan from possible invasion, American and Chinese Communist interests were conspicuously opposed. Furthermore, when United Nations troops crossed the 38th parallel and marched toward China's border on the Yalu, it is now clear in retrospect that China felt directly threatened and was willing to take risks in order to remove that threat. After more than two years of war in Korea, it was inevitable that it would take many years before either side might come to regard the other as anything but an enemy.

We do not mean to suggest that the United States could or should have behaved differently. Furthermore, to say that conflict between a revolutionary China and the United States was inevitable, even if the word Communism and the ideological predilections it implies were absent, is to overstate the case. Such a conflict was a plausible outcome, however, given a China interested in expanding or even only securing its power and a United States committed to maintaining the status quo or simply restricting the expansion of Chinese power.

If one accepts the Sino-U.S. conflict as a collision of national interest,[1] many of China's other activities in the foreign arena can also be interpreted in these terms. One could see Chinese attempts to remove

[1]The Conference participants never reached a consensus as to what constituted the true motivations of Sino-U.S. conflict, but different national interests were considered a fundamental element.

the influence and power of the United States from Southeast Asia as nothing more, in Chinese eyes, than a move to secure China from hostile attack on its southern borders.

The fact that the method used to remove the American presence is exploitation of the revolutionary temper so prevalent in Southeast Asia doesn't prove that national interest is not paramount. This just happens to be the most effective tool available to the Chinese Communists. They do not have a significant nuclear arsenal at present. Their navy is only a coastal defense force. Their air force, although apparently recovering from its decline of 1961-1963, is still no match for the U.S. air force. Only their army is a substantial force, but it is probably of limited use in removing the United States from Southeast Asia; the Chinese must always fear that such action would lead to American employment of nuclear weapons or at least to a long costly war that might result in conventional bombing of China and defeat of the Chinese offensive force. It does not follow that the Chinese army is useless in this area, but its primary functions are as a deterrent to certain American actions and as a threat that "neutralist" regimes take seriously because they question the U.S. will to intervene or her ability to do so without involving them in a nuclear war (see Chapter VI). Nor is Chinese economic aid and trade likely to be a very effective tool, given the underdeveloped state of China's economy (see Chapter III). The only remaining methods likely to prove successful in removing American presence, therefore, are revolutionary propaganda and activity.

Other Chinese foreign policy acts can also be explained in terms of Chinese national interest with little or no reference to ideology. The invasion of Tibet, in Chinese eyes, was no more than the re-establishment of what were considered to be traditional Chinese rights and sovereignty over the area and as such was endorsed by the Kuomintang on Taiwan (although the Kuomintang did not endorse the use of force to attain these ends). Removal of special Russian rights in Sinkiang and Manchuria was hardly necessary if Communist solidarity were unbreakable, although one can argue that it wasn't necessary under such circumstances for the Russians to maintain these rights either. Chinese Communist acceptance of Outer Mongolia as an independent sovereign state, on the other hand, is slightly more difficult to explain in terms of Chinese national interest. One wonders, however, whether the Kuomintang, too, would not have bowed to the inevitable, particularly if Russian friendship or hostility toward China depended to some degree on the outcome.

Chinese trade and diplomatic policies are consistent with a national interest interpretation of Chinese motivations. In general, China buys where goods are cheap and sells where they are dear. The Korean War embargo usually explains any exceptions.[2] In the diplomatic field China has recognized everyone who has recognized her and withdrawn recognition of the Kuomintang. Statements that she will not exchange diplomatic representatives with the United States are related only to the issue of Taiwan, not to conflict of ideologies.

None of the above policies conflict with Marxist-Leninist ideology, any more than they do with a national interest interpretation of Chinese motivations. In Marxist terms, Chinese Communist activities toward Taiwan, Southeast Asia, and even Tibet can be interpreted as removal of the last vestiges of British and American "colonialism" in the area and the first steps in an Asian Communist revolution. This lack of conflict leads many analysts to state that one cannot differentiate between ideology and national interest because there is little substantive difference.[3] Even the Chinese recognition and often diplomatic support of nations whose governments are anti-Communist at home (de Gaulle's France and Nasser's Egypt) can be justified in ideological terms as an exploitation of the natural and inevitable conflicts between capitalist and imperialist powers. The difficulty is that almost anything can be justified in Marxist-Leninist terms, except a questioning of the inevitable course of history and the eventual triumph of Communism. Just because anything can be justified, however, it does not follow that Marxism-Leninism (-Maoism) is simply a terminological cloak for Chinese national interest.

One of the problems is that national interest is not always as obvious as in the cases cited above. At times one can understand these less obvious cases if one has a clear picture, if such is possible, of the urgency that the Chinese Communists attach to their desire for power and security. At other times, however, Communist ideology provides much more than simply an *ex post facto* justification of events.

## MARXIST-LENINIST GOALS (SINO-SOVIET DISPUTE)

That part of Peking's foreign policy which is most difficult to fit into a national interest framework is also the most important, the Sino-Soviet dispute. To some degree, of course, the Chinese Communist posture of seeking more active support of world revolution from the Soviet Union

[2] This is discussed at greater length in Chapter III.

[3] This position was held by several conferees at Airlie House.

results from the lack of alternative means for exercising influence on the international scene. In part the dispute is undoubtedly also a product of different ideas on how Communism can best be achieved, i.e., of different perceptions of the world in which the revolution is to be achieved. [4] If one analyzes the implications of the dispute for both China and the Soviet Union, however, neither of these explanations appears to suffice. Although the evidence presented below does not support the popular notion that the Russians have become bourgeois while the Chinese have remained inflamed revolutionaries, it does suggest that there are real shades of difference between their goals.

The Sino-Soviet dispute began out of differences in objectives and in interpretations of the significance of such events as the first Soviet Sputnik in 1957-1958. [5] Probably the turning point came when Khrushchev, after his meeting with President Eisenhower at Camp David, flew home by way of Peking with kind words for the Americans and their intentions. From that point on the conflict became increasingly bitter and more and more open. In 1960 the Soviet Union withdrew all Russian technicians from China. The Chinese allege that earlier the Soviet Union had torn up military cooperation agreements, including one to aid China's development of an atomic bomb. In the Party press the dispute began with China attacking the Soviet Union indirectly through criticism of Yugoslavia and the Soviet Union attacking China through Albania. This culminated in direct attacks by each on the other.

The existence and bitterness of the dispute is no longer in doubt. The more difficult question (and the one most relevant here) is what each side hoped to gain from taking the positions that led to the dispute. China, of course, wanted Russian support and the protection of the Russian nuclear shield to deter an American attack and provide a cover for offensive action. Anger over not receiving this support, however, does not lead logically to a decision to bring about a dispute in which the credibility of the Soviet nuclear shield is left in some doubt even for the defense of the Chinese homeland. This would hardly be the action of a China whose only concern was the fundamental security of the state. Nor does the dispute make much sense if China's only concern were domestic economic development. Soviet aid in the sense of grants (if any) and loans had been completely cut off by the end of 1957. Nevertheless,

---

[4] This is discussed in greater detail below.

[5] There was general agreement on this point among the Airlie House conferees.

over a thousand Soviet technicians remained in China, and their help, including the plans and complete plants which they brought along with them (all of which China paid for in full), was important to China's economic development. Perhaps in 1958 and 1959, under the euphoria of the "great leap forward," Peking felt it could get along without this help, but it is unlikely that the authorities felt this way in 1960 when the economy was nose-diving into a crisis.

The only thing which China could gain from the crisis, and to some extent did gain, was greater freedom of action to promote revolutionary movements around the world, even where such actions involved direct opposition to Soviet policies. In addition, in support of these actions, China created an image of herself around which all radical movements could rally. Whether Peking was genuinely interested in speeding up the pace of world revolution or was only taking this stance as a means of raising Chinese prestige and power in world affairs is a subject which will be considered in greater detail in connection with Chinese behavior toward specific revolutionary movements.

Russian motives in the split are somewhat easier to explain in pure nationalist terms. For example, although the Soviet Union's extreme characterization of the Chinese position on nuclear weapons is primarily a propaganda ploy, there have been so many Soviet statements to the effect that limited war is likely to escalate into all-out war that one is led to believe that this feeling is more than just a propaganda maneuver. Such sentiment, however, hardly constituted sufficient justification for promoting a split.

In order to argue that the Sino-Soviet split was little more than a conflict of national interests that were narrowly conceived, one has to assume (provided the foregoing arguments are correct) that it was the Russians and not the Chinese who pushed the split. This assumption is not borne out by the facts, since it seems that Peking's attitude has been the more provocative of the two. It is conceivable to argue that a bitter quarrel, particularly one that involves ideological issues, has a logic of its own. Once started it becomes increasingly bitter, even when a rational calculation of each party's gains and losses would cause the leaders to try to cover over differences.[6] There undoubtedly is some of this kind of irrationality in the Sino-Soviet dialogue, but the rational elements involved appear to be more important. If that is the case, then popular

[6] This argument was presented by more than one conferee.

characterization of the split as occurring between a Russia grown conservative by virtue of its wealth and power and a China that is less conservative in its willingness to take risks to promote revolution is not completely inaccurate.[7]

Is China's willingness to take such risks in support of revolutionary activities attributable to Peking's deeper belief in Marxist-Leninist ideology? Are the Chinese, in fact, taking any real risks at all? On close analysis, much of the evidence used to support the notion that Communist China is willing to take greater risks in order to promote revolutionary activities tends to support the opposite conclusion. For example, the Sino-Indian border conflict was carried out in such a way that the risk was minimal. Only a few divisions were involved, virtually all the fighting took place in mountains that were inaccessible to India, and the action was just long enough to be decisive but not long enough for any major power to help India retaliate. Furthermore, the Chinese withdrew from those areas where their attack had generated the most publicity (in the Northeast Frontier Agency) while remaining in the region that really mattered to them, the Aksai Chin area of Ladakh.

Peking's support of revolutionary movements outside Asia has been less vigorous than the publicity engendered would imply. The Chinese Communists usually counsel caution to potential revolutionaries who come to them for advice (there are exceptions, such as the case of Brazil). They are urged to return home to build an effective organization and to wait for an opportune time. Chinese technicians sent overseas are often although not always under orders not to engage directly in any way in stirring up local political activities. Instead they are supposed to observe and establish contact and work with potentially useful individuals (particularly through the bribery of local police), with reference to future rather than present action.

However, the significance of this caution as an indicator of the preeminence of either nationalist or Marxist-Leninist ideological motivations in Chinese behavior is more complex than the above discussion would suggest. In fact, the caution furnishes support for the notion that China is interested in world revolution for its own sake and not simply as a means of furthering national goals that were narrowly conceived.

If China's primary aim were to seize power within Communist Parties throughout the world in order to use those Parties to advance Chinese national goals, whatever the ultimate effects on world revolution, then

---

[7]On the other hand, some Conference participants held that there was no essential difference between Russia and China on this score.

indiscriminate promotion of revolution might make sense. Such a policy would appeal to the radical elements which make up a large part of Communist Parties, at least those outside Western Europe. It would underline the "bourgeois betrayal" of the Soviet Union and, provided it were carried out in such a way as not to lead to a series of revolutionary disasters, might eventually bring China leadership of the world Communist movement rather than just the Asian branch.

In fact, although the Chinese Communist Party has been happy to have other Communist Parties think of it as being more radical, it has taken no action to enhance this image that would undermine long-run revolutionary progress.[8] Stalin was quite prepared to use non-Russian Communist Parties not only for Russian but even for personal power goals, regardless of the ultimate effects on those Parties; this attitude nearly finished the Chinese Communist Party in the 1920's. To some degree, China's contrasting behavior has been dictated by the fact that Peking's control over its supporters within various Communist movements around the world is not comparable to what Stalin's was, but this is certainly not the only motive for China's unwillingness to exploit these movements for her own narrow nationalist goals. At least in part, the Peking regime's cautious promotion of world revolution tends to support the argument that China is interested in the success of these movements for their own sake (i.e., because they contribute to the sweep of world progress as envisaged by Marxist-Leninist ideology).

Two possible qualifications, however, need to be made. First, the split and rivalry for control between the two major Communist nations has left Communist Parties around the world in disarray. Even if the Chinese motive in the split was to speed up the pace of revolution, the initial effect was to weaken the movement, and the ultimate effects are yet to be determined. If, however, the Chinese are right and the Russians really have been "selling out" the revolution, then one can argue that China took the only possible course.

---

[8]This statement and the arguments around it are probably the most controversial in the chapter. In part this is a result of the authors' desire to make the point simply without adding a half-dozen qualifying clauses which would have enhanced the statement's accuracy but not its clarity. It is, of course, true that China has counseled caution or actively supported the government in power where prospects for revolutionary success were far from dim (Burma, Cameroons), but it is not clear that this inhibited Communist progress in the world as a whole (in contrast to impeding revolution within these specific countries). But there is nothing to match Stalin's treatment of the Chinese and Turkish Communist Parties, and less obvious shades of difference can be found in many other instances.

Second, the injection of "racism" into the Sino-Soviet dispute makes one question the Marxist-Leninist "purity" of Chinese motives. Like so many other issues in the dispute, this one also derives in part from Soviet statements about what the Chinese are doing, statements made in an attempt to discredit the Chinese position. There is considerable debate as to whether or not the Chinese are racist or are using racism as a means of seizing leadership over Communist Parties and other revolutionary movements in areas where the issue is important.[9] China's racism, if it exists, takes the form of a feeling of cultural superiority, not of inferiority. Racial hatred of the "white man," therefore, cannot be an important ingredient in Chinese motivations, if it exists at all. If Peking has been using race as a tactic to outmaneuver the Soviet Union, particularly in Africa, it is a tactic and little more.

The extent to which China may actually be using this tactic is not at all clear. Apparently low-level delegations to Afro-Asian conferences have on occasion used racial arguments to exclude Soviet participation, but more commonly they have argued that Russia is a European rather than an African or Asian power. Furthermore, Peking has conspicuously advertised its good relations with the New Zealand and Australian Communist leadership, not to mention Albania. If the Chinese are attempting to inject racial issues, one suspects it is more to tar the Russians as being white racists than to take any anti-white stand of their own. One certainly cannot make out a case that Peking is trying to split the Communist movement along racial lines in order to speed their own attainment of supremacy over the non-white half.

Although the above arguments are not conclusive, China's behavior in the Sino-Soviet dispute and in some of the issues surrounding it is most easily explained by a genuine and substantial interest by the Chinese leadership in the fortunes of the world Communist revolution, a revolution that may not always be the surest way of promoting the security and development of the Chinese state. The conflict between Marxist-Leninist goals pursued for their own sake and narrower Chinese power and security goals is not, however, very great. In most of the areas discussed, Chinese capacities are limited, and so are the risks involved in any actions they might undertake.

---

[9]There was considerable debate on this point at Airlie House, but no general consensus was reached.

## MARXIST-LENINIST GOALS (SOUTHEAST ASIA)

The one area of Chinese activity where the risks to China are far from slight is Southeast Asia. It is also an area where her capacities to act are considerable. The most interesting cases for the purpose of ascertaining China's foreign policy goals are Burma, Laos, and Vietnam.

There is fairly general agreement that China desires to see Communist governments ultimately established throughout Southeast Asia. Whether the Chinese expect those governments to be their satellites in the manner of Eastern Europe under Stalin, or truly independent regimes still basically loyal to China in the manner of the suzerain relationships of traditional China, is impossible to say. There is no evidence to suggest that the Chinese have followed the Stalinist pattern in dealing with North Korea, even though the Chinese army was in Korea for several years in sufficient numbers to enforce many of the desires China might have had. North Vietnam is not as relevant because China has never been in a comparable position there.

The more interesting question concerns the pace with which Peking hopes to establish these Communist governments. From the Chinese policy toward Burma, one could find support, although not proof, for the argument that China does not really care whether Communist governments are ever set up, that all that matters is the removal of United States power.

Burma is a country where two Communist rebellions have been under way for over a decade. In addition, there are the Shan and Kachin rebellions and a built-in excuse for Chinese intervention in the form of scattered groups of former Kuomintang troops in northern Burma. Yet China has made no real effort to exploit this situation. She negotiated and signed a border agreement with Burma without acrimony, and she has made no special effort to enhance the capabilities of those Communist rebels under her control. On the other side, Burma has bent over backwards not to offend China, has at times refused all aid from the West and thrown out a number of Western organizations from Burmese territory, and has promoted socialist slogans and actual socialization of the economy. Nevertheless, Burma is also an independent, non-Communist regime which, among other things, signed the Test Ban Treaty. One could infer from this that the Chinese Communists, for the present at least, are satisfied with an essentially suzerain (i.e., compliant) relationship with non-Communist but "neutral" and pro-Chinese Southeast Asian governments.

One could draw similar conclusions from China's policy toward Sihanouk's Cambodia and Sukarno's Indonesia. These cases are less convincing, however, if only because China has few alternatives at present.

Sihanouk's popularity in Cambodia makes any effective revolutionary movement impossible. In Indonesia the army may still be too strong for the Indonesian Communist Party to challenge it openly. In any case, China's ability to control the Indonesian Communist Party is quite limited.

The case that tends to undermine this theory (assuming a degree of Chinese control over or approval of the situation) is Laos. China could hardly have asked for a weaker, more "neutralist" government with a pro-Chinese bias than that of Souvanna Phouma. True, it was a coalition government, one element of which was a right-wing, anti-Communist group, but the Communist Pathet Lao controlled over half the country anyway. The coalition government was in no position to interfere with activities important to the Communists in many other areas, including the supply, through Laotian territory, of insurgent groups in South Vietnam. Yet the Communists by their actions against the neutralist faction, including pushing them off the Plaine des Jarres by military force, accomplished the otherwise improbable result of driving Souvanna Phouma into an anti-Communist stance.

Laotian action, of course, is closely related to far more important insurgent actions in South Vietnam. A Communist takeover in Laos would greatly accelerate the collapse of the American-supported South Vietnamese regime. A strong anti-Communist regime in Laos conversely might materially hamper the Communist effort in South Vietnam, but there is little likelihood of such a regime's gaining power. The important question for this discussion is to try to determine just what kinds of risks the Chinese Communists are willing to assume in order to enhance Communist revolution on the former Indochinese peninsula.

Two issues are involved. The first is the degree to which China really can control the Vietnamese situation (and hence the Laotian situation). The second consists of what constitutes the risks they perceive. As to the first, it is clear that operational command in both Laos and South Vietnam comes not from China but from North Vietnam. All foreign troops in Pathet Lao areas, with minor exceptions, are North Vietnamese. All indications are that the National Liberation Front in South Vietnam receives its basic policy direction from North Vietnam, although in day-to-day operations the Front apparently acts with a high degree of independence, as any successful guerrilla organization must. Peking's position, therefore, is primarily one of either encouraging or discouraging the North Vietnamese from taking any particular action.

Initially the Chinese position consisted of not discouraging the North Vietnamese, but by the summer of 1964 this had evolved to the point where China publicly and explicitly stated that she would come to the aid of North Vietnam in case of attack. Although this does not constitute proof of all-out support of North Vietnamese actions, it and other Chinese statements would seem to point in that direction. The Soviet Union, in contrast, apparently has attempted to restrain the North Vietnamese, particularly in Laos.

Although Peking probably does not foresee that its support of North Vietnam could jeopardize the existence of the Communist regime in China, there is reason to believe that it does anticipate significant risks. It certainly sees air attacks on South China by the United States as a distinct possibility, particularly now that targets in North Vietnam have been bombed. Some kind of involvement by Taiwan is also a possibility. In the first half of 1964, South Vietnam sent no fewer than four high-level military missions to Taipei, and the Chinese claim that Secretary of State Dean Rusk's visit to Chiang Kai-shek in April, 1964, was to plan for a North Vietnam operation. Whether or not there is any truth in these beliefs, Peking apparently thinks there is sufficient risk to justify generating public attitudes in and out of China which might deter the use of Chinese Nationalist forces. In attempting to appraise Chinese perception of the risks involved, it is useful to recount that since the Korean War Peking has always tended to overrate what, to the United States, are incredible kinds of contingencies, such as the re-invasion of mainland China with Kuomintang troops. It seems fairly clear, therefore, that Communist China has been willing to accept rather considerable risks in choosing to support North Vietnam. [10]

The proponent of the national interest and power view of Chinese foreign policy can point out that China took these actions in order to solidify her position among the North Vietnamese leadership vis-à-vis that of the Soviet Union. Certainly Peking had to offer something in return for the Viet Minh decision, apparently taken at their Central Committee meeting in December, 1963, to give down-the-line support to the Chinese position in the Sino-Soviet dispute, including refusal to sign the Test Ban Treaty. On the other hand, the Russian position was such that Peking could have simply not discouraged Hanoi. Instead, as pointed out above, the Chinese took a number of actions, including several statements of support in case of attack, which one can only interpret as active encouragement of the North Vietnamese.

One can also, with much truth, interpret Chinese actions as a vigorous

---

[10]There was far from unanimous agreement on this point at the Conference. A minority contended that there were no real risks to China, while others contended that the risks were readily controllable.

attempt to push the United States out of Southeast Asia. If this were the only motive, however, one might expect a more concerted effort to get the United States to accept a de Gaulle type of neutralization solution. Instead, the Communist position appears to be one of pressure for all-out victory within a few years, with neutralization only a device to pave the way for that victory. If the Chinese were sincerely interested in a viable neutralist regime, one would expect a somewhat different behavior in regard to Laos. One would also expect some interest in renewed negotiations on a meaningful basis. By all appearances, no such interest has been indicated by either China or North Vietnam.

## CHINA'S PERCEPTION OF THE WORLD

China's perception of the world in which she is attempting to achieve her foreign policy goals is a subject as vast as analysis of the goals themselves. Certain Chinese Communist perceptions, however, are particularly important in reinforcing Peking's interest in revolutionary movements and her aggressive behavior in general.

First of all, a good case can be made that Peking and Moscow do genuinely differ over which tactics are likely to work best. Chinese Communist experience with the Kuomintang alliances (unlike Bolshevik experience in the Kerensky government of 1917) was not a happy one or one calculated to produce undue confidence about the usefulness of future alliances between Communist Parties and powerful bourgeois military groups. Nor is it likely that Peking gives much credence to the argument that the world will turn to Communism if only Russian per capita gross national product surpasses that of the United States. They have repeatedly stated that no Communist government ever has or ever is likely to come to power except by use of force. There is no reason to believe they are insincere in this contention, particularly since history has tended to support it.

In the areas where they lack direct or extensive personal experience, the Chinese Communist leaders tend to fall back on Marxist-Leninist ideology. This, on the whole, has served them rather poorly in the sense that it often appears to have led them toward incorrect policy conclusions.

Sino-Japanese relations in 1958 appear to provide one of the better examples of how the Chinese view of the outside world is distorted by ideology. The Kishi cabinet, then in power, was considered by Peking to be highly conservative and pro-Kuomintang and thus unlikely to take any steps to restore formal relations with China or otherwise act favorably toward Chinese interests. The Chinese hoped somehow to bring pressure on the Kishi government and perhaps topple it, or at least alter its policy toward China. In 1958 they thought they had the means. Both Japan and the United States were undergoing economic recessions, and the time was thought ripe to exacerbate class differences, already sharply antagonistic. By cutting off trade between China and Japan, the Chinese believed that many capitalists, thus deprived of an opportunity for gain, would join with the "progressive" forces (the Japanese Socialist and Communist Parties and the intellectuals) and that a united front of all forces opposing the government would be formed. That front would be sufficient to topple the government immediately or to greatly weaken the Liberal-Democratic Party in the general elections that summer.

By all appearances, however, the Chinese miscalculated their ability to bring down the Japanese government in this way, in large part because of ideological influences. Marx has very little to say about the precise nature of the Socialist or Communist state, and so any good Communist can be quite flexible without conflicting with basic Marxist dogma. But *Das Kapital* analyzes at great length the evolution of capitalism, the nature of the class conflicts therein, and the economic crises which will gradually help bring those conflicts to a head. Japan is, of course, just such an evolving capitalist state.

The Chinese Communists image of the United States and the Western world is probably more distorted than their image of Japan, but less obviously so because Peking is under few illusions as to how much it can influence the internal politics of the West. When the Chinese Communists do not reveal by their actions how much of a particular situation they understand, it is not always easy to isolate what they really believe from the propaganda image that they hope to convey. Nevertheless, one is left with the impression that China's image of the Western society, if not taken straight from Dickens, is at any rate derived from nineteenth-century clichés. Such a picture appears to have led Peking to underestimate the domestic strength and staying power of the United States government.

## FUTURE CHANGES IN GOALS AND PERCEPTIONS

The main interest of this study, however, is not in what China's foreign policy goals and perceptions of the world around her are today but in what they are likely to be in the years ahead. Can we expect an evolution in attitudes similar to that which has already occurred in the

Soviet Union, changes different in nature, or no changes at all? Although everything that can be said on the subject is highly speculative, there are reasons for maintaining that China's basic foreign policy goals and to a lesser degree her perceptions of the world are likely to change rather slowly, perhaps even more slowly than in the Soviet Union.

That some change will occur is inevitable. The top level of Chinese leadership today is old and could be gone within a decade. Even if Mao and his senior colleagues are unlikely to change their ways, their successors may be different. [11] But what direction will change take? We can suggest some answers to this question, if only rather vague ones, by looking at the past experiences of the new generation of leaders and at what their future experiences are likely to be. To what degree were they involved in the revolution before 1949? What jobs have they held since 1949? What social classes they came from, their formal educational background, and other childhood experiences are undoubtedly also relevant but of little use for prediction, since our present knowledge of how these elements influence the behavior of national leaders is limited.

The new generation of leaders will not be so much younger than the present generation that it will have had only modest or no experience with the Chinese Communist revolution. Perhaps few will have experienced the Long March, but most will have fought with the Communists throughout the 1940's and perhaps the late 1930's as well. The revolution will have been the meaningful event during some of the most formative years of their lives.

What jobs the probable leaders of the 1970's will have held since 1949 is not as obvious because it is not clear just who they will be. Conceivably they could come from either the bureaucracy or the Party organizations (in either case they would be Communist Party members of long standing). If they come from the bureaucracy, it is possible that years of having to produce machinery, run an army, or whatever will have tempered their view of the role of ideology and politics in decision making. If Soviet experience and an understanding of the nature of Communist Party organization are any guide, however, it is more apt to be those active in the Party organization itself who come to power.

No matter who comes to power, however, one can make out a case that the Marxist-Leninist-Maoist ideological content in Chinese foreign policy goals and perceptions is likely to diminish. The argument is based on the premise that any dogma that relies on a distorted picture of the world of

[11]This is held by the authors to be most probably the case.

a past century is bound to fail rather consistently and thus undergo modification to bring it into line with experience. The problem is, however,
that foreign events are never easy to interpret, and failure is a relative
term subject to a variety of explanations: for example, the Chinese can
chalk up whatever failures they suffer to their present, if temporary,
weakness vis-à-vis the forces of capitalism.

Domestic failures are not so easily explained away. Many past failures,
particularly the communes and the "great leap forward," were quite
clearly the result of incorrect or misapplied ideological precepts. Failures
have not led the regime to revise its attitude toward the relevance of
Communist dogma in any significant way, but continual failures (which
are likely to occur whenever ideology is applied with a high degree of
literalism) will probably change this, just as they have in the Soviet
Union. [12] It does not automatically follow that a domestic failure based
in ideology will have any effect on its role in foreign affairs. However,
Marxist ideology is a consistent framework within which all phenomena
are to be judged. If the leaders in Peking become accustomed to thinking
in different terms in dealing with domestic problems, this change must
affect their thinking in other areas.

Nevertheless, modifications of ideology will not necessarily occur in
China at a pace comparable to that of the Soviet Union. Except during
the period of war Communism, ideology has perhaps never played as
large a role in Soviet decision making as it has in China during the past
few years. Furthermore, the shock of World War II and the desperate need
for survival caused the Soviet leadership to abandon ideological appeals
in favor of the far surer effects of Russian nationalism. Once doctrinal
punctilio was abandoned there was no easy road back. Finally, Stalinist
terror was the major fact of life for all Russians regardless of rank. In
fact, the higher one got, the greater was the probability of being affected.
De-Stalinization was, in part at least, an attempt by the new leaders to
change this way of doing things, for their own benefit. Once so important
a cog in the system was removed, it would have been difficult to prevent
new ideas from entering elsewhere, even if the will to do so had been
there.

Neither the Russian experience in World War II nor with Stalinist terror

---

[12]During a small group meeting at the Airlie House Conference, a substantial
majority of the group felt that ideology was bound to be greatly modified if
not rejected in part under bombardment from reality, but at least one participant
felt that the group was greatly underestimating the staying power of Communist ideology. See Chapter III for further discussion of this point.

applies to China. The Chinese Communists' period of desperate struggle for survival in the 1920's and 1930's was one in which the role of ideology was solidified. Circumstances may be different today, but the prospects of anything comparable to the German invasion of Russia are not great. Nor is the Chinese Communist system of control much like that in the Soviet Union, particularly as it affects the higher levels of leadership (see Chapter II).

Although Peking's goals and perceptions in foreign policy will be subject to only some of the same pressures present in the Soviet Union, there may be other events that will have an even greater impact on China. One major determinant of future Chinese actions in the area of insurgency, for example, will be how much success this measure meets with over the next few years. The same can be said about the role of force in general in Chinese foreign policy and about virtually every other tactic used by Peking. Ultimate goals, however, are much less subject to change than tactics to achieve those goals. Even the tactics themselves, the important ones anyway, are likely to change only slowly. A failure in Vietnam, for example, is not likely to lead Peking to abandon insurgency.

On the other hand, the Chinese Communists have shown a measure of flexibility in their use of tactics in the past, and there is no reason to expect any less flexibility in the future. "Peaceful coexistence" with non-Communist countries (not including the United States) was a tactic used extensively by Peking long before it became so popular in the Soviet Union. That China severely limited the use of this tactic, which was then generally referred to as the "spirit of Bandung," from 1958 on does not mean that they will never return to it. Nor does their present belligerent stance preclude any number of other future changes in tactics. Nevertheless, certain well-tested tactics, particularly insurgency, are likely to remain key weapons in Peking's arsenal for a long time to come.

Another way in which outside events might influence Communist China's goals and tactics is by forcing the regime to choose between narrow national interests and Communist revolutionary interests. To date, as pointed out above, such conflicts have been few in number, and it is doubtful that the regime is fully and consciously aware of the possibility of such conflict. An example of such a set of alternatives would be a choice between supporting a pro-Chinese (non-Communist) government or a Communist revolution whose leaders are likely to act independently. Such alternatives have already appeared, and if they become more frequent and the choice more clear-cut, the effects could be profound.

## IMPLICATIONS FOR ARMS CONTROL

If the above analysis is generally correct, then the implications for possible arms control agreements involving China are considerable. China is not today interested in anything that would appear to be a détente with the West, nor is her attitude in regard to this likely to change much for some time. Any benefits to Chinese national security arising from an arms control arrangement would have to be weighed against the effects such an agreement would have on China's image as a leader of the "anti-imperialist" forces and on her actual capabilities as such a leader. In contrast, these kinds of considerations have apparently played little part in Soviet calculations. In fact Khrushchev was probably much more interested in the détente aspects of the limited Test Ban Treaty than he was in its security element.

China's foreign policy goals and her perception of the world around her, therefore, do not dispose Peking favorably toward arms control arrangements. These goals and perceptions are not the only ingredients in her calculations. Other major components are discussed in subsequent chapters. Furthermore, these goals and perceptions can and will change. The changes that will occur, however, are likely to be slow and determined by factors, in part at least, beyond the influence of American policy. United States actions may be able to change China's perceptions regarding the use of insurgency, and they may force Peking to make uncomfortable choices between pursuit of revolutionary and narrow national power goals. Soviet policies are likely to have a comparable or even greater impact on Chinese perceptions. American actions that affect Soviet behavior, in fact, may ultimately have more effect on China than United States efforts aimed directly at China. Most, although not all, of the actions that come to mind, however, seem to be beyond the purview of arms control and disarmament, but this is a conclusion that cannot be supported without further evidence presented in subsequent chapters. The one major exception to this would appear to be Soviet-American arms control agreements designed consciously or otherwise to inhibit Peking (see Chapter XIII).

# II DOMESTIC POLITICS AND FOREIGN POLICY

The relationship between domestic and foreign policies, for Peking, as for most nations, is complex. In China, most connections between actions in the two arenas arise from economic considerations. It is economic capacity, for example, that limits a nation's military strength and the influence it can exercise through trade and aid. These relationships are discussed at length in Chapter III. There are also those, however, who purport to have discovered interaction in areas having little to do with economics, interaction which is essentially political in nature. This chapter attempts to see if that type of relationship exists in this case.

It is popular to compare simultaneous major shifts in Chinese domestic and foreign policy and to argue that any relationship is causal, not simply coincidental. The period of the Korean War coincides with land reform and the harsh measures taken against landlords during land reform, as well as with the "three" and "five-anti" movements against the bureaucracy and the bourgeoisie. The years between the Korean truce and the next major shift in policy toward the end of 1957, years which included the Geneva Conference and Indo-China truce of 1954 and the Bandung Conference of 1955, were years in which peaceful coexistence was stressed by the Chinese Communists at least in their relations with the underdeveloped world. In the domestic arena, repression was modified and a degree of free speech unprecedented in a Communist state was reached toward the end of the period, during the "hundred flowers" movement. Then, at the end of 1957 and early 1958, the regime switched to a harder line on foreign policy and, of course, initiated the "great leap forward" and the communes.

Coincidences, however, are often spurious. It is possible, for example, to develop an almost exact correlation between major shifts in economic policy in China and those in Hungary and Poland. The exact content of the policies differed, but their timing was almost identical. Although these shifts were not always in the same direction in the two areas in the sense of "hard line versus soft line," they usually were. But this proves nothing except that both areas were grappling with somewhat similar problems and using generally similar tools.

Close examination does not support the view that the relationship between Chinese domestic and foreign policies is causal.[1] The "Bandung
Spirit," or policy of peaceful coexistence, does coincide with the period
of the First Five Year Plan (1953-1957), and 1953-1954 were years of
comparative relaxation in domestic tensions, as was the last half of 1956
and early 1957. But 1955 and early 1956 marked a period of tight Party
control and strong pressures throughout the society in conjunction with
the drive to complete the socialization of industry and commerce and,
more importantly, to collectivize agriculture.

Nor does an examination of the period since the end of 1957 indicate
causality in the relationship between foreign and domestic affairs. In
foreign affairs, the period can be said to start with the Soviet launching
of an ICBM, which the Chinese interpreted as signaling the attainment of
military superiority by the Communist bloc. Peking felt that the bloc
should press its advantage and took the initiative itself in the Quemoy
crisis of 1958. When the Soviet Union played down the significance of its
missile accomplishments as a basis for more aggressive posture around
the world, Peking was less than pleased. As the Russians moved toward a
partial understanding with the United States, the Chinese line not only
hardened toward the non-Communist world but became increasingly bitter
toward the Soviet Union as well.

There was a close correlation between a hardening foreign policy line
and a similar domestic policy in 1958, and perhaps even into 1960. The
"great leap forward" marked a major shift to the left. Radical reorganiza-
tions of the economy and society as a whole were undertaken, Party cadres
were under heavy pressure to prove their loyalty and ideological purity,
and non-Party "intellectuals" (which includes all non-Party technicians)
in China were shunted aside and openly attacked for rightist tendencies.

The correlation ends in 1960-1961. Foreign policy continued to harden
toward the Soviet Union as well as others, as evidenced by the attack
on India in October, 1962, but domestic policy took a turn toward modera-
tion or relaxation of controls. The communes were abandoned in all but
name, free markets and peasant private plots were restored in order to

---

[1]A close examination of the extent of correlation between domestic and foreign
policies was suggested by one Conference participant, but the group never
got around to a systematic discussion of the issue. This probably accounts
for a certain degree of ambivalence among Conference participants as to
whether such a correlation really exists, although most participants were
suspicious of the simpler types of correlation.

stimulate subsidiary agricultural output. Most important, from the stand-point of this discussion, technicians were restored to positions of in-fluence at operational levels, and intellectuals in general were even en-couraged to renew the "hundred flowers" campaign, albeit on a much restricted basis. In early 1964 there was some evidence of another harden-ing in domestic policy with a call for factories and other units to emulate the army, particularly with respect to Party influence and organization. Again there was no move in the international sphere which was obviously comparable.

A lack of exact correlation between domestic and foreign policies does not constitute proof that there is no connection, only that whatever connection exists is more complex. The remainder of this chapter is devoted to an analysis of these complexities.

Communist China is ruled by a highly centralized political organiza-tion, the Chinese Communist Party. The phrase used by the regime to describe the nature of its control is "democratic centralism." Democratic centralism means that all levels of the Party, and even the polity, are supposed to discuss the merits and demerits of any particular issue and pass their ideas on up the chain of command to the top. It is the top, usually the Politburo of the Party, however, which alone makes the final decisions for major issues. After that decision is made, no further dis-cussion of it is allowed until the leadership so signals. This, of course, is a simplified picture. Many domestic policy decisions by their very nature must be made at intermediate and low levels, while others are made at the top without prior consultation with lower levels. Peking not only tolerates but actively encourages creative action by low-level Party cadres as long as the general policy line laid down from above is adhered to. The "great leap forward" and commune movement, for example, in-volved a substantial amount of decentralization away from Peking to provincial and lower-level cadres.

Because of decentralization of much domestic decision making, one can find many instances where central policies were modified almost be-yond recognition by the time they reached an operational level. However, there was often a high degree of consistency between widely disparate policies and geographic areas. This phenomenon was particularly pre-valent following "rectification" movements and resulted from heavy pres-sure on low-level Party cadres to prove themselves. Foreign policy decisions, however, have never been significantly decentralized.

In order to demonstrate a causal connection between foreign policy

and domestic political considerations, therefore, one must find that connection at the very top of the pyramid. The most obvious is that the same
people make both kinds of decisions. There is not one group within the
Politburo with sole responsibility for economic or political affairs and
another group for foreign policy. Individuals have areas in which they
are specially competent, but all are also generalists. Therefore, decisions
in both the foreign and domestic field are made within the same general
frame of reference. The same ideological and traditional predispositions
apply in one area as in the other. The locus of power within the Politburo
may, on occasion, shift.[2] Although Mao Tse-tung has always remained
more than simply "first among equals," he has never tried to operate as
a one-man dictator in the manner of Stalin. There are reasons to believe
that at times he has allowed policies to prevail which probably were
against his own better judgment. To say that there are cliques vying for
power within the top leadership is certainly to overstate the case greatly.
More often much of the uncertainty over alternatives takes place within,
rather than between, individuals. Nevertheless, there are probably some
people who tend to follow one point of view more regularly than another.
Those most clearly identified with a particular line occasionally have
even been dropped from favor along with the line they were espousing.
For example, the Minister of Defense, P'eng Teh-huai, was removed from
his post presumably for opposing the leadership's decision to push the
Sino-Soviet dispute regardless of how it affected such programs as the
modernization of the Chinese army. Vice Premier Ch'en Yun, the most
conspicuous advocate of a more pragmatic approach to economic matters,
disappeared from view during the "great leap forward" and was not restored to his position as Vice Premier until the December, 1964, meeting
of the National People's Congress. These extreme cases are probably
outward manifestations of shifts within the Politburo, if not of the locus
of directly usable power, at least of influence over those who do wield
direct power. It is natural that a particular ascendant style of operation
or group of individuals would affect both foreign and domestic policy.
And when the present top leadership is gone, one can expect shifts of
power and influence, although it is not possible to say in which direction
these shifts will tend.

Finally, there is the argument that Chinese Communist policy makers
strive for consistency between various types of policies for the sake of
being consistent. There is little evidence to support this view. There
are, of course, many instances where a particular action in one field can

[2]This was discussed at some length at the Airlie House Conference.

be carried out only if supporting actions are taken in another field. China's decision to enter the Korean War considerably narrowed the range of choices open to the regime in the domestic arena. Most of these relationships are economic and will be discussed in the next chapter.

In the political field, it is clear that certain foreign policy actions made various domestic political problems easier to solve. The Korean War was an excellent excuse for launching an attack on the bourgeoisie. Whether Peking ever takes foreign policy action in order to carry out domestic measures is another matter. The most commonly heard reason for any particular aggressive action by Peking is that the leaders had to do it to take the people's minds off their stomachs, to quiet dissatisfaction, etc. The obvious counterargument is that the regime would not dare take action when it is weak lest this jeopardize the security of the state. Neither theory seems to have much validity when applied to China. Peking's pose as the courageous leader of revolution in a hostile and dangerous world is undoubtedly useful in helping keep the Chinese population operating at a high pitch, when that is thought desirable, but there are too many other reasons for such a stance for this one to be considered very important.

Nor is there much reason for holding that domestic political actions are taken in order to influence foreign policy, although here, too, the actions in one arena certainly, on occasion, prove useful in the other. China's rapid economic development before 1960, the socialization of its economy, and many other actions greatly enhanced the regime's foreign image. The radical moves taken during the "great leap forward," particularly the communes, were useful to Peking in the Sino-Soviet dispute. But none of these measures were undertaken because of their foreign impact. One can argue that the propaganda barrage put out by the regime to herald the advent of the communes made it more difficult to abandon them once it became apparent they weren't working; actually, at most, this forced the regime to use more propaganda gimmicks, primarily that of continuing the commune organization in name while transferring most of its functions to smaller units, to cover up the fact that the communes were being abandoned.

This brings us to one of the fundamental reasons why the connection between domestic and foreign policy is so weak: the ability of the regime to manipulate the image it portrays, not only to the outside world, but to its own people as well. This ability is necessary to the centralization of political control but is not synonymous with it. It is a power which allows Peking to distort the outside world's image of China, at least that part of the outside world which is subject to any positive influence from China, and to distort the image of the outside world held by the average Chinese citizen. Complete control of all publications in China accounts for only part of the regime's power in this respect.

The more important part of the system is the regime's high degree of control over every level of Chinese society. It is a far more subtle and more effective form of control than the secret police plus labor camp of the Soviet Union. It is basically a system of mutual surveillance, the key cogs in which are the street committee chairmen, and *hsüeh-hsi* sessions (literally "study" sessions or discussions). Street committee chairmen are not so much policemen, and they are not at all secret, as they are local busybodies with access to higher authorities. In a sense, all party personnel and other activists are expected to play such roles wherever they are.

This system serves many functions, but one is that it allows Peking to carry out highly effective propaganda toward its guests, whether they are tourists or other kinds of visitors. These visitors can be allowed a quite free rein with little fear that they will get what, from the regime's point of view, would be the wrong impression. Buddhist guests from Southeast Asia can be taken to the one temple still in operation near Peking and leave with the impression that Buddhism is flourishing in China. Businessmen are introduced to a few "house capitalists" and gain the feeling they would be better taken care of by the Communists than by their own governments. A very selective visa policy keeps out, as far as possible, those people who might not respond or who might see through the façade.

China's foreign propaganda activities are run on a similar basis, although here Peking cannot completely control either the people propagandized or all the kinds of material which they receive. Here, too, the major effort is directed at those disinclined to be skeptical. It is an effort involving broadcasts, publication of textbooks, movies with propaganda themes of varying degrees of subtlety, and a few journals, such as the *Peking Review,* directed entirely at the foreign audience.

Monopoly of the press, however, does not allow the regime to control completely the kinds of information that go abroad. The regime publishes hundreds of journals and newspapers which are directed almost entirely at the domestic Chinese audience. There is general agreement among specialists that these journals are not written in order to mislead foreign analysts.

Chinese who read newspapers and journals may not be easily misled on domestic conditions, but they have no personal experiences to help them with foreign policy issues. Even here, however, the regime's publication policy is not as restrictive or conspicuously distorting as one might expect. They have published uncut speeches by President Kennedy, and they regularly published the Soviet statements during the Sino-Soviet dispute.

This occasional willingness to publish both sides of an issue in no sense constitutes a Chinese belief in freedom of speech. This publication policy is possible because the regime knows that the *hsüeh-hsi* sessions give it a high degree of control over the interpretation which readers will give to everything they read. Virtually everybody has to participate regularly in these sessions. The basic procedure is that each small group discusses a newspaper article, a day's event of national, international, or commonly of only personal significance. The Marxist-Leninist interpretation of that event is laboriously arrived at, with everybody actively participating in the discussion. One may question how effective this device is in creating genuine support for Chinese Communism, but studies of the process have indicated that it seriously affects what the population, particularly the more activist groups, thinks regarding any situation, especially in foreign policy.

Peking's power to separate its foreign policy actions from domestic opinion of those actions, therefore, is considerable, just as is its power to control its foreign image no matter what is actually going on. However, one should not exaggerate this. China cannot cover up major failures at home from foreign audiences any more than it can cover up for the domestic audience such things as the cost in lives of the Korean War. The United States and now even the Soviet Union are supplying alternative views, particularly for the foreign audience.

Nor could Peking shift to a policy which constituted a radical departure from established doctrine without paying a domestic political price for it. A shift to a policy of friendship with the United States would be difficult for the regime to explain in a manner which would not increase the skepticism with which the Chinese people hold the ruling ideology. Present hostility toward the Soviet Union has undoubtedly, in a similar manner, tended to promote nationalist tendencies among the people at the expense of ideology. Since the Chinese Communist leadership's view of its mission is not simply maintenance of power but is the creation of a nation (and a world) constructed along Marxist-Leninist-Maoist lines, any weakening of the domestic role of ideology is taken seriously. It is reasonable to assume that foreign policy actions that had such an effect would be undertaken only reluctantly. Nevertheless, the arguments above support the contention that foreign and domestic policies are, to a significant degree, determined separately. Peking's control over the channels of communication is a major reason why it does not have to join the two types of policies very closely. Equally important is the fact that decisions are made at the top in what is a highly centralized political system, i.e., where domestic political interests and groups have little influence on policy and where those making the decisions are not subject to pressures to prove their ideological purity and consistency.

The implications of this discussion for arms control arrangements with China would be more significant if a close connection between foreign and domestic action could be established. Whether such a close relationship would have predisposed China favorably or unfavorably toward arms control measures is impossible to say. On the one hand, increased domestic sensitivity to international affairs might mean that any lessening of tension between China and the United States would make it just that much more difficult to keep pressuring for extraordinary economic performance from the Chinese people. Conversely, increased domestic sensitivity to foreign activities might raise fears that a crisis situation could be used domestically to undermine the security of the state. Which of these considerations would predominate at any time would depend on how vulnerable the regime felt when the crisis occurred. In any case, the vulnerability of the regime to external acts certainly would be increased.

More important is the fact that Chinese domestic considerations, as well as international interests, would have to be taken into account whenever an attempt was made to assess likely Chinese reaction to any move or proposal. This is, of course, the case in the United States and any other democratic country, and the complexities of the interrelations between American domestic and foreign politics give some idea of the kinds of problems which would arise if a comparable relationship were to exist in Communist China. Complexity alone tends to be a bar to international agreement if for no other reason than that a country has difficulty sorting out what constitutes its own best interests, let alone attempting to guess what its adversary desires. This, however, is not China's problem, at least at present. Complexities in Chinese Communist foreign policy arise primarily from complexities in Chinese foreign goals and in the world in which they are trying to attain those goals.

# III THE ECONOMICS OF FOREIGN POLICY[1]

Economic issues enter into foreign policy decisions in many ways. The size of a nation's economy is the principal determinant of its economic and military power, and that power in turn has a major influence on a nation's ability to affect the actions of others. The pre-eminence of the United States and the Soviet Union in world affairs, for example, results in large part from the ability of these two countries' economies to sustain military expenditures substantially greater than those of their nearest competitors. Economic strength also enables a country to influence others with aid and trade. It is doubtful if either Cuba or Vietnam would be viable states under their present regimes if it were not for repeated injections of aid from the Soviet Union and the United States respectively.

Economic issues may also provide a nation with the basic motives for undertaking a given foreign policy. There are those who believe, for one example, that Communist China is interested in Southeast Asia primarily because of its surplus rice and natural resources. For another example, the desire or need to channel resources away from the military to more productive uses can provide a compelling reason for pursuing arms control and disarmament.

It is the intent in this chapter to analyze just what it is that China's present economic and technological capabilities allow Peking to do, as well as what the regime is actually doing, how these capabilities are likely to change during the next decade or two, and what implications any conclusions we make have for arms control arrangements with China.

## THE ECONOMICS OF MILITARY POWER

The close relationship between economic and military power is not absolute. In recent years, nuclear weapons and missiles have rapidly reduced to a matter of minutes the time available for mobilization. As a result, in a nuclear exchange, economic power will not mean military power except to the extent that it has already been used to support a military force in being. Furthermore, because it takes several years to convert civilian production into military space support industries, a country that is willing to devote a larger portion of its national product

---

[1] This chapter is based on a paper, "The Economics of Chinese Communist Foreign Policy," by Dwight H. Perkins, prepared for the Airlie House Conference, and on some of the discussion of that paper.

to military programs than another country may be able to achieve arms parity or superiority for a period of several years. However, military power still depends in great part on the size of a nation's economy and its technological capacity.

There are those who argue that nuclear weapons will make it possible for a country to have great power at low cost, but this remains to be proved. Bombs themselves may become less expensive, but costs of delivery systems have continuously increased. Although Communist China has exploded a nuclear device, it does not now possess either a large stockpile of weapons or the means of delivery.

The question for China is whether its economy and technical capacities are strong enough to allow it to develop a major nuclear and missile capacity or, barring this, whether it can achieve many of its goals through possession of a significant conventional warfare capability. Conventional warfare capabilities are also closely related to economic strength, but there are many ways in which this dependence can be reduced. Use of indigenous guerrilla forces is the least expensive of such measures. Substitution of manpower for firepower is feasible under certain circumstances, as was to some extent the case in Korea. Short and protected supply lines also reduce costs, as do limitations on the area in which conflict takes place. Short decisive actions which do not give the enemy and its allies time to bring their forces to bear (as in India) can often be accomplished with a minimum expenditure of materiel. Defensive actions often involve less strength than offensive. Actions where one's potential adversaries are likely to be divided reduce the strength which must be opposed. From China's point of view, it is most important that its adversaries refrain from using nuclear weapons, at least during the period when China lacks enough of such weapons to retaliate.

## THE SIZE AND CONVERTIBILITY OF CHINA'S ECONOMY

Before looking in detail into what kinds of nuclear development and conventional warfare capabilities can be sustained by the Chinese economy, let us examine the size of China's present economic and technological capabilities and their probable future development. Although China in per capita terms is one of the poorest nations in the world, its size makes it one of the largest economies in aggregate. Aggregate size is not the only criterion upon which the significance of economic strength for military capabilities should be judged, but it is not irrelevant. On the field of battle, it is not the opposing army's standards of living that matter, but the number of men, tons of steel, etc. which can be brought to bear.

International comparisons of gross national products are hazardous undertakings at best, even when the most sophisticated procedures are used, and for China these more sophisticated methods have yet to be used. In addition, the raw data for China are subject to numerous errors and distortions. Even if one allows for an enormous margin of error, however, comparisons between China and other nations show that Chinese GNP may be less than a tenth of that of the United States today or less than a sixth of that of the Soviet Union. But the Chinese GNP is also comparable in size to that of Germany or Japan in 1936, only a few years before those two countries were able to launch the largest war in history and to sustain it for years.

Fortunately, from the point of view of potential adversaries, there are reasons for holding that a much smaller portion of mainland China's gross national product is convertible into military capacity than was the case with either Japan or Germany in the late 1930's. This lack of convertibility is the result of China's low standard of living, the structure of its economy, with its heavy dependence on agriculture, and the low level of Chinese technological capabilities. Modern warfare requires more than the presence of well-fed troops on the battlefield; it requires that these troops be equipped with a wide variety of weapons, from rifles to jet fighters. These weapons require ammunition and often fuel. Furthermore, this equipment must reach the battlefield, which in turn requires trucks, fuel, and aircraft to protect supply routes. All of this equipment is produced by what can broadly be categorized as heavy industry and its supporting sectors. Generally, agricultural products, services, and consumers' goods industry (in China mainly food processing and textiles) cannot be directly converted into military hardware, although many of these goods can be exported in exchange for arms, if there is a country willing to make such an agreement. This, in effect, is how China paid the Soviet Union for most of the equipment used in the Korean War (other than that captured from the Japanese and Nationalists). Proceeds from trade, however, are limited in part by the fact that many products cannot readily be exported (most services, for example) and in part because there is a limit below which domestic consumption cannot be driven. There are those who believe that the lower limit was reached during the 1959-1961 agricultural crisis.

Technology constrains the convertibility of economic power into arms in two ways. In the first place, many modern weapons require that the country developing and producing them have a high degree of technological capacity. A country lacking sufficient capacity would be unable to produce the items at all or only at enormous cost. These weapons can always be purchased, but this again presupposes that there is someone willing to sell. Although Chinese capabilities are growing, they are still small.

Chinese expenditure of scarce foreign exchange on the purchase of transport aircraft from the U.K., France, or the U.S.S.R., for example, would not make much sense if China already could build this kind of complicated equipment economically and in quantity.

A second way in which technology restricts the convertibility of economic power is that it tends to accentuate specific as contrasted to general constraints. The recent literature on the economics of military power has quite rightly attempted to offset popular notions that such power depends heavily on a few key commodities (e.g., petroleum, manganese, etc.) rather than on general economic capacity. There are abundant examples to show how a nation can get around such constraints. The Germans, for example, were able to halve their copper and tin requirements at the same time they were raising the output of arms by several times, and Japan's super battleship *Yamato* made its suicidal sortie southwest of Kyushu powered by a refined soya-bean oil. These adjustments, however, required the efforts of a considerable number of talented scientists. It is doubtful that China today is in a comparable position.

Technological constraints, however, should not be overemphasized, particularly if one is talking not just about the present but about the next decade or more as well. Today, China has only approximately 2,200 people who have received advanced degrees in the natural sciences, 700 trained in the West and 1,500 in the Soviet Union. This is out of a total number of college graduates in the natural sciences of about 65,000. In engineering sciences the total number of college graduates has reached 390,000. Although the Sino-Soviet split and China's own educational policies during the "great leap forward" considerably slowed the development of scientific talent, by all appearances this slowdown was only temporary.

It will be many years before China is able to launch a balanced program in all the basic areas of science. It may be even longer before Chinese scientists contribute broadly and significantly on the frontiers of science. By concentrating on key areas and on adaptation of processes developed in the West or the Soviet Union, however, they can accomplish a great deal. A list of the top eight priorities in present Chinese scientific activities gives some idea of the effort they are putting in to overcome their backwardness in the military field:[2]

1. Atomic energy.
2. Electronics.
3. Jet propulsion.
4. Automation and precision instrumentation.
5. Exploration for petroleum and other minerals.

[2] This list is taken from the talk by Dr. John to the Airlie House Conference.

6. Alloy and metallurgical processes.

7. Fuel utilization and heavy organic synthesis.

8. Power equipment and heavy machinery.

Predicting the probable future course of development of the Chinese economy is even more difficult than predicting the pace of future technological developments. Even for the United States, economic predictions are subject to a wide margin of error. For China, forecasts are complicated by the short span of Chinese Communist economic experience and the total lack of institutional stability, not to mention the lack of reliable statistics. In more specific terms, the problem is one of deciding on the significance to be attributed to the four years (1960-1963), when the Chinese economy was relatively stagnant.

There are those who argue that stagnation is likely to be a long-run state of affairs. The Chinese Communists argue, in public at least, that the 1959-1961 crisis was temporary, brought on by bad weather and the departure of Russian technicians. More careful analysis suggests that the crisis resulted from a combination of temporary and long-run factors. The temporary problems would appear to include not only bad weather and the Russian pull-out but also disorganization resulting from unrestrained abandonment of central planning and controls during the "great leap forward" in 1958 and 1959.

A major long-run problem which actually began to appear long before the crisis of 1959-1961 is agriculture. The economic failure of the communes marked the final collapse of the regime's attempts to raise agricultural output without a major commitment of investment resources. If nothing unforeseen happens, a successful development program for China over at least the next two decades will require a substantial diversion of investment to agriculture. This need not reduce the value of such investment for future military potential. Fertilizer production requires development of a large-scale chemical industry, for example, and farm machinery producers can readily convert to military production.

Lack of investment in agriculture, however, is not the only long-run problem. Probably of even greater significance is the fact that the Chinese Communists have not only domestic economic goals but domestic political and ideological goals as well, and the latter often take priority over the former. Some, but not all, of the economic dislocations of the communes can be looked at in this light. And one can argue that socialist organization of agriculture is unlikely to be abandoned except under the most desperate circumstances, not only because of its desirable ideological character, but also because it provides an excellent means of political control over the rural population. Although there is no reason to expect much change in the priority given to political control, the same cannot be said of ideology.[3] If ideological prescriptions lead to economic reverses, this is bound to have its effect on the ideology. There are strong reasons for holding that Marxist-Leninist ideology is likely to have a detrimental effect on the economy, but it is not clear how quickly this will lead to a search for non-ideological solutions to economic problems. In any case, this is likely to occur only over the very long run.

None of these long-run problems, however, is likely to completely stall future Chinese economic development. There is no satisfactory way of estimating just how rapid that development is likely to be, but the probable range is between 3 and 7 per cent a year. At the lower figure, China would double its GNP in a little over twenty years. At the higher figure, GNP within twenty years would be four times its 1964 level. The increase in the convertible sectors of the economy undoubtedly would be even more rapid.

Two qualifications, however, must be made. Converting potential military power into actual arms and equipment will in itself tend to lower the rate of growth. This will be less true as per capita income rises, since the alternative of reducing consumption rather than investment will become more and more feasible. Second, other countries, including many of those among China's potential adversaries, will also be growing. In Asia, however, many countries are too small for growth to enhance their defensive capabilities, and others are not growing at all (Indonesia) or only very slowly (India). Unless Japan rearms more than it has to date or India grows more rapidly and at the same time builds significantly larger armed forces, the ability to deter Chinese military activities will rest even more heavily on the United States than in the past. Furthermore, China's ability to make American military options, short of all-out nuclear attack on the Chinese mainland, costly both in lives and money will tend to increase rapidly regardless of what happens to the American economy.

## COSTS OF ALTERNATIVE MILITARY PROGRAMS

It will be fruitful at this point to turn to some specific considerations of the range of military options now open to the Chinese Communists or likely to be open in the next two decades. A Western observer half a world away from China and without access to data on Chinese military costs is,

---

[3]One cannot completely separate political control from ideology, since the former to a degree depends on the latter, i.e., maintenance of cadres' political loyalty depends in part on the strength with which they hold the official ideology. There was some degree of agreement on this point at the Airlie House Conference.

of course, able to make only the roughest approximations. Nevertheless, the following calculations do give some idea of the range of possibilities.

In estimating costs of nuclear armament for China, one must start by differentiating between ability to construct a single atomic bomb or a few such bombs a year, ability to develop a modest nuclear strike capability complete with delivery system and a modest stockpile of nuclear weapons, and, finally, achievement of nuclear parity with the U.S. or Russia. Of the three alternatives, only the first puts little significant strain on the Chinese economy. The cost of producing enough plutonium for one or several bombs a year involves a capital investment of less than U.S. $100 million and an annual fuel (uranium and heavy water or graphite) and operating cost of perhaps U.S. $30 million per year; the cost of producing uranium 235 is somewhat higher. Even when allowances are made for much higher costs for China in construction of reactors and a plant for separation of plutonium or a gaseous diffusion plant, necessary annual expenditure constitutes less than 1 or 2 per cent of China's gross national product.

Development of a modest nuclear strike capability will be more expensive but not prohibitively so. The French *force de frappe* is presently costing about U.S. $300 million a year, although this is probably not an accurate picture of what a comparable capability (i.e., being able to inflict some meaningful damage on the major potential adversary, in China's case the United States) would cost China. Chinese costs are likely to be substantially higher than for France, which is technologically a highly developed economy. The cost of more sophisticated delivery systems rises rapidly. Development of an intercontinental bomber today costs U.S. $500-1,000 million, while the cost of developing the Atlas or Titan ICBM is between $1-2 billion each, exclusive of procurement costs. Furthermore, this does not include many billions of dollars that went into raising American missile capabilities to a level necessary to develop an ICBM. Even a medium-range missile capability of use only in Asia involves many of these same costs. China may be able to cut some corners by copying, but, in the end, lack of a highly sophisticated industrial base will probably raise costs well above what they have been in the U.S.[4]

---

[4]Costs in China's producers' goods industry tend to run well above comparable costs in the U.S.S.R. or the U.S. (based on scattered data collected by Dwight Perkins for other purposes). One must, however, differentiate between costs involved in mass producing an item such as trucks and the costs in designing and individually constructing a few dozen bombers or missiles which cannot be mass produced anywhere. Limited managerial and labor skills tend to raise costs in an underdeveloped country's industrial sector in the former case but may be sufficient for the more limited requirements (in terms of numbers) of

Therefore, China's development of a *force de frappe* may cost well over U.S. $1 billion a year and have as dubious capabilities as those of France.

Willingness to spend over a billion dollars a year, however, will not of itself be enough. China will still have to train enough scientists to accomplish these tasks. This takes time and is likely to restrict Chinese nuclear capabilities more than the cost involved. Technical and scientific personnel required for the production of atomic bombs comes to approximately 1,300 engineers and 500 scientists (only a few of whom must hold a doctorate or its equivalent), or about 2 per cent of the scientists and engineers in specific categories, a significant but not overpowering cost even if one takes into account that these personnel are presumably among the best available in China.[5]

Technological requirements for development of many types of delivery systems, however, are more formidable. One possible choice for a Chinese *force de frappe*, a nuclear submarine with Polaris-type missiles, is also the most sophisticated of all weapons systems. Its cost may not be prohibitive (procurement cost is U.S. $105-110 million), but even the French probably will not have a comparable system in operation before the early 1970's. By the time China has attained the necessary technical proficiency, it is unlikely that economic factors will be a major deterrent, unless China's rate of growth is, let us say, 3 per cent or less and concentrated in agriculture and consumers' goods industry.

If, however, China settles for a nuclear capability which can be used in a limited nuclear war in Asia, this will involve only medium-range missiles or even cruder delivery devices, an objective well within China's present economic and technological capacity.

Difficulties involved in making estimates of costs of various conventional warfare options open to Communist China are much greater than for nuclear options, primarily because alternatives available for attainment of any particular objective and uncertainties regarding their probable effectiveness are so much greater. Rather than go through these calculations here, it is useful simply to present the conclusions arrived at from analysis elsewhere.[6]

the latter. It is possible that the opportunity costs of using one's best scientists on military projects may be high, but it is also possible that an underdeveloped economy has only a very limited need for highly trained theoretical scientists.

[5] These estimates are taken from a paper on Chinese military capabilities prepared for the Airlie House Conference by Allen Whiting.

[6] The complete analysis appears in the paper mentioned in n. 1.

The key conclusion is that the Chinese economy is capable of supporting a major conventional land action on China's borders, provided that it does not involve long lines of supply and particularly if the supply lines are not subject to air interdiction. Once the logistics problem becomes a major one (as in a large invasion of India) or significant naval power is required (as in an invasion of Taiwan), the costs become prohibitive. Peking, therefore, has little to gain from a crash program designed to double or triple the size and strength of the nation's conventional military power, barring a major threat to the existence of the regime itself. It is also apparent that the leadership of the Chinese Communist Party has come to this conclusion.

## CHINESE MILITARY EXPENDITURES

Military expenditures reported in the budget reached a peak of 6.5 billion yuan in 1955 and declined to 5.0 billion yuan in 1958. As a percentage of the total budget, the decline during the early years of the regime is dramatic, from 42.5 per cent in 1951 to 11.0 per cent in 1959. It is generally believed, however, that only a portion of total military expenditures gets reported in the budget. Such items as defense industries and scientific research in the military field apparently are included under other categories, especially during the past few years. It is possible, therefore, that total Chinese defense expenditures have been rising while the budgeted figure has fallen. If true, this would indicate a shift in emphasis toward the development and production of modern weapons for smaller (in terms of numbers of men) but more efficient armed forces. Up to and including 1961, however, it nevertheless appears that the Chinese Communists kept a tight lid on total as well as budgeted military expenditures, although perhaps not as tight as the budget figures indicate.

This appraisal is supported by fragments of information available on the size of various branches of China's armed forces. The army was reduced from a force of 4-5 million men to approximately 2.5 million, but in the process, probably less than 10 per cent of the 2.5 million were organized into armored, heavy artillery, and anti-aircraft divisions, the remainder being equipped with modern standardized infantry weapons rather than the hodgepodge of captured Japanese, American, and Russian arms used during the Korean War.[7] The air force grew from a force of 650

---

[7] E. Joffe in a paper prepared for the Airlie House Conference, "China's Conventional Warfare Capability," estimates the total number of armored division at between two and four, with a comparable number of artillery divisions.

planes at the beginning of the Korean War to over 1,500 by the end of that war and to 2,500-3,000 aircraft at present (including naval aircraft), 1,800-2,000 of which are jets. If these figures are accurate, the Chinese Communists have purchased aircraft at an average rate of 200 to 300 planes a year from the end of the Korean War through 1959, as compared to a rate of 800 to 1,000 a year during that war. The Chinese navy is made up to 28 submarines, 4 destroyer escorts, and 800 other vessels, a force which could not have accounted for more than a small portion of the total defense budget.[8]

## CHINESE DEFENSE EXPENDITURES[a]

|      | (1,000,000 yuan) | % of total expenditure |
|------|------------------|------------------------|
| 1950 | 2,830 | 41.5 |
| 1951 | 5,060 | 42.5 |
| 1952 | 4,370 | 26.0 |
| 1953 | 5,680 | 26.4 |
| 1954 | 5,810 | 23.6 |
| 1955 | 6,500 | 24.1 |
| 1956 | 6,120 | 20.0 |
| 1957 | 5,510 | 19.0 |
| 1958 | 5,000 | 12.2 |
| 1959 | 5,800 | 11.0 |
| 1960 | 5,800 | 8.3 |
| 1961 | less than 5,800[b] | — |

[a]The 1950-1958 data are from *Ten Great Years* (Peking: Foreign Languages Press, 1960), pp. 23-24. The 1959 and 1960 budget data are from *Second Session of the Second National People's Republic of China (Documents)* (Peking: Foreign Languages Press, 1960), pp. 50, 58, 60.

[b]"Report on Work of Rear Services Departments in Entire Army," *Work Bulletin*, No. 30 (August 4, 1961).

It is useful here, however, to make a distinction between expenditure on conventional military forces-in-being and expenditure on development of the capability of producing advanced conventional weapons systems. China's apparent recently acquired ability to manufacture MIG-21's indicates that the regime was making a strong effort to develop its capabilities in this and other conventional spheres with the help of the Soviet

[8]Institute for Strategic Studies, *The Military Balance 1964-65* (London: Institute for Strategic Studies, 1964), p. 10.

Union before the cutoff of Soviet military support in 1960.[9] It is doubtful, however, that the amount of money (and number of technicians) involved in this operation was sufficient to require a major change in the relative priority given to defense.

This picture of limited military expenditure together with priority for economic development must be further qualified for the years since 1961. China's inability to purchase military equipment from the Soviet Union since 1960 has greatly increased her need not only for research on advanced conventional weapons systems, but also for actual production of many such weapons in order to supply forces-in-being. Simply to maintain the relative strength of Chinese conventional forces as constituted in 1959, therefore, required a significant increase in military expenditures. Increased expenditures in 1960 and 1961, however, probably would have met with a fate not unlike that of expenditure in non-military fields, although perhaps not to the same degree, i.e., disorganization in planning and control, ensuring that a substantial portion of any additional funds would have been wasted.[10] Such was undoubtedly no longer the case after 1961 in the military fields, and indications are that Peking is making considerable efforts to overcome what deterioration in conventional forces had taken place.

Even if the situation since 1961 is taken into account, however, it is still possible to argue that the Chinese Communists have not attempted to raise their conventional military strength as rapidly as possible but instead have given priority to economic development. If they had done otherwise, they still would not have been able to launch any major offensive operations in any area where they were likely to be opposed by the United States, at least not with any hope of success. Defense against nuclear attack was also impossible. On the other hand, their forces were already adequate for defense of the homeland and other key areas of vital interest to them and whose borders were contiguous with China. Military grounds alone, therefore, have generally militated against any substantial sacrifice of future for present military potential. When other domestic

---

[9]*New York Times*, December 30, 1964, p. 1.

[10]Evidence that military production did not escape the effects of disorganization during the "great leap forward" can be found in *Work Bulletin*, No. 30 (August 4, 1961). In the first half of 1961, for example, state factories attained only 15.9 per cent of the planned output in the manufacture of weapons, equipment, accessories, and parts. The *Work Bulletin* is a secret military journal published by the Chinese Communists, twenty-nine issues of which (all from 1961) were released by the U.S. Department of State and are available in the Library of Congress.

political and economic objectives are taken into account, the argument against a rapid military buildup is even more convincing. These priorities could, of course, change, as they already have in a limited sense. As their economy and technological capabilities develop, the number of potential military options open to the Chinese will increase and the regime may then undertake a much more substantial armaments program. Even if expenditures on the military were held at a constant percentage of the total budget, there would be a significant increase in Chinese military power. Barring a sharp increase in international tensions around the borders of China (a genuine fear of major escalation in Vietnam, for example), however, it is unlikely that China will find it desirable to shift its priorities radically against economic development and in favor of the military during the next decade or two.

The implications of this analysis for China's attitude for arms control measures are direct. The regime has shown a clear interest in transferring a substantial quantity of resources out of arms and into economic development. However, although the last known official military budget (that of 1961) took only approximately 5 per cent of GNP, an amount which if channeled into investment might raise the growth rate by as much as 2 per cent, and the true budget is probably even larger, it is doubtful that the Chinese Communists would risk any further reductions. To do so, Peking would have to be confident that Kuomintang and American retaliatory capabilities had been eliminated from Asia, and this is unlikely. Even then a sufficient military force would have to be maintained as security against any domestic eventuality and to deal with the military establishments of such countries as India, Korea, and perhaps Japan.

At the same time, Peking would presumably welcome any move that made it unnecessary for China to increase its military expenditure greatly. As already pointed out, Peking's military expenditures are likely to rise as China develops increasingly sophisticated delivery systems and enters into their production. At most, however, Chinese economic capacity will limit production (and probably even development) to one or two particular systems at any given time. Under no circumstances could the regime attempt to match United States developments in the field of nuclear weapons and delivery systems in quantity, quality, or variety. On the other hand, as we shall point out at greater length in subsequent chapters, the political (and to a degree military) advantages that Peking ultimately hopes to gain from its nuclear program are substantial.

Specifically, the Chinese Communists probably expect to be able to deter the United States from various kinds of military actions against China by being able to threaten the destruction of one or several American cities. To do this under present conditions, the Chinese will have to acquire Polaris-type submarines or enough ICBM's to make a convincing threat. Although Peking may settle for a lesser capability in the immediate future such as a delivery system useful only against Asian targets, it is unlikely that this limited capacity will remain acceptable to them over the long run.

China undoubtedly would prefer to achieve these political and military goals by less expensive means. A program designed to deter the United States even in the above described limited way will take expenditures that could be put to more economically productive uses. The political-military aims that deterrence of the United States will help China to achieve, however, are so basic to Peking that it is unlikely that the regime would see any advantage in transferring funds from the military budget to economic development. The principal way in which the American government could encourage such a reduction in Chinese arms expenditures would be by action that would allow China to achieve its key aims with a lesser expenditure or conversely to make it prohibitively expensive to attain those goals. Prohibition of all nuclear weapons, a step Peking has consistently advocated, would be an inexpensive way for China to accomplish its desires in the military sphere. An effective American defense against any particular weapons system would probably discourage the Chinese from going into production unless the same system could also achieve a more limited effect elsewhere in the world. In no case, except in the unlikely event of a complete prohibition on nuclear weapons, would Chinese research and development efforts be affected. Only the decision of whether or not to go into actual production of a particular system would be involved. It is conceivable, therefore, that the Chinese Communists might see some advantage in an agreement whereby the United States would abstain from defensive arrangements in exchange for a Chinese decision not to produce a particular weapons system since presumably a settlement along these lines would not affect the military balance at all. Such an agreement would presumably interest the two parties involved principally only if each wanted an agreement for political reasons not directly related to the specific military issues involved, but for China there would be the added incentive of some reduction in military expenditures.

## ECONOMIC WARFARE THROUGH TRADE AND AID

Economic factors influence the prospects for arms control agreements in another way as well. Any arms control agreement which shifted the contest for Southeast Asia or the underdeveloped world in general away from the military-political action (including insurgency) to the economic sphere (i.e., trade and aid) would put China at a maximum disadvantage vis-à-vis the economically developed nations.

Unlike military strength, trade and aid capacities depend not only on the size of national product or the product of the producers' goods sector but also on differences between the economies of trading partners. Most of the nations that China might desire to bring under its influence are underdeveloped, just as is China. Their trade, like China's, primarily takes the form of sale of agricultural products and raw materials in exchange for manufactured products. Three-quarters of China's exports are agricultural products or processed agricultural products (textiles and other industrial consumers' goods), and most of the remaining quarter takes the form of mining products such as tin and tungsten. Until the recent agricultural crisis forced China to import large quantities of grain from Australia, Canada, and France, all but 6 to 8 per cent of China's imports consisted of industrial producers' goods.

Not surprisingly, therefore, most of China's trade has been with industrial nations of the Soviet bloc, Western Europe, the United Kingdom, and Japan. Since 1960, the reduction in trade with the Soviet bloc has continued, but the shift has been toward non-Communist developed nations rather than the underdeveloped world. Furthermore, much of the trade carried on with the underdeveloped world is with Hong Kong and Southeast Asia. Trade with Hong Kong is of only limited direct political use since China has many other means of bringing pressure on the colony any time it should so desire. Trade with Southeast Asia is also of limited political use, but for different reasons. China has a large export surplus with this area (and with Hong Kong) primarily in consumer commodities which are not of vital importance to these countries. These are also goods for which China has to meet severe competition from consumers' goods industries of other newly developing nations. On the other hand, China imports few of the goods for which the Southeast Asian nations have greatest difficulty finding adequate export markets. Ability to bring political pressure through trade measures, therefore, lies more with the Southeast Asian nations than with China. Exceptions would occur if China were to become a major importer of rubber or rice. The former commodity is not likely to be sought in large quantities until China's economy has developed far more than at present, and the latter would be wanted only if China proved incapable of solving its agricultural difficulties. (China has imported Burmese rice during the past three years, but most of it has been re-exported.) Trade between China and Latin America and Africa, two areas where Chinese political activities in recent years have risen sharply, is negligible and is not likely to become significant during the next decade or two.

This general discussion perhaps has tended to belittle more than is justified China's ability to use its international economic relations as a weapon of foreign policy. By concentrating a trade offensive in a single area or against a single nation, China might be able to bring enough economic power to bear to influence a particular situation. It is also possible that China will be able to continue to use the promise of large future markets as a lure even if that trade never materializes. Finally, there is the whole question of aid, as differentiated from trade. The most valuable economic aid comes from developed countries with the most highly developed techonology as does much of the most useful military aid (jet aircraft, tanks, etc.), but there are many other types of aid in which China does not operate at such a disadvantage.

The ability of China to affect an isolated situation by concentrating its resources is often exaggerated by pointing to examples where China has taken the market for a specific product away from Japan or some other nation. The flow of Japanese foreign aid and private investment alone to the developing nations is almost as great as total Chinese exports to those countries. Even if the Chinese were to undertake to dump large quantities of goods in Southeast Asia, therefore, it is doubtful that they could do more than force Japan to curtail its aid to the area for a year or two, a sacrifice of little economic significance to Japan but bought at considerable cost to China. China's trade warfare capabilities are also severely hampered by its not being a member of GATT. There is nothing to prevent raising of discriminatory tariffs against Chinese goods, a step which would undoubtedly be quickly taken by most developed countries if they discovered that Chinese dumping was damaging politically friendly trading partners.

Nor would China have the ability to break a boycott or embargo on trade of a country such as Indonesia, if such an embargo or boycott were to be imposed, for example, in an attempt to stop "confrontation" with Malaysia. Indonesian petroleum production is over 20 million metric tons a year, while Chinese imports of petroleum have generally ranged between 2 and 3 million tons during the past three years. Tea, tobacco, and tin, three of Indonesia's major exports, are also exported by China.

The lure of China's 400 (now 700) million customers has remained powerful for more than a century, without being dampened by the reality of China's poverty and its, hence, meager trade. The Communists have been able to exploit this lure by hinting at major trade deals if only the country in question would be more reasonable in the political sphere (grant recognition, etc.). This argument has had the most impact on developed nations that depend heavily on trade, particularly Japan and the United Kingdom. For such countries, the actual prospects for increased trade are not negligible, although usually not as substantial as apparently anticipated. For underdeveloped nations with surplus primary products which they would like to be rid of, the lure also exists and has been exploited. The potential for such efforts by the Chinese Communists in these areas, however, is considerably reduced by the almost total lack of Chinese capability or willingness to import such commodities on anything but a token basis. Exceptions such as the importation of Cuban sugar and Burmese rice do not alter the fact that, except during the recent agricultural crisis, only 5 to 6 per cent of Chinese imports have been consumers' goods.

China's trade, therefore, does not provide it with a very powerful tool for attaining its foreign policy objectives. China's aid program is subject to some of the same limitations. One of the major objectives of United States economic aid, for example, is to raise the recipient's rate of growth of national income. United States aid helps primarily because it provides the country being aided with otherwise unattainable foreign exchange which it can use to import machinery and the like from a developed nation. China's trade position is much too weak for it to dissipate its small foreign exchange reserves on aid. As a result, China must and does tie much of its aid to the purchase of Chinese products, but China, unlike the United States, does not produce many items which the receiving nation most needs. The main function of Chinese aid in the economic sphere if it were given on a large scale, therefore, would be as a substitute for domestic savings and capital formation by the recipient. Even in this sphere, there is a real possibility that, if Chinese aid were greatly increased, the increase would simply allow the aided country to raise its level of consumption.

In the area of technical support, Chinese aid is of more potential value. Chinese technicians may lack certain skills, particularly in the building of heavy industry, but, unlike technicians from more advanced nations, they also possess recent practical experience in development problems. China may well be more able to help Cambodia build and operate three light industrial plants efficiently than could either the U.S. or the U.S.S.R.[11] This kind of technical support would be of little use to areas at approximately the same stage of development as China, such as India, Egypt, most of Latin America, and even much of Southeast Asia, but it

[11]The textile plant and cotton and paper mills set up by the Chinese in Cambodia have not generally met the targets set for them, but this probably reflects the problems involved in setting up any industrial establishment in Cambodia more than it does any comparative disadvantage of Chinese technical support. When the Czech cement and tire plants and sugar refinery are completed and put into operation, however, one will have a better basis for comparison.

could be helpful to the less advanced (Africa south of the Sahara, Cambodia, Indonesia, etc.).

Chinese military aid is also of little use to nations which can produce the same items themselves, although, if substantial enough, such aid might allow them to divert resources to economic development rather than arms production. It is probable that Chinese military technology will increase more rapidly than that of most other developing nations, and this may increase these nations' interest in Chinese arms. The discussion in the first half of this chapter, however, makes it clear that China will continue for some time to operate at a disadvantage in this sphere vis-à-vis the developed world.

The above analysis started from the premise that China desired to use its aid to assist an established government to develop its economy or military power.[12] This presumably is the case with aid to North Korea and North Vietnam. The analysis goes a long way toward explaining why China could not hope to replace the Soviet Union's position in Cuba, no matter how much both Castro and the Chinese might desire it. Outside of the Communist bloc, however, Chinese objectives more often are to weaken and eventually destroy the existing government. Even where the objective is to support one non-Communist government (presumably favorably disposed toward China) against its opposition, there is no incentive for the Chinese to make that government any stronger than is necessary for the attainment of immediate goals. These considerations put a premium on small arms aid for insurgent groups and projects designed to enhance the prestige of the existing pro-Chinese government (and the prestige of China itself), regardless of their ultimate effect, if any, on the economy.

The ability of China to produce the necessary small arms is obvious, although the ability to deliver them to the desired destination is subject to some limitations. Individual bribes and other similar uses of aid are also well within Chinese capabilities, although China is no match for the developed countries in this regard. Chinese capabilities in the prestige project sphere are not so obvious. Many of the most prestigious projects are those which China itself has had to obtain foreign assistance to build (steel mills are the prime example). Nevertheless, there are prestige projects which are feasible for China. The three factories in Cambodia can be thought of primarily in this light. The road in Yemen is another project which China was able to handle easily. The Cambodian factories, however, point up one of the difficulties of such prestige

---

[12]The ultimate purpose of such aid from China may be simply to win over a supporter in the Sino-Soviet dispute, but, to be effective in doing this, the aid must serve a positive economic or military function.

projects; they must operate fairly efficiently, or their prestige value is quickly dissipated.

One may conclude that the chief purpose of Communist China's foreign trade has been to benefit the Chinese economy, not to further the international political objectives of the regime. The major political influence on China's trade has come from actions directed by others against China, rather than those initiated by China. The Korean War embargo, for example, forced China to turn to the Soviet bloc as its major supplier of industrial products, and vestiges of that embargo still limit the nations from whom China can purchase key materials.

Aid, as contrasted to trade, has been motivated primarily by political rather than economic factors, although there have been exceptions. The bulk (71 per cent) of this aid, which has totaled over U.S. $1.2 billion exclusive of military aid, has gone to Asian Communist neighbors, North Korea, North Vietnam, and Mongolia, with lesser amounts (7 per cent) to Albania and Hungary and to non-Communist countries (22 per cent). Aid to some bloc countries is one price China has had to pay in an attempt to gain these countries' allegiance in the Sino-Soviet dispute. Foreign exchange costs of bloc aid are probably not large, either directly or indirectly, since the aid apparently is tied to Chinese products that would probably not otherwise find a market abroad. China has also given small amounts of aid to Cuba. Cuba's needs, however, are not generally ones which can be met by Chinese products. An attempt to replace Soviet aid to Cuba, therefore, would involve China in a loss of foreign exchange which could run at several hundred million U.S. dollars annually, a cost which it cannot afford.

Outside of bloc countries, the Chinese Communists have extended slightly over U.S. $100 million in outright grants and somewhat more in loans. The bulk of this aid has gone to Burma, Cambodia, Ceylon, Nepal, Indonesia, Morocco, Yemen, Egypt, Guinea, Ghana, and most recently to Syria, Somalia, and Zanzibar.

The first thing to notice is that most of China's aid went to very small countries where a relatively small sum might be expected to have a significant impact. The exceptions are loans to Indonesia and Egypt which were not large and which in the former case were closely tied in with trade considerations. A second fact is that most of the aid, as already mentioned, is tied to specific projects to be built with Chinese products and Chinese technicians. Cash grants have been made, as in the case of Nepal, where several million dollars was given for no obvious economic purpose, but these have been very small. Total cash grants to Zanzibar before the recent merger with Tanganyika, for example, have been estimated at only U.S. $500 thousand. The foreign exchange cost of this aid, therefore, has been negligible.

As for China's future aid-giving capabilities, there are two conflicting considerations. On the one hand, it soon will have completed repayment of all Soviet credits. During the past several years, China's export surplus with the Soviet Union generally has been between U.S. $100 and $200 million dollars. After 1964 these funds will be available for other purposes. Offsetting this, however, has been the need of China to import large quantities of grain because of domestic crop failures. Food purchases reached U.S. $360 million in 1961, and have fallen only moderately since. If necessity for these imports should disappear, China's ability to extend aid, even where that aid involved a loss of foreign exchange, would be enhanced.

Peking, therefore, would not welcome any international agreement that placed competition between China and the United States (or the U.S.S.R. or Western Europe) in the arena of aid and trade. It is possible, nevertheless, that the Chinese leadership might accept an agreement effectively barring all outside aid, economic and military, to either side in a dispute. The examples of Chinese agreement to such conditions for Korea and Laos, however, do not constitute proof of this position since it is quite clear that Peking never had any intention of abiding by these agreements (which applied to military aid only).

Finally a word must be said about the vulnerability of the Chinese economy to a trade embargo and the extent to which that vulnerability can be exploited by the United States or others. If an embargo were to be designed to hamper Chinese economic development, it could be successful only in a limited way even if it included all of the industrialized world, a highly improbable occurrence. China is not like Cuba. The Chinese economy is much less dependent on trade in general and trade with the United States in particular. The American embargo has been in existence for fourteen years with no obvious economic effects of any great significance. A general embargo, even with support of the Soviet Union and all other industrialized nations, would probably not bring the Chinese economy to its knees in terms of sharply reducing the standard of living or even entirely halting economic growth. An embargo by all countries on certain strategic items, however, would undoubtedly limit China's military capabilities. The relevant strategic items are those which China is incapable of producing herself because she lacks the necessary technological capability. To all appearances, an effective embargo on these items for China has already been in effect since 1959 or 1960 and has resulted in a temporary, although fast disappearing, decline in Chinese airpower. One can also make out a case that a similar embargo on petroleum imports would constrain Chinese military capabilities. This case is less convincing except in the short run, because China has been rapidly expanding domestic petroleum production from 436 thousand metric tons in 1952 to a reported 6.5 million tons in 1963.[13]

One must also differentiate between the question of whether measures such as those described above would have an effect on the Chinese economy and the question of whether the Communist regime would refrain from certain actions because of these effects. The disadvantage of an embargo is that it is certain to be carried out with great publicity and would make any subsequent Chinese concessions appear forced upon them. To be effective, these measures might have to be made clearly contingent on some future Chinese action, rather than in response to an existing situation, or in a desire to force China to take some specific action, such as signing the Test Ban Treaty.

In appraising the potential effectiveness of any such actions as these, it is useful to keep the Chinese Communist leadership's basic priorities in mind. Economics in Peking's eyes is more a means to various ends than it is an end in itself. If a choice comes down to a selection between attainment of international political goals or domestic economic development, it is by no means clear that China will always opt for the latter.[14]

---

[13]This capacity could be increased by one-third if refining capacity purchased abroad were matched by domestic oil discoveries.

[14]It would be somewhat more accurate to say that China would be willing to sacrifice a certain amount of economic development in order to attain international political goals, how much development depending on the size and importance of the political gain. The point is that political goals do have a very high priority.

# IV NUCLEAR STRATEGY [1]

It is apparently popularly held in the West that the Chinese have an unrealistic view of nuclear warfare and do not recognize the great destruction that it would cause in China as well as in the rest of the world. Frequently the Chinese are said to believe that even if half their population were destroyed they would still be able to dominate the world. The most extreme form of this view takes the position that the Chinese actively desire a general nuclear war and in fact are likely to try to trigger an all-out nuclear exchange between the United States and the Soviet Union. The more moderate view, widely held by some journalists, commentators, and apparently some Western government officials, is that the Chinese, while not actively desiring a nuclear war, would not be unhappy if one were to take place and that they contemplate its outcome with relative equanimity.

This image of the Chinese Communists fits in with the general Western view that the Peking regime is irrational and aggressive. (That the Chinese are in an earlier stage of their revolution than the Soviets, who are coming to be more "bourgeois," is sometimes given as support for this opinion.) The Chinese themselves contributed to this view by numerous statements issued up until 1962 that appeared to underrate American nuclear power. For example, in October, 1960, a People's Liberation Army (PLA) official declared: "The issue of a future war will not be decided by guided missiles or atom bombs. It will still be decided by man. Atom bombs will never be able to destroy mankind or the world.... The revolutionary people are always able to find ways and means for overcoming every kind of modern weapon." [2] However, the main impetus for the widespread notion of Chinese indifference to nuclear warfare seems to stem from a deliberate effort of the Soviet Union to create this impression in the minds of the leaders of Communist Parties as well as Western leaders and peoples. Khrushchev, in a number of statements to Western visitors, alluded to Chinese irrationality concerning nuclear warfare, and the Russians have repeatedly returned to this theme in their polemics against

[1] For more extended discussion, see Morton H. Halperin, *China and the Bomb* (New York: Praeger, 1965).

[2] *People's Daily*, October 6-7, 1960; quoted in Alice Langley Hsieh, "Communist China and Nuclear Force," R. N. Rosecrance (ed.), *The Dispersion of Nuclear Weapons: Strategy and Politics* (New York: Columbia University Press, 1964), p. 164.

the Chinese over the past two years. For example, in a statement issued
on August 21, 1963, commenting on the Chinese attitude toward the nuclear test ban, the Soviet government stated:

> No Leninist-Communist could help experiencing a feeling
> of natural disgust at this attitude towards thermonuclear war:
> that there is nothing wrong even if half of humanity, if 300
> million Chinese perish, for on the other hand imperialism
> would be erased from the face of the Earth and those who
> survive would rapidly create on the ruins of imperialism a
> new, a thousand times greater civilisation. This very attitude
> to thermonuclear war has more than once been reflected in the
> pronouncements of high-ranking Chinese representatives.
> Even if the PRC Government makes not two but a hundred and
> two statements that it is longing for the prohibition and de-
> struction of nuclear weapons, that its only concern is the
> interests of the peoples, it will not be able to wash away
> the shame of staking the lives of hundreds of millions of
> people, including Chinese people, in a thermonuclear war.[3]

The Russian government is accusing the Chinese of favoring nuclear
warfare. However, as discussed below, the dispute between the Russians
and the Chinese is really over how likely a thermonuclear war is and not
how destructive it would be. In fact the public positions of the Chinese
and the Russians on thermonuclear war seem to be remarkably similar
despite the assertions of the Russians that they are very different. Both
sides agree that general nuclear war can be avoided, and they agree that,
should it nevertheless occur, imperialism would be doomed but Communism
would survive. While laying more and more emphasis on the destructiveness of nuclear war, the Soviet Union has not abandoned the notion that
such a war would mean only the end of capitalism and not the end of
Communism or of world civilization.

The question of whether to stress the destructiveness of nuclear war
or the fact that Communism would nevertheless survive it has been one
with which Peking, as well as Moscow, has grappled since 1945 without
any unanimity of views. In what is apparently the first Chinese Communist statement on nuclear warfare, Mao Tse-tung took the following
line:

---

[3]Translation in *Moscow News;* reprinted in *Peking Review*, VI, No. 36 (September 6, 1963), pp. 21-22.

... Can atom bombs decide wars? No, they can't. Atom bombs
could not make Japan surrender. Without the struggles waged
by the people, atom bombs by themselves would be of no
avail. If atom bombs could decide the war, then why was it
necessary to ask the Soviet Union to send its troops? Why
didn't Japan surrender when two atomic bombs were dropped
on her and why did she surrender as soon as the Soviet
Union sent troops? *Some of our comrades, too, believe that
the atomic bomb is all-powerful;* that is a big mistake....
The theory that "weapons decide everything", the purely
military viewpoint, a bureaucratic style of work divorced
from the masses, individualist thinking, and the like—all
these are bourgeois influences in our ranks.[4]

In 1946, in an interview with Anna Louise Strong, Mao declared that
"the basic question is the consciousness of the people." "In the end,"
he said, "the bomb will not annihilate the people. The people will annihilate the bomb."[5] This downgrading of the role of nuclear weapons
(but not, as we shall see, of the possibility of avoiding nuclear war)
was plausible in view of the very small stockpile of fission weapons
which existed on both sides in the early years of the atomic age. However, by 1950, at the time of their entrance into the Korean War, the
Chinese seemed to have developed, if anything, an exaggerated opinion
of the destructiveness of nuclear weapons. The Chinese Communists apparently estimated that if the United States used atomic weapons on them,
they might suffer several millions of casualties.[6] This was probably an
overestimate, given the limited American stockpile and the likelihood
that much of it would be saved for use against the Soviet Union in Europe,
if needed there. Nevertheless, the Chinese were very much concerned

---

[4]"The Situations and Our Policy After the Victory in the War of Resistance
against Japan," dated August 13, 1945; printed in *Selected Works of Mao
Tse-tung* (Peking: Foreign Languages Press, 1961), IV, 21-22, italics added.
There is reason to believe that this statement was not written until sometime
in the 1950's.

[5]Anna Louise Strong, *Dawn Out of China* (Bombay: People's Publishing House
Ltd., 1948), p. 155.

[6]K. M. Panikkar, *In Two Chinas* (London: George Allen and Unwin, 1955),
p. 108.

that atomic bombs might be used, and they attempted to prepare their troops who were being sent into the Korean battle for such a contingency.[7] At the same time, the Peking regime began to emphasize in its propaganda and, apparently, in its internal calculations the strong possibility that the United States would be deterred from using these weapons.

The Chinese have been quite cognizant of the tremendous expansion of nuclear power both by the United States and by the Soviet Union, particularly with the development of fusion weapons by both sides. Thus their original dread of the destruction that atomic weapons would cause now fits the facts, and they lay greater stress than ever on the need and possibility of avoiding nuclear war.

If Chinese action through the early and mid-1950's suggested that they were aware that the United States might use nuclear weapons, that they feared the use of such weapons, and that they were determined to avoid provoking such use, it is also true that they were by no means ready to give up the initiative in foreign policy. In some statements they continued to disparage the possible role of nuclear weapons, even though there was apparently growing dispute within China as to the extent to which nuclear weapons might be decisive in warfare.[8]

Addressing a closed session of the Moscow meeting of Communist and Workers' Parties on November 18, 1957, Mao Tse-tung argued for a more aggressive line by the international Communist movement, according to a Chinese version of the speech released in 1963:

> At present another situation has to be taken into account, *namely, that the war maniacs may drop atomic and hydrogen bombs everywhere.* They drop them and we act after their fashion; thus there will be chaos and lives will be lost. The question has to be considered for the worst. The Political Bureau of our Party has held several sessions to discuss this question. If fighting breaks out now, China has got only hand grenades and not atomic bombs—which the Soviet Union has though. Let us imagine, how many people will die if war

[7]Herbert Goldhamer, "Communist Reaction in Korea to American Possession of the A-Bomb and Its Significance for U.S. Political and Psychological Warfare" (RAND RM-903, August 1, 1952); and by the same author, "Chinese Concern about the A-Bomb" (RAND, RM-987, November 7, 1952). The studies by Goldhamer are based on interrogation of Chinese and North Korean prisoners of war.

[8]Alice Hsieh, *Communist China's Strategy in the Nuclear Age* (Englewood Cliffs, N.J.: Prentice-Hall, 1962), pp. 15-75.

should break out? Out of the world's population of 2,700 million, one third—or, if more, half—may be lost. *It is they and not we who want to fight;* when a fight starts, atomic and hydrogen bombs may be dropped. I debated this question with a foreign statesman. He believed that if an atomic war was fought, the whole of mankind would be annihilated. I said that if the worst came to the worst and half of mankind died, the other half would remain while imperialism would be razed to the ground and the whole world would become socialist; in a number of years there would be 2,700 million people again and definitely more. *We Chinese have not yet completed our construction and we desire peace.* However, *if imperialism insists on fighting a war, we will have no alternative but to make up our minds and fight to the finish before going ahead with our construction.* If every day you are afraid of war and war eventually comes, what will you do then? First I have said that the East wind prevails over the West wind and that war will not break out, and now I have added these explanations about the situation in case war should break out. In this way both possibilities have been taken into account.[9]

The Russians have alleged that this is a "corrected" version of Mao's statement. The Soviets conceded that the Chinese statement accurately quotes the substance of Mao's remarks, but they noted that he had changed the emphasis in order to suggest a greater Chinese desire to avoid nuclear war than there actually was. They claim, for example, that Mao's statement in relation to construction in China actually read as follows: "In China construction has not got under way in earnest. If the imperialists impose a war on us, we shall be prepared to terminate the construction; let us first have a trial of strength, and then return to construction."[10]

[9]"Statement by the Spokesman of the Chinese Government—A Comment on the Soviet Government's Statement of August 21." Dated September 1, 1963; translation in *Peking Review*, VI, No. 36 (September 6, 1963), p. 10, italics in *Peking Review*. Reprinted from same source in William E. Griffiths, *The Sino-Soviet Rift* (Cambridge, Mass.: M.I.T. Press, 1964), Document 9, p. 376.

[10]"A Reply to Peking-Soviet Government Statement." Published in Moscow newspapers on September 21 and 22, 1963, in reply to the Chinese statement of September 1, 1963; translation published as *Soviet Booklet No. 122* (London: Soviet Booklets, 1963), pp. 20-21. Reprinted from *Soviet News*

Perhaps the most optimistic statement of the outcome of a nuclear war was published by the Chinese in *Red Flag* on November 8, 1960. In an article titled "Long Live Leninism," they declared:

*We consistently oppose the launching of criminal wars by imperialism,* because imperialist war would impose enormous sacrifices upon the people of various countries (including the people of the United States and other imperialist countries). *But should the imperialists impose such sacrifices on them,* we believe that, just as the experience of the Russian revolution and the Chinese revolution shows, those sacrifices would not be in vain. The victorious people would very swiftly create on the ruins of imperialism a civilization thousands of times higher than the capitalist system and a truly beautiful future for themselves.[11]

After quoting these two statements the Chinese Communists, in an exchange with the Soviet Union on the issue of the nuclear test ban, went on to insist:

The meaning of these words is very clear:

1. China wants peace, and not war;
2. It is the imperialists, and not we, who want to fight;
3. A world war can be prevented;
4. Even in the eventuality that imperialism should impose a war on the people of the world and inflict tragic losses on them, it is the imperialist system, and not mankind, that would perish, and the future of mankind would still be bright.[12]

The Chinese asserted that the Soviets shared the view that socialism and not imperialism would survive a nuclear war:

(September 23-24, 1963), in Griffith, *The Sino-Soviet Rift,* Document 12, p. 445. It seems very unlikely that eight years after the establishment of a Communist regime in China, Mao would state that construction had not yet gotten under way.

[11]Quoted in "Statement by the Spokesman of the Chinese Government—A Comment on the Soviet Government's Statement of August 21," *Peking Review* (September 6, 1963), p. 10. The complete text of "Long Live Leninism" is reprinted in G. F. Hudson, Richard Lowenthal, and Roderick MacFarquhar (eds.), *The Sino-Soviet Dispute* (New York: Praeger, 1961), pp. 82-112.

[12]*Peking Review* (September 6, 1963), p. 10.

While propagating the theory of the annihilation of mankind, they say that the people of the world will bury imperialism if imperialism forces a nuclear war on them. For instance, the Open Letter of the Central Committee of the C.P.S.U. of July 14 declared, "It stands to reason, of course, that if the imperialist madmen unleash a war, the peoples will sweep away capitalism and bury it." But people are bound to ask, if according to your theory all the 3,000 million people in the world will die if imperialism unleashes a nuclear war, then who would remain to bury imperialism?[13]

The Chinese rendition is accurate. However, the Soviet statement goes on to say: "The Communists, representing the peoples, the true advocates of socialist humanism, are called upon to do everything they can to prevent another world war in which hundreds of millions of people would perish."[14]

It seems clear that the Chinese are not now making any attempt to capitalize on the West's belief that they are irrational and do not have an appropriate fear of nuclear warfare. In fact, the Chinese have gone out of their way in the items quoted, as well as in their radio broadcasts throughout the world and in their propaganda journal the *Peking Review,* to stress that they are not bad men who welcome a nuclear war. There seems to be very little doubt that the Chinese recognize the destruction that would come to China in the event of a nuclear war and that their policy is geared to prevent such an attack. At a press conference in Somalia during his African trip in 1964, Chou En-lai, when asked whether it were true that "in the event of a nuclear war China feels she is less vulnerable than any other country on the globe and that she would hope to emerge victorious from such a war which might destroy the rest of the world," replied that "this is fabrication, pure and simple. . . . If a nuclear war breaks out, China would lose more people than would other countries

---

[13]*Ibid.*, pp. 10-11.

[14]"The Open Letter of the Central Committee of the Communist Party of the Soviet Union to Party Organisations and All Communists of the Soviet Union," *Pravda,* July 14, 1963; translation published in *Current Soviet Documents,* I (August 5, 1963), p. 18. Reprinted from *Soviet News,* No. 4872, in Griffith, *The Sino-Soviet Rift,* Document 3, pp. 300-301.

.... It is with ulterior motives that the imperialists and certain other persons unscrupulously have distorted China's position and made widespread propaganda about it."[15]

The difference in emphasis, with the Chinese stressing that Communism will survive a nuclear war and the Russians stressing the destruction in nuclear war, probably stems from the fact that the Chinese, being themselves without the means to deter a nuclear war, are reluctant to put all their emphasis on deterrence. They find it necessary to proclaim that even should the West launch nuclear aggression, the Communist system in China and throughout the world would still survive. The Chinese themselves have been quite candid in the past few years in discussing their dilemma about stressing the destructiveness of nuclear war:

> We hold that in order to mobilize the masses of the people against nuclear war and nuclear weapons it is necessary to inform them of the enormous destructiveness of these weapons. It would be patently wrong to underestimate this destructiveness. However, U.S. imperialism is doing its utmost to disseminate dread of nuclear weapons in pursuit of its policy of nuclear blackmail. In these circumstances, while Communists should point out the destructiveness of nuclear weapons, they should counter U.S. imperialist propaganda of nuclear terror by stressing the possibility of outlawing them and preventing nuclear war; they should try and transmute the people's desire for peace into righteous indignation at the imperialist policy of nuclear threats and lead the people to struggle against the U.S. imperialist policies of aggression and war. In no circumstances must Communists act as a voluntary propagandist for the U.S. imperialist policy of nuclear blackmail. We hold that the U.S. imperialist policy of nuclear blackmail must be thoroughly exposed and that all peace-loving countries and people must be mobilized on the most extensive scale to wage an unrelenting fight against every move made by the U.S. imperialists in their plans for aggression and war. We are deeply convinced that, by relying on the united struggle of all forces defending peace, it is possible to frustrate the U.S. imperialist policy of nuclear

[15]Interview with Agence France Presse, February 3, 1964. Text in *Peking Review*, VII, No. 7 (February 14, 1964), p. 16.

blackmail. This is the correct and effective policy for achieving a ban on nuclear weapons and preventing a nuclear war. [16]

## THE LIKELIHOOD OF NUCLEAR WAR

There has been perhaps as much misunderstanding of the Chinese view on the likelihood of nuclear warfare as on the question of the consequences of nuclear warfare for the future of Communism. The Chinese have never claimed that nuclear war is inevitable, but they have denied that peace could be attained by a policy of conciliation and disarmament rather than by a policy of building up military strength and practicing militant opposition to imperialism. They have also differed with the Russians on the possibility and desirability of avoiding local wars and on the relationship between local wars and the likelihood of a general war.

The earliest statement by Mao Tse-tung on the possibility of avoiding world war was apparently made in a speech delivered on December 25, 1947, in which Mao declared: "If everyone makes strenuous efforts, we, together with all the democratic forces of the world, can surely defeat the imperialist plan of enslavement, prevent the outbreak of a third world war, overthrow all reactionary regimes and win lasting peace for mankind." [17] The Chinese have made no efforts to conceal their belief that war could be avoided. They have explicitly accepted the Khrushchevian reinterpretation of Leninism which holds that the socialist camp is now strong enough to prevent imperialism from launching a world war. In an article published in the *Peking Review* on November 1, 1963, in fact, the Western press was taken to task for failing to recognize that China as well as Russia accepted this modification of Leninism. The article declared:

It doesn't take the "free" Western press long to catch on! After years of harping on the theme of China's supposed "warlike intent" and theory of the "inevitability of war" — a game of make-believe in which the Soviet press has more

[16]"The Differences Between Comrade Togliatti and Us," *People's Daily*, December 31, 1962; translation in *Peking Review*, VI, No. 1 (January 4, 1963), pp. 12-13.

[17]"The Present Situation and Our Tasks." Dated December 25, 1947; printed in *Selected Works of Mao Tse-tung*, IV, 173.

recently joined—both the London and New York *Times* on October 2 made a brilliant discovery of the obvious.

Taking up a Reuters dispatch from Peking the two eminent *Times* displayed shock headlines: "China Hints at New Attitudes to War" and "Red China Eases Stand on Inevitability of War." They found their "new attitude" in the National Day speech of Peking's Mayor Peng Chen, who said that with world unity, "a new world war can be prevented, world peace can be preserved and the future of mankind is infinitely bright." This, they said, quoting Reuters' man in Peking, was seen by "observers" as "a new formulation of the Chinese attitude to the future of the world."

All we can say is that, like the "observers" in Peking, the *Times'* China experts have neglected their homework rather badly. Where have they been for the last three years— and longer? What Peng Chen said on National Day should not be news to anyone remotely concerned with China. For years China's leaders and newspapers have been saying that "world war can be prevented if the peoples of the world unite." [18]

The article goes on to quote statements by various Chinese Communist sources in 1960, 1961, and 1962, as well as the foregoing statement by Mao Tse-tung in 1947, to demonstrate quite amply that China has not for some time taken the line publicly that world war is inevitable. What then has been the difference between the Russians and the Chinese over the inevitability of war?

While accepting the proposition that a nuclear exchange between the United States and the Sino-Soviet bloc is not inevitable, the Chinese have argued that neither local wars nor wars of national liberation can be avoided. Local wars, they define, as did Khrushchev in his widely quoted speech of January 6, 1961, as wars started by the United States. Wars of national liberation, they define as wars started by indigenous Communist or nationalist forces. [19] Although Khrushchev in that statement and elsewhere spoke of the need to oppose local wars and to support wars of national liberation, the Russians have tended to argue that a very high probability of even wars of liberation exploding into general

---

[18]*Peking Review*, VI, No. 44 (November 1, 1963), pp. 19-20.

[19]The Khrushchev speech has been widely reprinted, as, for example, in Hudson, *et al.*, *The Sino-Soviet Dispute*, pp. 207-21. In this translation the discussion of kinds of war appears on pages 211-14.

nuclear war. The Chinese, on the other hand, have argued that this is
impossible:

> But it is one thing to prevent a world war and another to
> eliminate all wars. Imperialism and the reactionaries are the
> source of war. In conditions where imperialism and reac-
> tionaries still exist, it is possible that wars of one kind or
> another may occur. The history of the 17 postwar years shows
> that local wars of one kind or another have never ceased.
> Oppressed nations and oppressed people are bound to rise in
> revolution. When imperialism and the reactionaries employ
> armed forces to suppress revolution, it is inevitable that
> civil wars and national-liberation wars will occur. Marxist-
> Leninists have always maintained that only after the imperi-
> alist system has been overthrown and only after all systems
> of oppression of man by man and of exploitation of man by
> man have been abolished, and not before, will it be possible
> to eliminate all wars and to reach a "world without war." [20]

Thus the Chinese have two serious points of disagreement with the
Russians on wars below the level of general nuclear war. The Chinese
argue that the Sino-Soviet bloc must be prepared to give aid to groups
fighting wars of national liberation against imperialist and neo-imperialist
regimes. They also argue that it is necessary for the Sino-Soviet bloc to
counter any Western intervention in such conflicts with intervention of
their own. The Chinese appear to have specifically argued these points
in relation to the Algerian revolution and to events in the Middle East in
1958. They accuse the Soviets of being cowards who believe that a single
spark could ignite a nuclear war and therefore that it is necessary to
avoid intervention in any local war situation and to seek revolution by
peaceful means. The Chinese deny that nuclear weapons have changed
the basic obligations of socialist regimes:

> The leaders of the C.P.S.U. hold that with the appearance
> of nuclear weapons there is no longer any difference between
> just and unjust wars. . . .
> They hold that with the appearance of nuclear weapons
> the oppressed peoples and nations must abandon revolution
> and refrain from waging just popular revolutionary wars and
> wars of national liberation. . . .

[20]"The Differences Between Comrade Togliatti and Us," *Peking Review*
(January 4, 1963), p. 15.

> In short, according to the leaders of the C.P.S.U., with
> the emergence of nuclear weapons, the contradiction between
> the socialist and the imperialist camps, the contradiction
> between the proletariat and the bourgeoisie in the capitalist
> countries, and the contradiction between the oppressed
> nations and imperialism have all disappeared. . . . They regard
> the contradictions in the contemporary world as boiling down
> to a single contradiction, that is, their fictitious contradiction
> between the so-called common survival of imperialism and
> the oppressed classes and nations on the one hand and their
> total destruction on the other. [21]

Wars of national liberation must be supported, the Chinese argue,
because they are the only way in which Communist regimes can be in-
stalled. The Chinese point to the fact that Communist regimes have never
been established by peaceful takeover and that therefore to abandon
violence is to abandon the spread of revolution. They also argue that the
Russians very greatly overestimate the danger that any war of national
liberation or Soviet intervention in a local war would lead to general nuclear war. They say that the pressures against all-out war are very great
and that the Russians are being cowardly in retreating in the face of
Western action. The danger of nuclear war, the Chinese contend, can be
avoided through resolute and united action by the socialist camp but not
through an effort to appease the imperialist powers or to stress the importance of peaceful coexistence and the possibilities of disarmament. [22]
They claim that history in the postwar period has borne them out on this
point:

> In recent years, certain persons have been spreading the
> argument that a single spark from a war of national liberation
> or from a revolutionary people's war will lead to a world con-
> flagration destroying the whole of mankind. What are the
> facts? Contrary to what these persons say, the wars of

---

[21] "Two Different Lines on the Question of War and Peace—Comment on the
Open Letter of the Central Committee of the CPSU (V)." Dated November 19,
1963; translation in *Peking Review*, VI, No. 47 (November 22, 1963), pp.
11-12. Reprinted from same source in Griffith, *The Sino-Soviet Rift*, Document
16, p. 485.

[22] By putting the "united" in their formula for action, the Chinese leave themselves free to criticize the Soviet Union for "adventurism," as they did in the
Cuba crisis, and to advocate the spread of nuclear weapons to China, as
discussed in a later section.

national liberation and the revolutionary people's wars that
have occurred since World War II have not led to world war.
The victory of these revolutionary wars has directly weakened
the forces of imperialism and greatly strengthened the forces
which prevent the imperialists from launching a world war
and which defend world peace. Do not the facts demonstrate
the absurdity of this argument? [23]

Local wars and wars of national liberation, then, Peking argues, are
not only inevitable but desirable and necessary to expand the area of
Communism. History demonstrates, say the Chinese, that, instead of
being as dangerous as the Russians have suggested, "popular" wars do
not lead to general nuclear war. On the contrary, the failure of the Sino-
Soviet bloc to take an aggressive stance only encourages the Western
powers and makes war more likely. General nuclear war, the Chinese
agree, can and must be prevented by the unity and action of the socialist
camp. Other forms of warfare are desirable, and it is only an absurd fear
of their explosion into general nuclear war which keeps the Soviets from
rendering the proper assistance to national-liberation movements.


## THE ROLE OF THE STRATEGIC BALANCE

Far from deprecating the role of nuclear weapons in influencing the
course of international politics, the Chinese, if anything, have tended
to overestimate the importance of the strategic nuclear balance. They
were apparently very conscious of the great danger posed for them by
the American atomic monopoly. They greeted the announcement of Russia's first nuclear test with obvious relief: "The Soviet Union has recently
declared that she had atomic weapons for some time already. This declaration is a heavy blow to the instigators of atomic war. Thus it is clear
that we will certainly have sufficient strength to pulverize all the criminal plots of the warmongers." [24] During 1951 and 1952, the Chinese

---

[23]"A Proposal Concerning the General Line of the International Communist
Movement: The Letter of the Central Committee of the Communist Party of
China in Reply to the Letter of the Central Committee of the Communist
Party of the Soviet Union of March 30, 1963." Dated June 14, 1963; translation
in *Peking Review* VI, No. 25 (June 21, 1963), p. 14. Reprinted from same
source in Griffith, *The Sino-Soviet Rift*, Document 2, p. 274.

[24]Radio Peking, International Service in English Morse to North America,
October 4, 1949.

apparently became increasingly nervous because of the signs of development of a U.S. thermonuclear capability. It was with great relief that the
Chinese were the first to announce openly the Soviet H-bomb test in
August, 1953, breaking a three-year silence about hydrogen weapons.
Even then, recognition of continued American superiority in nuclear
weapons from 1955 on led to growing public discussion and apparently
official concern about the ever-increasing American stockpile of strategic
nuclear weapons.

The period of extreme Chinese fear of the nuclear imbalance came to
a halt suddenly in 1957 with the launching of a Soviet Sputnik and the
Soviet ICBM test. The Chinese concluded that a fundamental change had
taken place in the psychological balance of power and would soon take
place in the military balance, so that the East wind was now prevailing
over the West wind. Addressing the Moscow Conference on November 18,
1957, Mao declared:

> It is my opinion that the international situation has now
> reached a new turning point. There are two winds in the world
> today, the East wind and the West wind. There is a Chinese
> saying, "Either the East wind prevails over the West wind
> or the West wind prevails over the East wind." *It is char-
> acteristic of the situation today,* I believe, *that the East
> wind is prevailing over the West wind. That is to say, the
> forces of socialism are overwhelmingly superior to the forces
> of imperialism.* [25]

Beginning in 1957, the Chinese urged the Soviets to take advantage
of the changing strategic balance and to press on for the victory of
socialism. By 1960, the Chinese began to have second thoughts about the
effect of the change in the strategic balance in 1957. It was not that they
doubted that a fundamental change in the strategic situation had occurred.
Rather, they came to recognize that the Soviets were not inclined to share
the radical Chinese estimate of the change in the strategic balance and
were not prepared to press the political advantages that seemed to stem
from the new military situation. On the contrary, the Russians seemed to
be moving toward a détente with the West, using their new military strength
as a means of effecting a political settlement which would leave unful-
filled the Chinese demands for Taiwan and recognition as a major world

---

[25]Quoted in "Statement by the Spokesman of the Chinese Government—A Comment on the Soviet Government's Statement of August 21," *Peking Review*
(September 6, 1963), p. 10, italics in *Peking Review.*

power and would materially undermine the progress of revolutionary movements around the world. At the same time the Chinese were alarmed by the evidence that the United States was increasing the size of its defense budget and might soon redress the strategic balance which the Chinese believed incorrectly was then in the favor of the Soviet Union.[26]

It seems clear that the Chinese very much overestimated the change in strategic balance in 1957 and that they have never been informed in great detail by the Soviets as to the nature of the balance. The Soviets have in fact accused the Chinese of speaking out of ignorance:

> Of course we cannot now divulge such things as, for instance, the concrete results of the nuclear weapon tests we carried out in 1961-62, information on the calibres of the nuclear warheads in our arsenal, the purpose of specific nuclear combat devices of which the Soviet Union has an abundance, where these combat devices are deployed, and so forth. That would be against the security interests of the Soviet Union and of all the socialist states, including the security interests of the People's Republic of China.
>
> And if the Chinese leaders, in saying that in recent years the situation has not changed but the USSR policy on a test ban has, thus try[ing] in a way to provoke the Soviet Union to demonstrate clearly the changes in the balance of nuclear strength in recent years and for this purpose to divulge the defence secrets of USSR, we can tell them one thing only: *while you are talking about your concern to strengthen the defence of the socialist countries, you are in actual fact playing the role of those who do not cherish the security interests of the socialist community but are ready to play into the hands of the forces of imperialist reaction.* The Chinese leaders cannot be unaware of the fact that obtaining really reliable information on Soviet nuclear and missile

---

[26]This interpretation of the Chinese attitude in 1960, as well as the more general assertion of the significance which the Chinese attach to the overall strategic balance, is based on A. M. Halpern, "Communist China and Peaceful Coexistence," *China Quarterly*, No. 3 (July-September, 1960), pp. 16-31. The original RAND version of this paper bore the more descriptive title "Why Are the Chinese Nervous?" (RAND, P-1987, July 5, 1960).

weapons is exactly what the military staffs of certain powers and aggressive military blocs dream of.[27]

By 1963, then, in attempting to justify the decision to sign the nuclear test ban, the Soviets were arguing that the balance of military force had changed from the earlier period when they felt that a three-environment test ban treaty would not be in their interests. They argue that the change in the balance makes possible peaceful coexistence and economic and political competition for the underdeveloped areas, rather than the kind of aggressive policy urged by the Chinese. The Chinese, on the other hand, have now been put in the position of at least suggesting that there has been no change in the balance between 1961-1962 and 1963, when the Test Ban Treaty was signed.


## THE NEED FOR A CHINESE NUCLEAR CAPABILITY

The Chinese desire for a national nuclear capability stems fundamentally from the aspiration to make China a great power. More specifically, the Chinese leaders have been motivated by: (1) the wish to exercise greater influence within the Communist world, (2) the desire for a more credible deterrent against an American attack, (3) the feeling that the Soviets are not willing to capitalize on their capability to oppose the West and in particular are unwilling to support wars of liberation, and (4) the desire for an additional means for establishing Chinese hegemony in Asia.

In their first formal reaction to the Test Ban Treaty, in which they proposed the complete prohibition and destruction of nuclear weapons, the Chinese demonstrated their opposition to Soviet as well as American efforts to dominate the world by maintaining a nuclear monopoly:

> In the eyes of U.S. imperialism, the countries of the world are divided into two categories: those which possess nuclear weapons and those which do not. The few nuclear powers, as a matter of course, are the masters of the world, whereas the countries which do not possess nuclear weapons are, to quote Kennedy, irresponsible and unstable, so that

[27] "Statement of the Soviet Government." Dated August 21, 1963; translation in *Moscow News*. Reprinted in *Peking Review* (September 6, 1963), p. 19. Italics in *Peking Review* reprinted from the Chinese text appearing in *People's Daily*, September 1, 1963. Reprinted from *Soviet News*, August 21, 1963, in Griffith, *The Sino-Soviet Rift*, Document 8, p. 380.

they are by no means qualified to possess nuclear weapons, nor can they have any say in the matter. In other words, those countries which do not possess nuclear weapons and the broad masses of people of the world must be left for ever to the tender mercies of others, and doomed to be the object of nuclear blackmail and nuclear threats.

. . . . . . . . . . . . . . . .

To speak frankly, if in this matter in international relations the principle followed is righteousness and justice and not tyranny and brute force, then no nuclear power has any right to dictate to any non-nuclear power—it has only the duty to submit itself to the demand of the people of all countries of the world for the complete prohibition and thorough destruction of nuclear weapons.

There are more than 130 countries in the world. All countries, big or small, nuclear or non-nuclear, are equal. It is absolutely impermissible for two or three countries to brandish their nuclear weapons at will, issue orders and commands, and lord it over in the world as self-ordained nuclear overlords, while the overwhelming majority of countries are expected to kneel and obey orders meekly, as if they were nuclear slaves. [28]

The Chinese have accused the Russians of desiring not only to control all the nuclear weapons within the Communist camp but also, as a consequence, to monopolize the right to speak on questions of nuclear weapons and nuclear policy within the bloc.[29] The Peking regime has clearly decided that in order to have equal influence with the Soviet Union inside the socialist camp, China will have to develop an indigenous nuclear capability. It has concluded from observing Soviet pressure to prevent the Chinese development of such a capability, as well as the corresponding efforts by the United States to halt diffusion within the capitalist camp, that in fact even a small, primitive force of nuclear weapons serves as an important source of intra-alliance power.

[28]"People of the World, Unite! Strive for the Complete Prohibition and Thorough Destruction of Nuclear Weapons!" *People's Daily*, August 2, 1963; translation in *Peking Review*, VI, No. 32 (August 9, 1963), p. 8.

[29]"Statement by the Spokesman of the Chinese Government—A Comment on the Soviet Government's Statement of August 3." Dated August 15, 1963; translation in *Peking Review*, VI, No. 33 (August 16, 1963), p. 8. Reprinted from same source in Griffith, *The Sino-Soviet Rift*, Document 7, p. 340.

## DETERRING AN AMERICAN ATTACK

Another basic Chinese motive for acquiring a national nuclear capability is that it would reduce the likelihood of nuclear blackmail by the United States against socialist countries and in particular against China. The Chinese argument here in part is simply that the more socialist countries which have nuclear weapons, the more successful is deterrence likely to be—an argument analogous to that advanced by certain groups in Britain and France.[30] The Chinese have also quarreled with the Russians as to the extent of support which the Soviet Union has been willing to give to China in terms of nuclear deterrence in past crises. The Chinese are likely to seek to deter the United States by threatening to make nuclear attacks on Asian countries.

The Chinese argument that the spread of nuclear weapons to socialist countries other than the Soviet Union would increase deterrence and reduce the likelihood of nuclear blackmail was stated frequently, even before the time that it became clear that a nuclear test ban was in the offing. The *People's Daily,* on August 9, 1962, noted that China had consistently opposed nuclear tests and had favored the banning of nuclear weapons but was not foregoing such weapons for herself:

> We hold . . . that when imperialism is stubbornly hindering and opposing agreement on the suspension of nuclear tests and the prohibition of nuclear weapons and is using such weapons to threaten the people of the world, the socialist countries, to ensure the security of the socialist camp and defend world peace, naturally must possess nuclear weapons, and, moreover, nuclear weapons of better quality than those of U.S. imperialism.
>
> The socialist countries love peace; nuclear weapons in their hands and nuclear tests conducted by them are entirely different in nature from nuclear weapons in the hands of the imperialist bloc and nuclear tests conducted by that bloc. The possession of nuclear weapons and the carrying out of nuclear tests by the socialist countries can only be a telling blow against the imperialist policy of the nuclear arms drive and nuclear blackmail and therefore helps to prevent war; it will help force imperialism to accept some kind of agreement on the discontinuance of nuclear testing and the prohibition

[30]The Chinese have sometimes argued that *any* increase in the number of countries possessing nuclear weapons is desirable.

of nuclear weapons and so will help the cause of world peace.[31]

This is a position that would suggest that nuclear weapons are necessary for China not because of any breakdown in the Sino-Soviet alliance but merely because they add to the credibility of bloc deterrence. However, the Chinese have gone beyond this to argue that the Soviets have tried to use their nuclear dominance to control the socialist camp and have not put nuclear weapons at the disposal of the other socialist countries or cast a protective umbrella over wars of national liberations when they should. In addition, the Chinese have suggested that since the aim of the test ban agreement is apparently a détente with the West, in the future the Soviets are even less likely to be willing to use their nuclear strength to promote the aims of other socialist countries and perhaps to protect them against American nuclear threats. At present, however, the Chinese assert that Russia will in fact come to China's aid in the event of an American attack. Thus Chou En-lai told newsmen in Cairo in December, 1963, that "in the event of emergency, the Chinese and Soviet peoples will without fail stand by each other, shoulder-to-shoulder, hand-in-hand."[32]

[31]Abridged translation in *Peking Review*, V, No. 33 (August 17, 1962), p. 10.

[32]Text in *Peking Review*, VI, No. 52 (December 27, 1963), p. 14.

# V PROLIFERATION

Preventing the proliferation of nuclear weapons was a major concern of the United States for many years before the first Chinese atomic explosion, and it remains so. The issue dealt with here is how the event of October 16, 1964, has affected American hopes with regard to the spread of these weapons of mass destruction. From the outset, it is useful to distinguish between three types of proliferation involving China: proliferation of nuclear weapons (including delivery systems) to China, proliferation around the borders of China, and proliferation from China to other nations.

The Chinese explosion of a nuclear device changed the character of the problem of proliferation to China but did not eliminate it. Now, of course, if indeed prevention was ever possible, China cannot be kept from possessing atomic and hydrogen bombs.[1] It is still possible, however, for China to receive outside support in the development of more advanced bombs and delivery systems. Such support could lower costs and eliminate technological bottlenecks in various advanced weapons programs and thus greatly accelerate China's attainment of a substantial nuclear capability.

The fact that Peking has already joined the "nuclear club" might actually make it easier for a country like France to justify nuclear assistance since it could be put in the context of mutual assistance between existing atomic powers on the Anglo-American model. This is not the place to discuss whether sharing of this type is likely to be in the interests of France or any other nation, nor is it a proper context in which to analyze how a country with such proclivities can be influenced to abstain from proliferation to China. This is a job for specialists on France, the Soviet Union, etc. Here it is only worthwhile pointing out that non-proliferation agreements properly worded, with or without the participation of China herself, still have relevance to the Chinese situation.

## PROLIFERATION IN ASIA

Of more immediate interest is the question whether Peking's possession of nuclear weapons will make more likely the development of

[1]This discussion does not consider the question of whether or not China's nuclear capacity might be removed by means other than an international agreement, because that subject does not come under a discussion of arms control.

atomic capabilities by other nations, particularly in Asia. Closely related to this is the issue of whether opposition to the further spread of nuclear weapons in Asia continues to be in the interest of the United States.

At present, and probably for the next decade or two, there are only three Pacific-area nations capable of developing nuclear weapons on their own: India, Japan, and Australia.[2] Any of these countries could want a nuclear capability for reasons of military security, national prestige, or a variety of other factors, rational or otherwise. What they do want or are likely to want in the future is the subject for other studies, but there are several calculations that they may make which are particularly relevant to China and to American policy toward China.

The first such calculation has to do with whether possession of nuclear weapons would increase or decrease the military security of any Asian nation vis-à-vis China.[3] The legitimacy in the French position on their need for a nuclear capability is based on the fear that the United States, under certain circumstances, may not be willing to risk its own total destruction in order to come to the aid of Europe. This argument in turn depends on the existence of a nuclear stalemate between America and the Soviet Union or at least a Soviet capacity to destroy much of the United States. But no such stalemate exists now, or is likely to exist for some time, between the United States and China. India and the others need have no fear that American nuclear might will not be used in their defense, because China is unable to damage the United States significantly.

American nuclear power will be available to Asians, however, only insofar as coming to the aid of Asians is deemed to be in the American national interest. The defense of India against a major Chinese invasion would be clearly in the interest of the United States. In the case of Japan and Australia, the U.S. is obliged by treaty to come to their aid. However, Asian countries desiring to embark on aggressive policies of their own, vis-à-vis China, in contrast to simply deterring Chinese action, might find it necessary to have their own nuclear arsenal. An Indian government that wanted to recover the Aksai Chin area of Ladakh by force might find itself in such a position, although even with nuclear weapons the prospects for success of such an effort would be remote. Similar situations involving Japan and Australia and having some degree of realism are even harder to imagine. Real military security calculations,

[2]There is also a possibility that Indonesia may be able to develop an atomic bomb.

[3]This discussion is not concerned with such questions as whether possession of nuclear weapons would increase India's security vis-à-vis Pakistan, etc.

therefore, shouldn't loom large in any decision by these countries to favor development of their own nuclear weapons.[4]

Also weighing against proliferation will be domestic economic and political calculations. The cost of a nuclear weapons program may have more serious consequences for democratic India than it has ever had for totalitarian China. If India paid for an expanded program out of existing tax revenues, economic development expenditures would have to be cut back. If, alternatively, taxes were raised, there could be serious political unrest. The "opportunity" costs for Japan and Australia would undoubtedly be less, but there might be undesirable political consequences unrelated to economic cost.[5]

These, however, are speculations that cannot be pursued here. Suffice it to say that domestic economic and political calculations are likely to work against proliferation.

## NATIONAL PRESTIGE CONSIDERATIONS

A consideration that under certain circumstances could outweigh all the others is that of national prestige or the desire of a country to be thought of as a great power and treated accordingly. In this sphere the effects of the Chinese nuclear program and the response to it could be felt in varying degrees far beyond the borders of Asia. If the dozen or more powers that today, or within the next decade, could develop a nuclear capacity were to feel that only through such development could they expect to be treated as a great power, the impetus toward proliferation would be very great. It is just such a consideration that has kept Great Britain from abandoning its nuclear force and has caused France to build a *force de frappe*. It is also a prime impetus behind Chinese efforts. Treating China as a great power because of its possession of a *force de frappe* of its own would only accentuate this tendency to think of atomic capability and great-power status as synonomous.

There are two aspects to the issue: first, does a nuclear capability automatically make a country a great power; and, second, can a nation be

---

[4]This analysis in no way implies that essentially false military security arguments may not be made and listened to.

[5]It is still a question, for example, whether Japanese reactions to an attempt by their government to develop a bomb might have serious domestic political consequences. Several people at the follow-up Conference felt that Japanese attitudes had changed radically since the first Chinese explosion: others were not as sure the changes had been great.

a great power without a nuclear capacity? The answer to the first question depends on what one means by a "great power." Certainly a *force de frappe* does not give a nation the kind of power possessed by the United States and the Soviet Union, whatever de Gaulle might think. Canada or Australia with a hydrogen bomb is not thereby going to become a major force throughout the world, a fact of which Canada appears to be more aware than most others. Egypt with the bomb would complicate the Middle Eastern situation enormously, as would the more likely prospect of an Israeli bomb. Possession, however, would not give Egypt greater influence over events in Vietnam or probably even in South Africa. Similarly China with the bomb need have no more influence over events in the Middle East than it has at present.

The more interesting question is whether great-power status is possible without the bomb.[6] Superpower status, of course, requires hydrogen bombs and missiles in great quantity. If a few bombs do not allow a country to at least deter the superpowers from using their forces under some circumstances, then there is little but prestige and a very limited ability to influence one's immediate neighbors in having a few bombs. A small arsenal will not make it easier to exercise economic power in the world, and might make it even more difficult if the nuclear program is sufficiently expensive. Both Japan and India, for example, because of their size, and in Japan's case its high degree of economic development, have reason for desiring and expecting great-power status in the sense of having influence over major decisions taken in Asia or in any other area where their interests are affected. Neither country, however, can expect this influence because of its military power alone, with or without nuclear weapons. The key issue, therefore, is whether possession of nuclear weapons would cause Japanese and Indian voices to be heard when great decisions were being made.

The one way in which Japan and India can achieve the ability to influence world decisions is for those who are making decisions to take Japanese and Indian views into account. Many such decisions are made within the country involved, as is the case, for example, with many aspects of the revolutionary situation in Vietnam (the Diem government's policy toward the Buddhists, etc.). These decisions can be influenced from outside only by military and economic power and, on rare occasions, moral suasion brought to bear on the local scene. Other kinds of decisions, however, are taken by the superpowers. Since many of these decisions have wide ramifications throughout the world, the powers making them

---

[6]The conferees at Airlie House disagreed about this. Some thought it impossible; others thought it possible for certain countries.

often consult with their friends and allies before plunging ahead. Consultation is considered necessary because, without it, alliances would tend to fall apart and friendly countries might work at cross purposes. The extent to which any particular country is consulted in large part determines the power which that country can wield. There is no need for the extent of consultation to depend on a nation's possession of a small nuclear arsenal. Treating China as a great power because it possesses nuclear weapons, however, would tend to make other nations think this was the case and act accordingly. Such feelings could be partly offset by an active United States effort to treat the country without nuclear weapons as a great power by constant consultation.

The degree to which the United States and other powers can feasibly carry out such a plan, however, should not be exaggerated. Carried to its logical extreme it would mean not making any adjustments in policy whatsoever because of China's bomb. Efforts to bring China into a nonproliferation agreement, beyond simply presenting Peking with a paper which it could sign or reject, for example, could be ruled out on such grounds. Even if United States policy makers consistently ignore Chinese nuclear weapons, at least in public, others will not, for various reasons of their own. Whether or not great-power status is possible without nuclear weapons, other potential nuclear powers are certain to see that China's bomb has, in fact, enhanced her influence in world affairs, and this is bound to have an effect.

### NUCLEAR AID FROM CHINA

The third major problem with respect to proliferation in Asia, is that China might decide to aid others to develop their own nuclear weapons or give them weapons outright.[7] Peking will certainly have the capacity to do this within a few years and in some areas (training of nuclear scientists, etc.) could begin immediately. The more interesting question is whether there is a will as well as a way.

The answer to this latter question would appear to be a qualified yes. China has continually looked for areas in which she has a comparative advantage, guerrilla action, certain types of propaganda activity, etc. Supplying "less responsible" nations with nuclear weapons could

---

[7]Another possibility is that China might station nuclear weapons in a country, conceivably even without sufficient safeguards against their falling into local hands.

prove to be just such an area. What China would get in return would depend on circumstances, but a country such as Indonesia under Sukarno might be willing to pay a heavy price for Chinese help. Peking might even gain simply from the instability that such a move could engender. Egypt with nuclear weapons would have a clearly destabilizing influence on the Middle East without much increasing the danger to China. Pakistan's possession of the bomb would put great pressure on India, but the results in this case would not necessarily prove favorable to Peking. Many other examples could be cited. China's justification for such action would undoubtedly include the same arguments she has used to justify her own possession of nuclear weapons, i.e., the more socialist nations, "anti-imperialist nations," that have nuclear weapons, the greater will be the security of the world, since the main threat to peace comes from the "imperialists." In fact, the frequency with which Peking has used this argument might cause Mao's regime some embarrassment if it refused to give nuclear aid to its allies when asked.


## AMERICAN INTERESTS

Granted, therefore, that China's possession of nuclear weapons will significantly increase the possibility of proliferation, particularly in Asia, there remains the issue of whether opposition to proliferation is still in American interests and, if so, what the United States can do about it.

The reasons for arguing that opposition to proliferation continues to be in the American interest are numerous. Many are readily implied in what was said above. If the spread of nuclear weapons doesn't enhance military security in Asia, then it in no way supports other United States efforts directed to that end. The high cost of atomic programs means either reduced economic development in the region or more economic aid from the industrial powers (which may be harder to get because Congressmen and others who control the purse strings may take a jaundiced view of nuclear expenditures). There is also the probability that the spread of nuclear weapons, once started, will become a stampede as more countries feel they must match the military prowess of their neighbors and rivals.

Finally, proliferation could complicate American military actions in the Far East. The problem is not so much one of increasing the chances of all-out nuclear war. It is more a question of creating military situations in which the United States could be faced with several choices, all of them bad. For example, an attack by Chinese conventional forces on India, if successful, might cause India to use its nuclear weapons against

China. China might in turn retaliate by using nuclear weapons against India. An Indian rather than Chinese decision to escalate would create great difficulties for American policy makers. A blanket American guarantee to use nuclear weapons in the defense of India whenever India was under nuclear attack from China would give the Indian government the power to determine the use of the American nuclear arsenal. Even if the United States promised to defend India against China only if the latter were the first to use nuclear weapons, there would still be the problem of deciding whether an Indian first attack was deliberate escalation or an attempt to get in ahead of an expected Chinese attack. Another difficult situation, unlikely though it might be, would be one in which India launched a conventional attack against China and China replied with nuclear weapons in its own defense. None of these problems, except possibly the last, would arise if China were the only country possessing nuclear weapons. There would be no question of who was responsible for first use of nuclear weapons, although there would still be some question as to what the United States response should be in the last example cited. If China used an atomic bomb against an invasion force from Taiwan, for example, the American response is far from obvious.[8]

## AMERICAN POLICY

If it clearly remains in the interest of the United States to prevent proliferation in Asia, there is still the much more difficult problem of how. There are a variety of programs available.

One such program already discussed is that of playing down the significance of China's nuclear arsenal and taking steps to dissociate nuclear weapons from great-power status. To the extent the problem is one of military security, the U.S. can renew guarantees, make new ones, shift forces around to back up these guarantees or make them convincing, etc. In many cases, these steps are presently being taken. President Johnson's speech following the Sinkiang blast was in this general vein. As already indicated, however, these steps are not likely to be sufficient if the pressures for proliferation are great.

The measures with the greatest chance of success are those directed at specific countries on an individual basis. Such measures include everything from greater economic aid to a variety of economic and political

---

[8] Because of these considerations, there was a consensus among the conferees at Airlie House that proliferation of nuclear weapons in Asia was not the solution to security problems arising from China's possession of the bomb.

sanctions. What these should be and under what circumstances they should be used, however, is, as in several other instances mentioned above, a question for specialists on the countries concerned.

## A NON-PROLIFERATION AGREEMENT WITH CHINA

Finally, there is the whole question of dealing directly with China as a means of putting obstacles in the path of proliferation. The issue of dealing directly with China is, of course, not simply concerned with proliferation, but it is useful here to treat it as such. Furthermore, it is desirable to look only at the China-connected aspects of any contemplated agreement.

There are two key questions. Would it be to the advantage of the United States to have Chinese participation in a non-proliferation agreement, and would the Chinese be willing to participate? From the American point of view, if nothing else, the agreement would inhibit nuclear assistance from China to her friends and allies. Once signed, Peking might still consider violating the agreement's terms, but this would be difficult to do without detection. In addition, a formal treaty of this type might provide the Chinese with an adequate excuse for not giving nuclear assistance to others clamoring for it. If it did, such an agreement would presumably be in China's interest as well, at least on this ground.

Peking also might see an advantage in a non-proliferation agreement that clearly recognized China as one of the great powers. Such recognition, of course, could undermine United States attempts to play down the relationship between nuclear weapons and great-power status. From China's point of view, any treaty with the United States, particularly one directed specifically, although not exclusively, at the underdeveloped world, tends to undermine its revolutionary image, but these effects might be largely offset by the underdeveloped world's generally favorable reaction to all steps designed to control nuclear weapons. Lest too optimistic a conclusion be drawn from these remarks, however, it must be pointed out that China is presently on record as opposing all non-proliferation agreements (see Chapter IX).

Even if all the above suggested steps are taken, proliferation in Asia and elsewhere may still occur. The main problem, therefore, may not be prevention of proliferation so much as learning to live in a world where possession of nuclear weapons is widespread and where China is one of the countries with such weapons.

# VI CONVENTIONAL WAR

Despite the emphasis which the Peking regime has put on guerrilla warfare and the substantial resources that it is apparently devoting to the development of a nuclear capability, the Chinese, as indicated in Chapter III, have not neglected conventional forces. In terms of numbers of men under arms, China probably has the largest conventional army in the world, and China has developed the capacity to produce at least the essential weapons needed by its ground, air, and naval forces.

Mao's military doctrine is frequently emphasized as being a strategy of guerrilla warfare—providing a means by which a small but determined group, through protracted warfare, can take over a country. However, that this military doctrine calls at the end for conventional operations is frequently overlooked. Mao has recognized, in other words, that the culmination of a successful guerrilla operation is development of a force capable of engaging in conventional military warfare. This is the third stage, when the enemy is in retreat and the revolutionary group attacks and captures the country by conventional warfare. It is true that even in this stage Mao envisions using guerrillas and guerrilla operations, as was done in the Chinese Civil War. Nevertheless, Mao's doctrine itself and its implementation in China called for and led to the creation of large-scale forces more or less conventionally organized and employed in conventional ground military operations.

Thus, the guerrilla forces that Mao formed in the early days of the Chinese Communist Party were gradually molded into regular fighting units. The end of the Civil War saw the Peking regime in control of a very large force which had just won a substantial conventional war.

The Chinese had to regroup their armies and turn them to the new task of supporting a regime now fighting to maintain power and to industrialize the country. At the same time, the leadership was confronted with problems of maintaining military power in the nuclear age.

Despite substantial transformation that had gone on before 1949, these tasks required further and rapid modernization and professionalization of the People's Liberation Army, as it is called, in order to turn it into a regular and effective force. This process has produced a number of strains, both within the military and between the military and the Party, but through the twists and turns of internal debate and political maneuvering the Chinese have maintained a very large conventional military establishment. We now turn our attention to the Peking regime's uses of these conventional forces.

During the past fifteen years, the military has had a large role in China. The leadership of the Chinese Communist Party, it should be remembered, consists almost entirely of men who fought actively in the PLA, men who were soldiers as well as political leaders. Thus the Peking regime is in the habit of thinking and speaking in military terms. In addition, the leadership has had to look to the army for active participation in internal activities. At the same time, the army increasingly has performed traditional functions in relation to problems of external security.

The first use to which the Peking regime put the army was as a source for the recruitment of virtually its entire top leadership. In 1949, when the Communists took control of China, the Party and the PLA at the top level were inseparable. The top leaders of the army simply moved over and became the top leaders of the government, most of them leaving their military positions but others staying on to direct the army.

The Peking regime has also looked to the army to provide inspiration to the people as a symbol of the kind of devotion the leadership expects in its effort to turn China into a developed society. The army has also been used for civic action programs, similar in a way to the work performed by the Army Corps of Engineers in the United States. Conversely, many individuals in China have been incorporated into the militia, providing a civilian backup to the army, presumably for use in the event of a major invasion or internal threat.

The size of the Chinese standing army is difficult to explain without taking into account the substantial role it has played in insuring internal security. In the years after 1949 it was crucially involved in mopping up remaining resistance and suppressing potential resistance. The use of the army in this role suggests the limits to which the Chinese would be prepared to go in reduction of conventional forces. Even if no other problems stood in the way, the perceived need of the army for internal purposes and particularly for internal security would probably make the Chinese reluctant to accept any proposals for substantial reduction in their standing forces.

Undoubtedly, the most important task that has been entrusted to Chinese conventional forces is that of defending the territory of China against possible invasion, either by Chinese Nationalist forces from Taiwan, or by American forces, or by a combination of the two. Chinese military doctrine, as revealed in the secret *Work Bulletins*, places heavy emphasis on defensive training against enemy invasion of China, including apparently at least some training against invasion involving the use of nuclear weapons as well as biological weapons. The Chinese Communists have moved swiftly to crush any attempts of small-scale landings by the Chinese Nationalists and in 1964 demonstrated a willingness to move a very substantial number of conventional forces to Fukien Province in order to deter any possibility of a Chinese Nationalist attempt to land on the Chinese mainland. The Chinese army, therefore, appears to have been designed primarily for the roles of maintaining internal order and defending China against possible external attack. This is not to say, however, that the army has not been important as a positive instrument of foreign policy nor that the Chinese are not prepared to use force beyond their own borders when necessary.

In fact the Chinese armed forces have served as a major instrument, if a subtly employed one, of Chinese foreign policy. The reputation of the Chinese army, because of China's traditional position as the major land power of Asia, was further enhanced by the impressive Chinese Communist defeat of the Chinese Nationalist forces which had received substantial American aid particularly in the period 1946-1949. The Chinese ability to hold the United States to a standstill on the Korean peninsula also added substantially to the reputation of Chinese Communist conventional forces, as did the rout of the Indians in 1962 on the Sino-Indian border. Today the Chinese army is thought of as clearly the most powerful ground force in Asia, one which cannot be stopped, even with substantial assistance from the United States without using nuclear weapons. This "fact," although open to skepticism in relation to most of the territories bordering on China, has served as an important instrument in the implementation of China's policy of securing hegemony over her neighbors. The leaders of Asian countries, such as Burma and Cambodia, which border on or appear to be within easy reach of China, and even the leaders of Communist states, North Korea and North Vietnam, probably take it for granted that China can, with the use of her mass land army, move in and conquer their territory any time that she decides to do so. They assume that the only thing that could stop China would be massive use of American nuclear power, an action that might well mean destruction of their own territory. In addition, American policy has caused the leaders of at least Cambodia and Burma to conclude that the United States was probably not prepared to wage war in their defense. Thus the Chinese, while seldom threatening to use it, have managed to make their large standing army a major instrument of foreign policy.

Finally, it must be noted that the Chinese *have* on certain occasions been willing to use their conventional forces beyond the borders of China. However, before looking at these instances, and the rationale that may have been behind them, we shall examine the strong pressures which have limited such use to a very few cases.

The most important determinant of the caution with which the Chinese have used their very large conventional forces would appear to be the possibility of provoking an American nuclear attack against China. Certainly in the early years of the regime, the Chinese had some reason to fear that either as a result of action on their part, such as intervention in the Korean War, or simply as the result of the American alliance with the Chinese Nationalists, the United States would decide to launch a major attack on China, relying on its airpower and its nuclear weapons. The Chinese are probably less fearful now than they were in the past of an unprovoked American attack on China and less fearful that the United States would attack in order to support a Chinese Nationalist landing. They are undoubtedly still fearful of provoking the United States into military action, possibly by the development of a major nuclear capability, but most important has been their concern that their own conventional operations would lead to intervention and ultimately to an American attack on China.

The Chinese apparently took the massive retaliation threats made by John Foster Dulles and others in the Eisenhower administration much more seriously than either the Russians or most American commentators. The Chinese saw American policy as expressing actual willingness to employ nuclear weapons and perhaps to engage in attacks directly against the Chinese mainland in retaliation for Chinese support of local military actions. This may account for Chinese pressure on the North Vietnamese to accept at the 1954 Geneva Conference less than they had won on the battlefield. Since at least 1954 the Chinese have been very sensitive to American nuclear deployment in the Pacific.

Another reason that the Chinese have been relatively restrained in using military forces beyond their borders may be that they perceive that such use is not very valuable. Maoist doctrine places great emphasis on internal conditions within any country and the need to wait for the proper moment to attempt a revolution. The Chinese would agree with the current Soviet view that revolution cannot be exported, at least not exported by a conventional military force.

Nevertheless, the Chinese have resorted to the external use of military force on several occasions, and their objectives at these times should be explored. A distinction should be made between relatively minor use and major use of Chinese conventional military power. The Chinese have resorted to relatively minor use of military force or explicit threats of the use of minor military force in the Taiwan Straits on several different occasions and during the Sino-Indian border clashes. These uses appear to be related to very specific political objectives. They show that the Chinese are willing to use military force in a limited

way for political purposes, provided they do not run great risks of provoking the United States and do not use large economic resources in the
endeavor.

The objectives behind each of the Chinese Communist uses of limited
force will be explored briefly.[1]

The Chinese Communists launched heavy military action against the
offshore islands of Quemoy in 1949, 1954-1955, 1958, and 1960. In 1962
they raised the threat of such action by mobilizing very large numbers of
troops opposite Taiwan and the offshore islands. The first instance of
Chinese military action in 1949 was simply a continuation of the Civil
War and an effort by the Chinese Communists to bring as much Chinese
territory as possible under their control while destroying Nationalist
forces. The defeat of the Chinese Communist forces attempting to take
Quemoy was the only substantial military victory for the Nationalists
during 1949 and focused the attention of both Chinese Communists and
Nationalists on the offshore islands.

In 1954-1955, the Chinese launched their first major artillery barrage
against the offshore islands. This action was apparently in some sense a
response to the formation of the SEATO alliance by the United States. In
addition, in the aftermath of the Geneva Indochina armistice negotiations
of 1954, the Chinese Communists wanted to remind the world that there
still were unsolved political disputes in which they were prepared to use
military force. The Chinese action coming at the time the U.S.-Chinese
Nationalist Security Treaty was being negotiated also may have been intended to remind the American government, Congress in particular, of the
dangers and problems that might be involved in such an arrangement.

In 1958, the Chinese launched what was apparently their most determined effort to capture the island of Quemoy. At that time they acted with
the apparent expectation that the capture of Quemoy, if it could be
accomplished without American intervention, might so undermine morale
on Taiwan that it would make possible a takeover of Taiwan by some
form of political subversion. At the end of this crisis the Chinese in-
stituted two procedures which they have followed ever since. The first is
the issuing of "serious warnings" about violation of Chinese sea or air
spaces by American forces. The second innovation was the Chinese
announcement that they would fire on the offshore islands only on odd
days. This practice has also been continued; the Chinese do not fire on
the offshore islands on even days, and they merely fire propaganda shells

---

[1]Obviously, no attempt can be made here to provide a detailed or definitive
interpretation of either the Taiwan Straits crises or the Sino Indian border
clash.

on some odd days. While the motives for these devices have never been fully explained, they both suggest a willingness on the part of the Chinese to use military force or the threat of military force in apparently bizarre ways in order to accomplish what they perceive to be valuable political objectives.

In 1960, at the time of President Eisenhower's visit to Taiwan, the Chinese fired a large number of shells against the offshore islands, apparently simply as an expression of their displeasure at the visit and their attempt again to remind the world that the China issue was unsettled and that the Chinese Communist government still considered Taiwan to be a part of China which should come under its control. In 1962, the Chinese moved very large numbers of troops opposite Taiwan and the offshore islands. While they did not at this time institute any military action against the islands, they raised the fear in the West that they would do so. This had the effect of producing a statement by President Kennedy which clarified the American attitude toward Taiwan and the off-shore islands and strengthened the still ambiguous commitment of the United States to the defense of the islands.[2] In response to this, the Chinese secured from the Russians the strongest declaration of support that they have received since the Sino-Soviet dispute began to become public. All of this the Chinese achieved while at the same time accomplishing their primary objective of guarding against a possible Chinese Nationalist landing by moving their troops to Fukien Province.

The Chinese have also used military force very selectively on a number of occasions along the Sino-Indian border, and they conducted a relatively major operation there in 1962. However, here again, their use of force was relatively limited and apparently closely connected to specific political objectives. In this case, military action apparently solidified control over that part of the disputed territory that was considered to be of strategic importance, while at the same time demonstrating that the Chinese army was still a formidable conventional military fighting force despite the economic setbacks that China suffered between 1959 and 1961.

As was noted above, the Chinese have been quite reluctant to engage conventional military forces except under very special circumstances. The first of these situations was the Civil War, where the army destroyed all Chinese Nationalist power on the mainland. In addition, they were clearly preparing for invasion of Taiwan until the United States intervened. Second, the Chinese used major military force in order to subjugate Tibet, which they considered to be an integral part of China. Finally, in 1958

[2]*New York Times*, June 28, 1962, p. 1.

they appeared to be willing to use relatively large-scale artillery and naval forces to blockade the island of Quemoy, another piece of territory that they consider part of China. In each of these cases force was used against areas that the Chinese clearly believe are part of their own country and in a way which was not likely to bring about Western involvement.

The only other time that the Chinese have used large-scale military force was, of course, the Korean War. The Chinese objectives here, however, appear to have been almost entirely defensive. That is, the Chinese intervened only because they felt not to do so would pose a larger threat to their own existence than to intervene. The Chinese apparently believed that the United States, if allowed to capture all of North Korea and destroy the North Korean regime, might well not stop at the Yalu and might be encouraged by the success of this military operation to begin to give aid to the Chinese Nationalists for a return to the mainland. However, they did fight to preserve some of the territory under North Korean control.

For the next several years at least, it would seem extremely unlikely that the Chinese will change their basic approach to the use of conventional military power. It will continue to be important for internal reasons and as an implicit threat in their dealing with countries on their border. At the same time, the likelihood of their using this force would appear to be sharply reduced because of the growing belief in the West that an attack on China might not trigger a retaliatory attack by the Soviet Union. Therefore it is much more likely that the United States might intervene with a nuclear attack on China in the event of major Chinese conventional aggression.

In addition, the Sino-Soviet rift has meant that the Chinese have not been able to secure Soviet military supplies and parts for their military equipment. Since the Chinese domestic armaments industry, although growing, is still limited, this has meant a very substantial reduction, particularly in the capabilities of their air and naval forces over the past few years. This reduction in capability will continue until the Chinese are able to develop large numbers of ships and planes on their own (see Chapter III).

Finally, with the possible exception of Indochina, there does not appear to be any region in which large-scale military action might prove useful to the Chinese Communists. They no longer have any doubt that the United States would intervene massively if they attempted to capture either the offshore islands or Taiwan. There would appear to be little scope or value for additional military action on the Sino-Indian border. Along the rest of their boundaries the Chinese have concluded treaties defining the border and calling for peaceful relations in such a way as seemingly to preclude any present intention to employ conventional military force.

Vietnam remains a question mark. Here it would seem that the Chinese intervention is extremely unlikely except in the case of massive American involvement either with the landing of ground troops or extensive bombing of North Vietnam and Communist-held areas in Laos. In this situation it would be rash to predict Chinese behavior, but the introduction of ground troops cannot be ruled out as a possibility.

Finally, the Sino-Soviet border should be mentioned. Both sides have admitted that there have been limited military clashes on this border, and it may be the case that the Chinese Communist army will have to turn increasing attention to the protection of its borders with the Soviet Union in order to prevent border incursions or various other kinds of border activities by the Russians. If this occurred, it might occupy a substantial portion of the Chinese army and it is not inconceivable that this could lead to fairly large-scale fighting in Central Asia.

# VII ARMS CONTROL AND WAR

Certainly the most important forms of military interaction which have taken place between the United States and China were the Korean War and, by proxy, various other limited wars in Asia, including those in Indochina and in the Taiwan Straits. In these encounters, both sides refrained from using all their available military force against all possible military targets.[1]

Most of the limited wars with which the United States has been concerned in the postwar period have involved Communist China or allies of the Peking regime. During the course of these wars a very substantial number of tacit understandings about what is or is not appropriate in a limited war situation have developed. The extent to which these limitations have been consciously recognized by the two sides has been important in keeping these wars limited.[2] Both sides, for example, set sharp limitations on their objectives during the fighting. Many of the limitations on forces which have been observed by one or both sides in limited wars in the Far East in the postwar period can be divided into four main categories. In each category there has been a single limitation consciously recognized by both the United States and Communist China as crucial to holding the war within bounds.

The first limitation is that of geography and the recognized need to confine any war to a circumscribed area. All wars in the Pacific since 1949 have been confined to relatively small pieces of territory, usually within the confines of a single country. The second limit, in the area of targets to be attacked, is that supply lines, particularly supply lines beyond the battle, are not bombed or otherwise directly interfered with. What made American bombing in Laos and Vietnam in the winter of 1964-1965 unique was precisely the fact that it violated this limit.

The third limitation has, at least from the point of view of the Chinese,

---

[1]Under some definitions of the term "arms control," restraints observed in a limited war would be included; under others it would not. While such action will be considered here as arms control, the reader who prefers a different definition can simply choose to regard the chapter as one concerning restraint observed by the Chinese during wartime and on the problems of war termination.

[2]For an elaboration of the points made in this section, see Morton H. Halperin, *Limited War in the Nuclear Age* (New York: John Wiley & Sons, 1963), pp. 1-38.

been one-sided. It concerns the U.S. policy of refraining from using nuclear weapons. There have been other restraints by both sides in the general category of weapons limitation.

Finally, both the United States and China have been concerned with avoiding direct involvement in a local war situation. The troops of the United States have been used in major combat only in the Korean War, where they were part of a United Nations police force. In Indochina, U.S. ground troops are termed "advisors" or they guard U.S. "bases," and U.S. air forces have been used in limited ways, notably in attacks on North Vietnam and in strafing Pathet Lao positions in Laos. Chinese troops in Korea were officially labeled "volunteers" by the Peking regime. Some American troops have been used in other Far Eastern conflicts but in the form of advisers and not combat troops, and even this has been done hesitantly and where it was felt that there was no alternative. The Chinese have also not committed their troops, at least overtly (for example, in the actions in Indochina), although they were directly involved in what they called civil war activities in the Taiwan Straits. Although the role of some American "advisors" in Vietnam seems to be very similar to that which would be performed by combat troops, and although there may be some Chinese in South Vietnam, both sides are seen to prefer to at least downgrade, if not to ignore, the possibility that they may be engaged in direct combat with each other.

Related to the importance of not committing one's own troops, or disguising their commitment, is the fact that no state of war has ever been formally declared in any of the postwar military encounters in the Far East. Declaring war seems to have gone out of style in international politics in general. Certainly the United States and Communist China, although they have clashed both directly and indirectly on a number of battlefields, do not appear to have come close to the stage of declaring war on each other. The reasons for this are complex and varying, but one constant seems to be recognition both by the Peking regime and the United States that total victory would not likely be the outcome of a specific military encounter. Since at least on the United States side there is a strong presumption that when war is declared the outcome will be total victory, it has appeared advisable to refrain from a declaration of war.

Before looking at some of the limitations that the Chinese have observed in previous local war situations and attempting to speculate upon limitations in future wars, it is important to find out to what extent the Chinese have consciously engaged in war limitation, to what extent they have reached deliberate decisions to refrain from using particular weapons

or otherwise restrained their military action, and to find out what have
been their motivations for doing so. That is, do the Chinese have some
sort of theory of limited war?

There appears to be a good deal of evidence to suggest that the
Chinese are very conscious of the fact that they and their opponents are
limiting the use of their military forces, and that there would very likely
be reciprocal responses of some kind if they were to enlarge the war.
There are a number of elements of Maoist military doctrine which would
lead the Chinese to adopt a policy of war restraint. Perhaps the most
important is the notion of despising the enemy strategically but respecting
him tactically. The Chinese idea that the United States is a "paper
tiger" must be understood in these terms. The Chinese are completely
aware of the existence in the Pacific of a vastly greater American military power than the United States has ever used or thought of using. But
they argue that, in the long run, the United States and capitalism as a
whole will be defeated because of inherent weaknesses of the system.
They have also asserted on certain occasions that the United States
lacked the will to use the military force which it had. The Chinese were
conscious of the necessity to avoid provoking the enemy into using his
existing military force and conscious of the fact that certain kinds of
military actions were likely to bring corresponding intervention or increase in military action by their opponents. At the same time the Chinese
have been alert to the fact that they might effectively deter an increase
in the use of military force by the United States or its allies by threatening
a step-up in their own military activity. The Chinese interest in limitation
and their conscious awareness of the process of interaction can be illus-
trated by several Chinese acts of restraint in particular international
crises.

One of the most important and most interesting limitations observed
by the Chinese was their decision not to bomb South Korea during the
Korean War, although they had some, but limited, capabilities for bombing
operations.[3] The Chinese position, as was learned later from captured
documents, was that they would not permit their planes to take off from
bases in Manchuria and bomb South Korea. Rather, their position was
that any planes that were to carry out bombing missions over South Korea
must first touch onto bases in North Korea. The Chinese apparently believed that if the planes touched down in North Korea, the United States
would not retaliate by bombing Manchuria but would simply continue
extensive bombing of North Korea. On the other hand, they believed that,

[3]*Ibid.*, pp. 39-57.

if the planes did not touch down, the United States would bomb Manchuria. Since the United States air force kept all air bases in North Korea out of operation during the entire Korean War, the Chinese did not bomb South Korea.

This example is interesting for a number of reasons. First, it suggests that the Chinese are very conscious that an action of theirs is likely to lead to another action on the part of their opponent. Second, it indicates that the Chinese are aware that restraints and reaction to restraints need not be reciprocal. The United States was carrying out bombing raids on North Korea from aircraft carriers and from bases beyond South Korea, yet the Chinese believed that, if they carried on attacks on South Korea from bases beyond North Korea, the United States would retaliate by bombing their Manchurian bases, even though the Chinese were not attacking aircraft carriers by air or attacking other American bases beyond Korea. Finally, the example is interesting because the Chinese assessment was probably incorrect. The United States was prepared to bomb Manchuria if the Chinese engaged in bombing attacks on South Korea, but the United States does not appear to have been either attuned to or likely to be influenced by the fact that the planes touched down in North Korea. Thus, one of the most important limitations during the Korean War, that of targets bombed, resulted from a misconception, but at the same time a perception, by the Chinese, that action on their part was likely to lead to a response that would expand the area of war.

During successive crises in Vietnam, the Chinese, recognizing that the United States might consider it credible, have implied that, in the case of the introduction of American combat troops, it might be necessary to introduce Chinese ground forces. The Chinese have also apparently recognized that open intervention by them in South Vietnam or in Laos would make it much more likely that American forces, certainly air and naval forces, and possibly ground forces, would be employed.

In the Sino-Indian border clashes, one of the Chinese motivations for halting the actions was that they apparently recognized that any attempt to move into heavily populated regions of India might have brought British and American and possibly even Soviet intervention.

Thus it seems clear that Peking recognizes that limitations that it observes are noted by the other side and to some extent reciprocated, in that extensions of the war on its part are likely to lead to various extensions of the war by its opponent. The Chinese appear to have been only moderately adept at communicating their concept of the limitations being observed by both sides and the kind of retaliatory expansion in which they might engage.

Wartime communication is an extremely complicated and sensitive operation. On the one hand, one wants to communicate the restraints that one is observing in order to be sure that the enemy is aware of them and is taking them into account in making his own decisions about what military operations to carry on. At the same time, the communication of limitation may suggest weakness and encourage the enemy to expand his actions. It is also true that in some situations one wants to threaten possible expansion of war and to suggest that the war might get out of hand unless it is brought to a halt rather than to suggest that the war can be kept limited. These inherent difficulties, as well as the lack of many direct formal means of communication between the United States and Communist China, have hampered the Chinese in their efforts to stabilize local war situations by adequate and effective communication.

The Chinese have used several different means of communication during local wars. The first and most important have been their actual military actions. On numerous occasions they have not used all the force available to them, and this has been noted by the United States and its allies and had an impact on Western decision making. The extreme caution that the Chinese have used in avoiding direct encounters with American military forces, particularly in the Taiwan Straits, has served as a powerful means of communicating both the Chinese desire to limit the war and also—illustrating one of the problems involved—a relative lack of Chinese resolve, which the United States might more forcefully exploit in future crisis situations. The Chinese have also attempted to communicate via intermediaries, as they did through the Indian ambassador at the time of their entrance into the Korean War, and as they apparently have through other channels both during the Taiwan Straits crises and during the crises in Indochina. They also, of course, had direct communication with the United States at the bilateral ambassadorial talks in Warsaw.

The most important and successful Chinese communications strategy during local wars is the device of calling for the opening of diplomatic negotiations in order to get the enemy to curb his own military action by halting operations that are under way or refraining from expanding them.

The Chinese used this device on several occasions during the Chinese Civil War, and they have used it successfully since then. For example, it now seems certain that hints from the Soviet Union and the Chinese that they were willing to open negotiations leading to a Korean armistice came at the time when the Chinese army was close to disintegration. The United States had just begun a ground advance which, had it continued, might have been successful.[4] The Chinese, by proposing the opening of armistice negotiations, succeeded in getting the United States, which was already weary of the war and which was not aware of the extent of Chinese weakness, to agree to open the talks and at the same time to call off the planned offensive. A major objective of the Chinese in the early weeks and months of the Korean negotiations was to get an agreement on the armistice line which would be observed once the other terms of the armistice were settled, thus again substantially reducing the incentive to the United Nations forces to launch a major offensive. This device was successful and enabled the Chinese to turn the Korean War into a stalemate.

The Vietnamese Communists, perhaps with the advice of the Chinese Communists, used a slight variation of the same technique in 1954, at the time of the Geneva Conference on Indochina, when they engaged in a major offensive operation, the capture of Dienbienphu, just at the time that political talks were about to open. The Communists seem to have guessed correctly that the West was very unlikely to take the kind of major military action that would have been needed to restore the military balance in Indochina to the *status quo ante* while the political conference was in progress. The Chinese and Vietnamese Communists were able to give the impression that they were ready at the conference to settle for less than they had earned on the battlefield. The conclusion of an armistice agreement in Indochina prevented the possible massive introduction of American air and naval forces which might have occurred if the war went on. Since 1954, the Chinese have called for reconvening the Geneva Conference as a device either to deter increases in military effort by the West or to consolidate their own military advances.

At the height of the Taiwan Straits crisis of 1958, at a time when the Chinese may well have been afraid that the United States would step up the level of military action by permitting the Chinese Nationalists to bomb the mainland, the Chinese again called for the opening of diplomatic talks, in this case at the ambassadorial level between the United States and Communist China. The fact that the Chinese called for a reopening of the Warsaw talks has been singled out by many as a sign that they were prepared to end the crisis, perhaps by negotiations. In fact, the Chinese intended this communication for the same purpose as other calls for political conferences, that is, to prevent their opponent from substantially increasing the use of military force, thus leaving the Chinese free to continue to exert pressure at the same level.

[4]Robert Frank Futrell, *The United States Air Force in Korea: 1950-1953* (New York: Duell, Sloan and Pearce, 1961), pp. 341-45.

They used this technique again with effect in the Sino-Indian border crisis, when they proposed negotiations and actually pulled back their forces somewhat after scoring a successful military advance. Again, both their pulling back, carried out because their objectives had been accomplished, and the proposal for diplomatic talks made it extremely unlikely that the United States would intervene to force a major military encounter.

The Chinese have thus used a call for political negotiations as a successful device to prevent Western expansion of a local war and, at least in some instances, signaled their willingness to end the conflict or at least to call a temporary halt to overt employment of major military force. This leads, then, to the question of the kinds of war termination agreements the Chinese have been prepared to sign and the way in which these agreements have been observed.

The general Chinese attitude toward international agreements, including the armistice agreements which they have signed in Korea and over Indochina, will be discussed in Chapter XI and will not be considered in detail here. It is worth noting, however, that, with respect to the timing of negotiations, the Chinese have been extremely sensitive not only to international but also to domestic political conditions in the countries with which they were negotiating. In the Korean situation they seemed to recognize that, once the truce talks were opened, and particularly once there was an agreement on the cease-fire line, the United States was not likely to begin the massive ground offensive which the Chinese feared. The talks could then be extended almost indefinitely in the hopes of gaining better political terms. On the other hand, during the 1954 Geneva Conference, the Chinese apparently recognized that the United States might be ready to intervene decisively. In addition, the government of Pierre Mendès-France in Paris was apparently unlikely to remain in office in the event that no agreement could be reached quickly on ending the Indochinese conflict. In this situation, after the military victory at Dienbienphu, the Chinese and Vietnamese Communists were ready for quick negotiations, in which they gave away some gains from their military actions in order to secure an armistice, which in this case they may have felt was necessary to deter American involvement.

Where their own borders are involved, the Chinese have been willing to accept tacit agreements to stop military action. After the Sino-Indian border clashes, the Chinese withdrew from parts of the territory they had occupied. While they might have entered formal negotiations, they were willing instead to accept a *de facto* cease fire in the area. This left them in possession of much additional territory and forced the Indians either to accept the Chinese line or, alternatively, to launch an offensive and the start of "new war" to regain the lost territory.

In the Taiwan Straits, at the end of the crises of 1954-1955 and 1958, the unwillingness of the Chinese Communists and the Nationalists to enter into any diplomatic negotiations with each other made a formally negotiated cease fire impossible. Both crises ended without a formal agreement of any kind being signed and with a unilateral declaration by the mainland Chinese that they would stop their fighting. The 1958 crisis, of course, ended with the now well-known Chinese device of first announcing a two-week cease fire, then a one-week extension of the cease fire, and then the policy of shelling only on odd days.

One further issue which needs to be considered in connection with the problem of war termination is that of substantial arms control agreements that might emerge after a major military conflict, particularly one that involved nuclear weapons. Herman Kahn and others frequently make the point that the United States ought to have blueprints for the kind of arms control and peacefully controlled world that it would like to negotiate, or impose, or accept after a Soviet-American nuclear exchange. This is based on the assumption that it is extremely unlikely that a far-reaching arms control agreement and political settlement will be adopted, but, if it is at all, it is likely to be after the use of some nuclear weapons and perhaps only after a major nuclear war. Most of this line of reasoning has tended to assume either that the Soviet Union had enough control over China to force her into an arms control agreement of this kind or that the two superpowers would be prepared to use military force to press China and other nations into the agreement. However, it seems clear that, regardless of the damage done to China in a U.S.-Soviet nuclear war, if the current leadership is still in power in Peking, the regime is likely to resist any total settlement that would appear to it as an establishment of hegemony over the world by the two superpowers. Thus within the context of planning for comprehensive arms control, should it become feasible, some detailed plans for how the Chinese might be brought in must be developed. American planners need to project themselves into a time after Soviet-U.S. nuclear exchange, when there would be strong sentiment on both sides for substantial political and arms control settlement, and ask what conditions the U.S. would want the Chinese to observe and how these might be imposed.

In addition, there is the special problem of the kind of arms control arrangements and political settlements that one might try to negotiate or impose on the Chinese in the event of a major war involving only the United States and Communist China. It is clear that in this case, as well as perhaps in the case of the Russians, the overriding considerations and the overriding agreements would be political rather than concerned with military forces. Nevertheless, there certainly would be an arms control element included in any settlement that the United States sought to impose on the Chinese. This would include, for example, the questions of whether the United States wanted to demand the dismantling of any Chinese Communist nuclear weapons or nuclear production facilities, what the United States would try to do about Chinese assistance to revolutionary wars in Indochina or in Africa and in Latin America, and what might be done about the very large Chinese army, including the Chinese militia. A large-scale Chinese-U.S. war is of low probability. Any planning that was done for the end of this contingency would undoubtedly have only limited value because no one could predict the precise form the conflict would take. Nevertheless, there would appear to be some utility to thinking about this question, not only because these improbable events might come about but also because it might help to shed some light on America's long-run aspirations as to the evolution in Chinese foreign policy, tactics, and objectives.

The Chinese, as we have noted above, have been and remain committed to the use of force and the threat of force as a major instrument of foreign policy.[5] It is very likely that the kind of political-military maneuvering that was going on in Vietnam in the summer of 1964 will continue between the United States and China and its allies all along the periphery of China. This will require the United States to engage repeatedly in a test of will and nerve with the Chinese Communists in which an important component will be the need to communicate restraint combined with an indication of what the United States is prepared to do in the event of Chinese expansion of a local conflict or persistence in a local conflict in a way that seems detrimental to American interest. The statement made by President Lyndon Johnson in connection with his authorization of American attacks on certain specified targets in North Vietnam appears to reflect the kind of message the Chinese Communists should be given in connection with American military action. Secretary McNamara said afterward that he had in fact encouraged the President to make the speech before the attack but after the North Vietnamese might have time to make adequate defense preparations. This explanation was justified in terms of the need to reassure the Chinese that the attack was not against the

[5]No one at the Conference seemed to dissent from this view or from the belief that the Chinese were more committed to the use of violence than were the Soviets.

Chinese mainland but was limited to a few targets in Communist North Vietnam.

The record of past Chinese behavior in limited war suggests that they would be sensitive to all the implications of Mr. Johnson's and Mr. McNamara's remarks as well as to the massive buildup of American military force in the area. Both sides are perhaps now prepared to share a key understanding of the importance of communication and the problem of maintaining restraints on local war situations because the termination of any local war will still depend primarily on the internal political situation in the country in which the fighting is taking place as well as on the relative will of the main protagonists.

Thus we may expect the Chinese to continue to pursue a policy that seeks to limit any military encounter in which they are directly involved or involved by proxy and to be sensitive to signs and signals from the United States that suggest willingness to abide by certain rules and restraints in the military encounter or that imply a threat of American expansion of the military operations.

# VIII ARMS CONTROL AND INSURGENCY

Insurgency is a form of limited war. The key limitations involved, geographical confinement and, on occasion, the maintenance of at least the fiction of non-involvement by one or more of the major powers, were discussed in the previous chapter, as were the reasons for them. There remains the question of whether arms control measures have a role to play in either halting or altering the nature of insurgency itself.

Insurgency may be directed against a foreign invader, as was the case in China during the Sino-Japanese war (1937-1945); it may be a form of rebellion against an existing government wholly domestic in origin; or it may be an insurrection against an established government partially or completely controlled and supported from the outside. Insurgency differs from a civil war in that it does not involve conventional warfare, although it may lead ultimately to such warfare. In fact, it is basic Maoist dogma that the final stage of "wars of liberation" is open conventional warfare between the opposing sides (see Chapter VI).

The relevance of arms control for insurgency is at best marginal. Insurrections wholly domestic in origin and support clearly cannot be stopped by international agreement, although such agreements could affect the outcome if they aided or inhibited the flow of assistance to the established government. The primary area in which arms control arrangements may have relevance, however, is where insurgency is supported to some degree from outside the country, principally by the shipment of arms and cadres to the insurgents.

Although movement of weapons and cadres is, conceptually at least, an arms control problem, many other aspects of insurgency are not. Foremost among these are the local political, social, and economic conditions in which insurgency thrives. These conditions can be affected from outside but not by means normally within the framework of arms control measures, except in the sense that trained cadres can sometimes bring about (or make the populace aware of) conditions productive of popular discontent and rebellion. Nor is it a function of arms control as such to inhibit the flow of revolutionary ideology or guerrilla technology across national borders. In any case, such a task is only possible in a formal sense between totalitarian states which have complete control of communications crossing their borders.

## PROBLEMS OF DEFINITION AND VERIFICATION

An agreement to prohibit the flow of arms and men to insurgents, to government forces, or to both appears to be a logical way of checking insurgencies; yet such agreements are hard to define. What constitutes outside support? Prohibitions on the sale or delivery of all kinds of military aid run into the problem of defining what constitutes military aid. Does a tractor factory or a transport plane represent military or civilian aid? Both can be easily converted to military uses once obtained. Are civilian advisers really doing civilian work? Under such an agreement between the Communist Chinese regime and the United States, would the latter seek to prohibit student travel from countries with actual or potential insurgents on the grounds that the courses they take often are more relevant to political agitation than to more conventional activities? Would China also argue that foreign students studying in the United States acquire certain political orientations, and would it therefore call for a termination of American foreign-student training programs?

The problems of defining what the agreement should include may be surmountable, provided that two or more countries with insurgency problems are involved and that China (or the United States) favors the insurgents in one case but not in the other. In such a situation, which probably is impossible to define in negotiable terms, pro-American insurgents might be traded off against pro-Chinese insurgents. An arrangement involving a single country with insurgency problems, on the other hand, is difficult to define conceptually in terms which can be the basis of negotiation. In any single situation, an arms control agreement is likely to work to the advantage of one protagonist and against the other. During the early stages of a guerrilla campaign, for example, the insurgents may be dependent on outside support to sustain their movement. As their efforts begin to succeed, however, it may be the government, rather than the insurgents, that is in greatest need of external aid (as in Vietnam). Thus, counter-insurgency forces often depend on imported heavy modern equipment (helicopters, bombers, etc.), whereas guerrilla forces seldom do. Although it might be thought that an arms control agreement could be drawn up that prohibited both sides from carrying on a particular type of activity, this discussion indicates that the wide disparity in weapons and techniques between the two opposing forces means that any such settlement will favor one side over the other. With respect to the Chinese, for example, it is possible to conceive of an agreement in which the United States promised not to sell anti-insurgent government forces modern weaponry in exchange for a promise from China not to train guerrilla cadres, but this undertaking would be extremely difficult to negotiate due to difficulties in deciding just what constitutes a *quid pro quo*.

Far more serious than the problems of definition and negotiation, however, are the difficulties involved in effective verification of an agreement terminating insurgent connections with outside supporters. An insurgent action must by its very nature be a highly secret affair. If it is to have any hope of success against the vastly superior forces of a government, it must have an intelligence system which allows it to predict where government forces will be concentrated and a control network that ensures sufficient secrecy over its operations to prevent any comparable knowledge on the part of the government. An effective verification agreement, therefore, is almost certain to affect the insurgents adversely, if not destroy them altogether. Thorough inspection and verification measures under many conditions would require collaboration and assistance from the insurgent forces. Could this cooperation be expected from them under an agreement signed by foreign powers?

Nevertheless, one of the few feasible types of settlements which can be conceived is where two powers, such as the United States and China, each agreed to allow the other to establish itself in one area in exchange for non-interference in another area, i.e., "I'll sacrifice my insurgents if you'll sacrifice yours." The first objection to this is, not surprisingly, likely to come from those being sacrificed. In this case, if the great powers involved lack sufficient discipline over insurgent groups receiving their support, any agreement will come to nought.

## CHINESE INTERESTS

It was argued at length in Chapter I that the Chinese Communists are actively interested in insurgent operations in areas around the world where they believe the prospects for success are bright. Peking, therefore, is not at present likely to see any merit in an agreement designed simply to inhibit such operations. Nor is this attitude likely to change very rapidly even if American and other counter-insurgency efforts begin to succeed, although such successes over a prolonged period undoubtedly would damp Peking's interest in guerrilla actions. Arms control arrangements to halt or inhibit insurgency are likely to become of real significance to China only in the event that guerrilla actions launched against Chinese-supported regimes appear to be a real threat to the survival of these governments, and thus to the prestige and influence of the Chinese. [1]

Various attempts to undermine Communist regimes by means of counter-insurgencies (e.g., in Cuba and North Vietnam) have not been notably successful, primarily because these regimes have been able to maintain a high degree of control over their civilian populations and because they also have enjoyed a significant level of popular support, at least with politically important segments of the population. Insurgency operations are extremely difficult to get under way under the most favorable circumstances, and the circumstances in Cuba and North Vietnam have been far from favorable for opponents of the established revolutionary regimes in these countries.

This state of affairs, however, may not always exist. For example, were the Communists to take over Indonesia following the death of Sukarno, the Communist Party of Indonesia might lack sufficient power to establish full control over more than the island of Java, if that. It would then need and presumably seek outside support. Chinese difficulties arising from pressure and desire to support the Indonesian Communists might well alter Chinese attitudes toward measures designed to halt outside aid to insurgents opposing a Communist government in Indonesia. Whether, under the circumstances, an agreement designed to prevent Chinese assistance to the Indonesian Communists would be in the interests of countries opposed to China would depend on many factors, including what was happening in the rest of the world at the time.

At present all formal and informal arms control settlements designed to inhibit insurgency will have to overcome China's interest in maintaining its position as leader of revolutionary forces around the world. A drastic change in the Chinese position at this point appears to be a prerequisite for her willingness to accept arms control measures to limit her support of insurgent warfare. An agreement under which China was put in a position of totally sacrificing one group in order to save another, if such a situation can be envisaged, might severely damage China's ability to promote and lead insurgent groups elsewhere. But such an agreement almost surely would have unfavorable consequences for the United States or other parties to it as well.

Arms control arrangements, therefore, are not likely to play a major role in dealing with insurgency involving China for some time to come.

[1]This discussion does not consider the possibilities that China might become a *status quo* power or that China might desire to limit insurgency for fear that such action might escalate into a major war. The former possibility is very remote, while the latter was touched upon in the previous chapter.

Not only are they difficult to negotiate and almost impossible to verify, but there is little prospect of China becoming interested in them unless the United States or other Western powers are able to launch effective guerrilla operations against Chinese-supported regimes and are able to deal effectively with similar operations launched by the Communists against regimes supported by the West. But if the West is able successfully to launch guerrilla actions and to promote counter-insurgency measures, there is a real question as to whether arms control agreements inhibiting insurgency would be in Western interests. Perhaps there is some middle ground where agreement is feasible, but the prospects today seem quite remote.

During the period from 1949 to the mid-1950's, Peking tended to support the Soviet policy on major international issues, especially those that did not directly concern Far Eastern affairs.[1] The Soviet position on disarmament in particular met with much sympathy from the Chinese Communist leadership. The Soviet Union, confronted with virtually an American monopoly of nuclear capacity, pressed for elimination of nuclear weapons, without any proposals to eliminate conventional forces. The Chinese endorsed this position without reservations. They were as concerned as the Russians with trying to reduce the likelihood of American use of nuclear weapons.[2]

One of the earliest Chinese statements in support of the Soviet position came in the *People's Daily*, September 30, 1949, in a commentary entitled, "Act in Response to the Call of Vyshinsky." The article supported the Soviet proposal presented at the United Nations that called for a banning of atomic weapons and for a five-power peace pact which would include Communist China.[3]

It was only in the late 1950's, as the Sino-Soviet dispute sharpened and as the Soviets began to take specific decisions on arms control issues which appeared to conflict with the Chinese interests, that the Chinese began to adopt an independent line on questions of arms control and disarmament. The Chinese disagreement with the Russians came in the context of the general Sino-Soviet dispute and involved particular measures such as a nuclear-free zone in the Far East, the test ban, and

---

[1]The Chinese position on arms control is discussed in Alice Hsieh, *Communist China's Strategy in the Nuclear Age* (Englewood Cliffs, N.J.: Prentice-Hall, 1962); Hsieh, "The Chinese Genie: Peking's Role in the Nuclear Test Ban Negotiations" (RAND P-2022, June 20, 1960); A. Doak Barnett, "Inclusion of Communist China in an Arms Control Program," in Donald G. Brennan (ed.), *Arms Control, Disarmament, and National Security* (New York: Braziller, 1961), pp. 282-303.

[2]For a discussion of Soviet arms control policy during this period, see Alexander Dallin *et al.*, *The Soviet Union, Arms Control and Disarmament: A Study of Soviet Attitudes* (New York: Columbia University School of International Affairs, 1964)—also published as *The Soviet Union and Disarmament: An Appraisal of Soviet Attitudes and Intentions* (New York: Praeger, 1965), pp. 117-27—and the items cited in Dallin, p. 223n (hereafter cited as *Soviet Attitudes*).

[3]*People's Daily*, September 30, 1949, as reported by New China News Agency, September 30, 1949 (hereafter cited as NCNA).

the general Soviet line of first pressing for general and complete disarmament and more recently for specific arms control measures.

## THE NUCLEAR-FREE ZONE [4]

The first issue on which an independent Chinese position was publicly indicated was the possibility of a denuclearized zone in Asia and the Pacific. In their first statements on the question, the Chinese seemed to be fully supporting the Soviet proposal for a nuclear-free zone. In February, 1958, Chou En-lai supported what was described as a proposal by Indian Communists and Indian Prime Minister Nehru for the "establishment and expansion of an area free from weapons of mass destruction."[5]

The Chinese have continued to the present to support a nuclear-free zone in the Far East but increasingly in ways that have made it clear that they were not as enthusiastic about the proposal as the Russians may have been. In fact, even before the first Chinese statement endorsing the proposal, the president of the Chinese Academy of Sciences, Kuo Mo-jo, in an interview with an Italian Communist publication, tied his support in general for nuclear-free zones to a context of a series of agreements including a ban on the "manufacture, stockpiling and use of nuclear weapons."[6]

Khrushchev gave a major push to the possibility of a nuclear-free zone in his address to the Twenty-first Congress of the C.P.S.U. The Chinese, who had supported such proposals only in passing since mid-1958, delayed before endorsing his and then did so in a way which left no doubt about their lack of enthusiasm.[7] They have since indicated that during this period Khrushchev was trying to convince the Peking regime that China had no need to become a nuclear power and should instead seek to rely on Soviet nuclear guarantees, coupled with a nuclear-free zone that included withdrawal of American nuclear weapons from at least some areas in the Far East. The Chinese made it clear that they rejected these

---

[4] For a discussion of the Sino-Soviet disagreement on this issue, see Hsieh, *Communist China's Strategy in the Nuclear Age*, pp. 156-66.

[5] *Survey of the China Mainland Press* (U.S. Consulate General, Hong Kong), 1712 (February 13, 1958), pp. 1-7 (hereafter cited as SCMP).

[6] NCNA, February 4, 1958, and SCMP, 1708 (February 7, 1958); cited in Hsieh, *Communist China's Strategy in the Nuclear Age*, p. 105.

[7] For a discussion of the Chinese reaction to Khrushchev's proposal, see Hsieh, *Communist China's Strategy in the Nuclear Age*, pp. 154-66.

Soviet suggestions.[8] Thereafter the Chinese continued to give lip service to the nuclear-free zone proposal, apparently to keep up the pretense of Sino-Soviet cooperation and to capitalize on the popularity of the proposal, especially in Japan and particularly within the Japanese Communist Party.

In 1959, Chou En-lai in a report to the Second National People's Congress declared, "We advocate the establishment of an area free of atomic weapons, an area of peace, throughout the whole of *East Asia* and the Pacific region." It is possible, as Alice Hsieh has suggested, that Chou was suggesting that part of China might be excluded from such a zone.[9]

The following year, Peking switched to another track, suggesting not only that the whole of China should be included but the United States as well. In August, Chou En-lai declared that "we advocate that the countries of Asia and around the Pacific, including the U.S.A., conclude a peace pact of mutual nonaggression and join the whole of this area into a nuclear-free area."[10] This linking of a pact of non-aggression with a nuclear-free zone has not been continued in Chinese propaganda, but the condition that a nuclear-free zone include the United States has apparently been repeated in all the Chinese statements on the subject that have been made since the beginning of August, 1960.

In an editorial released shortly before the signing of the Test Ban Treaty, the Chinese reaffirmed their support for a nuclear-free zone including the United States:

> We are in favour of achieving a total prohibition of nuclear weapons stage by stage. This goal may be attained by following the procedure mentioned above, or its attainment may be promoted by the establishment and extension of nuclear weapon-free zones. Both methods hinge on the fact that countries possessing nuclear weapons must undertake practical obligations. The Chinese Government proposed long ago that

---

[8]"Statement by the Spokesman of the Chinese Government—A Comment on the Soviet Government's Statement of August 21." Dated September 1, 1963; translation in *Peking Review*, VI, No. 36 (September 6, 1963), p. 9.

[9]Chou En-lai, "The Report on Government Work." Delivered to the first session of the Second National People's Congress on April 18, 1959; translation in *Current Background* (U.S. Consulate General, Hong Kong), 559, (April 23, 1959). Quoted in Hsieh, *Communist China's Strategy in the Nuclear Age*, p. 160.

[10]SCMP, 2314 (August 10, 1960), pp. 136-38.

Asia and the Pacific region be turned into a nuclear weapon-free zone. The proposal clearly stipulates that the United States must be included and undertake the same obligations. We consider the establishment and expansion of other nuclear weapon-free zones to be helpful in diminishing the scope of activity of the nuclear powers and helpful to the prevention of nuclear war. But, inasmuch as nuclear weapons and their delivery vehicles have been developed as they are today, it is only when the nuclear powers undertake obligations that show respect for the nuclear weapon-free zones that the aspirations of the people there can be fulfilled.[11]

In the disarmament proposals released by the Chinese after the signing of the Test Ban Treaty, Peking went even further to propose the establishment of a "nuclear weapon-free zone of the Asian and Pacific region, including the United States, the *Soviet Union*, China, and Japan."[12] In an interview with a Japanese journalist in 1964, Mao reportedly said that if the Chinese proposal for a nuclear-free zone were accepted, "no military base will be liberated Taiwan."[13]

The Chinese have never clarified what they mean by including the United States and the Soviet Union in a nuclear-free zone in the Far East. If the proposal simply means that no American or Soviet weapons could be stationed in the designated area, then this would seem to be implicit in any notion of a nuclear-free zone. The Chinese position may be taken to mean that no nuclear weapons may be stationed anywhere in Asia or the Far East, even on territory of the countries owning nuclear weapons. This presumably would mean the Soviet withdrawal of nuclear weapons to the Urals and American withdrawal of nuclear weapons from bases in the Far East and Pacific, including perhaps Hawaii. However, it seems extremely unlikely that China would be prepared to forego nuclear weapons simply in return for withdrawal of American and Soviet nuclear weapons from Asia. If the proposal is taken literally to mean inclusion of all the Soviet Union and all of the United States as well as the entire territory of China, then, if accepted, it would leave Britain and France as the only nuclear powers in the world.

[11]Translation in *Peking Review*, VI, No. 30 (July 26, 1963), p. 48.

[12]"Statement of the Chinese Government advocating the complete, thorough, total and resolute prohibition and destruction of nuclear weapons, nuclear weapons zone, and proposing a conference of the government heads of all countries of the world." Dated July 31, 1963; translation in *Peking Review*, VI, No. 32 (August 9, 1963), p. 7, italics added.

[13]*Tokyo Shimbun*, August 4, 1964.

In the disarmament proposals they put forth immediately following their first detonation, the Chinese continued to indicate their support for a nuclear-free zone, but they concentrated on other first steps. On November 22, 1964, in a major statement on disarmament, to be discussed more fully below, Peking indicated that it was no longer willing to accept an Asian nuclear-free zone unless a ban on the use of nuclear weapons was already in effect:

> Many countries at present are keenly interested in the establishment of nuclear-free zones. However, to really free the nuclear-free zones from the threat of nuclear war it is first necessary for the nuclear powers to undertake not to use nuclear weapons. Otherwise, the establishment of nuclear-free zones would be impossible and even if they be set up in name, all it means is that the non-nuclear countries would be deprived of their legitimate right to develop nuclear weapons to resist the nuclear menace and be bound hand and foot, while the nuclear powers would in no way be affected in their continued production, stockpiling and even use of nuclear weapons. Consequently, the sole result would be: the larger the nuclear-free zone, the graver the U.S. imperialist nuclear threat to the non-nuclear countries.[14]

## PARTICIPATION OF CHINA IN DISARMAMENT NEGOTIATIONS

Another Chinese deviation from the Soviet line on disarmament came in January, 1960 and was contained in an NCNA dispatch under what had been until then a typical form of heading: "NPC (National People's Congress) Standing Committee Support Soviet Disarmament Appeal." After noting Chinese support for the Soviet disarmament position, the dispatch went on to say: "China will unhesitatingly commit itself to the international obligations to which it has agreed. However, it must be pointed out that any international disarmament agreement which is arrived at without the full participation of the Chinese People's Republic and the signature of its delegate cannot, of course, have any binding force on China."[15]

---

[14]"New Starting Point for Efforts To Ban Nuclear Weapons Completely." Translation in *Peking Review*, VII, No. 48 (November 27, 1964), pp. 12-14. The translation is reproduced here as Appendix A.

[15]SCMP, 2185 (January 27, 1960), p. 4.

At almost the same time, presumably in response to private Chinese statements making this point, Khrushchev told the Supreme Soviet of the U.S.S.R. on January 14, 1960:

> True, there have been isolated pronouncements, notably in certain small countries, expressing apprehensions lest the great powers, in agreeing among themselves, jettison the interest of small nations and disregard the views of states not represented at the conference. Permit me to state that these apprehensions are absolutely unfounded. As far as the Soviet Government is concerned, now as in the past, it has no intention of reaching an agreement behind the backs of other states on questions in which their interests are directly involved. We believe that any attempt to obtain unilateral advantages at the expense of other states is in general contrary to the objectives of the forthcoming meeting [i.e., the ten-nation disarmament conference], the results of which benefit universal peace and, consequently, all nations, big and small.[16]

The Chinese position was reiterated by the Chinese observer at the February, 1960 meeting of the Warsaw Treaty Organization, who warned: "The Chinese Government has to declare to the world that any international disarmament agreement and all other international agreements which are arrived at without the full participation of the Chinese People's Republic and the signature of its delegate cannot, of course, have any binding force on China."[17]

Several months later, Chou En-lai made it clear that this was not simply a Chinese bid for an invitation to the disarmament talks. He indicated that China would not attend such talks unless it had already been admitted to the United Nations.[18] This need for Chinese participation in any agreements that they would accept was to be a recurring theme and was to mark one of the first points of emerging Chinese views on arms control and disarmament independent of the Soviet position. China would participate in arms control talks—or at least those even vaguely under the sponsorship of the United Nations—only if she were recognized and

[16]N. S. Khrushchev, "Report to the Supreme Soviet of the U.S.S.R.," English translation in *Supplement to New Times*, No. 4 (January 30, 1960), p. 21. Quoted in Dallin, *Soviet Attitudes*, p. 241.

[17]Quoted in Dallin, *Soviet Attitudes*, pp. 243-44.

[18]SCMP, 2260 (May 18, 1960), pp. 40-44. As indicated below, the Chinese repeated this assertion following their nuclear detonation.

admitted to the United Nations. She would abide only by any arms control agreement that she participated in negotiating and formally signed.

Publicly the Soviet Union appeared to be ignoring this Chinese position when on March 16, 1960, at a meeting of the Ten-Power Disarmament Committee in Geneva, the Soviet delegate proposed that:

> As a significant measure in the first stage of the program of general and complete disarmament it would seem advisable to provide for the reduction of the armed forces of the Soviet Union, the United States of America, and the Chinese People's Republic to a level of 1,700,000 men, of the United Kingdom and France to a level of 650,000 men, and of all other states to levels that would be agreed upon at a special session of the United Nations General Assembly, or at a world-wide conference on general and complete disarmament. The figures proposed for the reduction of the armed forces of the Great Powers were, as will be remembered, listed earlier in the documents presented also by the Western Powers, and even in the program for partial disarmament measures, and therefore, and in our view, should not evoke any objections from those powers.[19]

The proposal made no reference to the need to secure the support of the Chinese People's Republic and, in suggesting the acceptability of the General Assembly meeting to approve the figures, left open the possibility that they would be negotiated without the participation of Communist China.[20]

[19] *Verbatim Records of the Meetings of the Ten-Power Disarmament Commission,* Cmd. 1152 (London: HMSO, 1960), p. 37.

[20] One observer has argued that in fact it was this action by the Soviets which precipitated the Chinese publication of the statement "Long Live Leninism." See Harold Hinton, "The Sino-Soviet Dispute and the West: The Chinese Aspect" in Arnold Wolfers (ed.), *Changing East-West Relations and the Unity of the West* (Baltimore: Johns Hopkins University Press, 1964), p. 82. *Long Live Leninism* has been published as a pamphlet of the Peking Foreign Languages Press.

## GENERAL AND COMPLETE DISARMAMENT[21]

The introduction of the issue of general and complete disarmament (GCD) into international negotiations marked not only a major turning point in Soviet strategy but also the beginning of a major dispute between the Soviet Union and Communist China over the role that GCD should play. The Chinese and Russians have disagreed both over the possibility of obtaining GCD prior to the elimination of capitalism and also over the relative priority which would be given to support for GCD as opposed to the need to support wars of national liberation.

The Soviet campaign for GCD began with a speech by Premier Khrushchev to the United Nations General Assembly on September 18, 1959.[22] In the following month, the Standing Committee of the National People's Congress heard a report by Foreign Minister Chen-Yi on the Soviet proposals and, according to NCNA, passed a resolution expressing full support for the Soviet plan.[23]

The Chinese, however, were already unhappy about the Soviet emphasis on GCD, and their disagreement with this position was to become increasingly public. Nevertheless, following his visit to the United States, Khrushchev journeyed to Peking and declared publicly the choice before the world was now between "peaceful co-existence or war with its catastrophic consequences."[24] During this visit, the Soviet Premier, according to the Chinese, "went so far as to try to sell China the U.S. plot of 'two Chinas,' and at the state banquet celebrating the 10th Anniversary of the founding of the People's Republic of China, he read China a lecture against 'testing by force the stability of the capitalist sys-

---

[21] Debate about general and complete disarmament has played such a central role in the Sino-Soviet dispute that general works on the Sino-Soviet conflict are directly relevant. The most recent such study is William E. Griffith, *The Sino-Soviet Rift* (Cambridge, Mass.: M.I.T. Press, 1964), which contains a comprehensive listing of the most relevant earlier works. For a documentary discussion, see "The Disarmament Issue in the Sino-Soviet Dispute: A Chronological Documentation," in Dallin, *Soviet Attitudes*, pp. 237-76.

[22] Text in *Documents on Disarmament 1945-59* (Washington, D.C.: GPO, 1960), II, 1452-60.

[23] Text in SCMP, 2120 (October 21, 1959), pp. 1-5.

[24] Text of speech in G. F. Hudson, Richard Lowenthal, and Roderick MacFarquhar (eds.), *The Sino-Soviet Dispute* (New York: Praeger, 1961), p. 62. Quoted in Dallin, *Soviet Attitudes*, p. 240.

tem.' "[25] The Chinese also alleged that as a gift to Eisenhower before Khrushchev's visit to the United States, the Soviet Union "unilaterally tore up the agreement on new technology for national defense concluded between China and the Soviet Union on October 15, 1957, and refused to provide China with a sample of an atomic bomb and technical data concerning its manufacture."[26]

Beginning in 1960, the Chinese began publicly to make clear their disagreement with the Russian emphasis on the need for disarmament to prevent nuclear war. While the *People's Daily* editorial of January 16 declared that "the Chinese People have always cherished peace and stand for universal disarmament," the National People's Congress Standing Committee, in supporting the Soviet position five days later, made it clear, as indicated above, that China would only accept agreements which she had participated in negotiating.[27] In a speech before the Warsaw Treaty Organization in February, 1960, the Chinese observer, Kang Sheng, not only reiterated the need for Chinese participation in negotiations but also took a rather pessimistic view about the possibilities for disarmament:

> As to the disarmament question, a certain measure of agreement has also been reached on procedural matters. The Chinese people and all other peace-loving people and countries the world over rejoice at this. The emergence of such a situation is not accidental. This is the result of repeated struggles waged by the Socialist forces, the national revolutionary forces and the forces of peace and democracy against the imperialist war forces, the result of the East wind prevailing over the West wind . . . .
>
> . . . At the present time universal disarmament is an important question relating to the defence of world peace. Since World War II, the Soviet Union has time and again made positive proposals for disarmament, the banning of atomic

[25]"The Origin and Development of the Differences Between the Leadership of the CPSU and Ourselves—A Comment on the Open Letter of the Central Committee of the CPSU [1]," *People's Daily*, September 6, 1963. Translation as pamphlet (Peking: Foreign Languages Press, 1963), p. 27.

[26]*Ibid.*, p. 26. See also "Statement by the Spokesmen of the Chinese Government—A Comment on the Soviet Government's Statement of August 3." Dated August 15, 1963; translation in *Peking Review*, VI, No. 33 (August 16, 1963), p. 14.

[27]Translation in SCMP, 2181 (January 21, 1960), pp. 42-44; SCMP, 2185, pp. 1-2.

weapons, and the ending of nuclear weapons tests. The Soviet Union and other Socialist countries have, on their own initiative, reduced their armed forces. Not long ago, the Soviet Union proposed general and complete disarmament at the U.N. General Assembly. It later adopted a law at the Supreme Soviet session, again slashing its armed forces unilaterally by 1.2 million men. These facts convincingly demonstrate the sincerity of the Soviet Union and other Socialist countries for peace and their confidence in their own strength.

Although U.S. imperialism dare not oppose disarmament in so many words, it has always in fact sabotaged universal disarmament. Whenever certain U.S. proposals were accepted by the Soviet Union, the United States always concocted new pretexts for a retreat from its original position, creating all kinds of difficulties and preventing by every means the reaching of agreement on the disarmament question. U.S. actions prove that it will not abandon its policy of the arms race. Therefore, the struggle for universal disarmament is a long-term and complicated struggle between us and imperialism.

The Chinese Government and the Chinese people have always stood for universal disarmament, and actively supported the proposals concerning disarmament made by the Soviet Union and the other Socialist countries. Since 1951, the Chinese Government has on its own initiative again and again reduced its armed forces. The present Chinese armed forces are less than half their original size. We shall continue to work tirelessly for universal disarmament together with the Soviet Union and other Socialist countries. We hope that the countries concerned will reach agreement on this question of universal disarmament. [28]

In April, 1960, the Chinese launched their public attacks on the Soviet position. In "Long Live Leninism," published at that time, the Chinese argued that the only way to preserve peace was to oppose the United States actively. They reiterated there, for the last time in a major statement, that in the event of nuclear war, "the victorious people would create very swiftly a civilization thousands of times higher than the capitalist system and a truly beautiful future for themselves."[29]

[28] Translation in Hudson *et al.* (eds.), *The Sino-Soviet Dispute*, pp. 73-74.

[29] Translation in *ibid.*, pp. 93-94.

In June, 1960, continuing the tradition of ostensible support for the Soviet positions, the Chinese government issued a statement headed "Chinese Government Supports the Soviet Government Disarmament Proposals." The Chinese statement actually argued that the Soviet proposals would simply present a test of the willingness of imperialist countries to accept peace and predicted that the imperialists would reject the Soviet proposals. The statement then went on to declare: "Only with the peoples of all countries of the world waging unremitting struggles and isolating to the greatest extent the imperialists with the U.S. at the head, would it be possible to impel the imperialist countries to sit down to earnest disarmament talks, to put off, even stop, imperialism's plan for starting a new world war, and to insure world peace."[30]

Also in June, 1960, the meeting in Peking of the World Federation of Trade Unions (WFTU) marked the first public Sino-Soviet clash over disarmament at an international front meeting.[31] The chief Chinese delegate, Liu Chang-sheng, challenged the Soviet position in a speech in which he declared that it was unrealistic to expect that the United States would agree to general disarmament. According to the text released by NCNA, he said:

> We support the disarmament proposals put forward by the Soviet Union. It is of course inconceivable that imperialism will accept the proposals for general and complete disarmament. The purpose of putting forward such proposals is to arouse the people throughout the world to unite and oppose the imperialist scheme for arms drive and war preparations, to unmask the aggressive and bellicose nature of imperialism before the peoples of the world in order to isolate the imperialist plot headed by the United States to the greatest extent, so that they will not dare unleash a war lightly. But there are people who believe that such proposals can be realized when imperialism still exists and that the "danger of war can be eliminated" by relying on such proposals. This is an unrealistic illusion. As the view that after disarmament, imperialism would use the funds earmarked for war purposes for "the welfare of the laboring masses" and for "assisting

[30]SCMP, 2277 (June 2, 1960), p. 30.

[31]There have been many such clashes since. In fact, the issue of the relative roles of disarmament and support for wars of national liberation has become the focus of debate between the Chinese wing and the Soviet wing in front organizations.

underdeveloped countries" and that this would "bring general progress to people as a whole without exception"–this is downright whitewashing and embellishing imperialism, and indeed this is helping imperialism headed by the United States to dupe the people throughout the world.

Liu Chang-sheng declaimed that only when socialist revolution is victorious throughout the world can there be a world free from war, a world without arms. Such a world is inconceivable while imperialism still exists. This is not a question of whether socialist powers want peace or not. According to Liu, the imperialists will never lay down their arms of their own accord, because they want to suppress the people of their own countries, and they want to suppress the colonies. They will not lay down their arms so long as they scheme to carry on expansion and aggression against other countries. History has confirmed and will continue to confirm this, Liu maintained, and then he stated:

> To win world peace, the struggle of the world's peoples and diplomatic negotiations carried out by the socialist countries should go hand in hand. It should not be supposed that since diplomatic negotiations are needed, the struggle of the peoples can thus be dispensed with. On the contrary, diplomatic negotiations must be backed up by the united struggle of the world's peoples. To win world peace, we should mainly rely on the struggles waged by the peoples of various countries.[32]

The key issue, then, as laid down by the Chinese, was whether disarmament was to be attained at the negotiating table or by resolute struggle against imperialism.

The next round of the Sino-Soviet debate over arms control came at the Bucharest Conference in late June, 1960, when, during closed sessions, the Russians vigorously supported their disarmament position and criticized the Chinese for bringing the disagreement out into the open at the Trade Union Conference. The Chinese delegate, Peng Chen, defended the Chinese position, arguing that he did not accept the view that the United States was not prepared to start another war. He argued that it was necessary to oppose the enemy in order to prevent war.[33]

---

[32]Translation in Hudson *et al.* (eds.), *The Sino-Soviet Dispute*, p. 126.

[33]Edward Crankshaw, *The New Cold War: Moscow versus Peking* (Baltimore: Penguin, 1963), p. 105.

During the latter part of 1960, in the period of preparation for the Moscow meeting of Communist parties at the end of the year, the Chinese apparently became convinced not only that the Soviet Union was advocating general and complete disarmament as the tactical line for the International Communist movement but also that the Soviets had perhaps come to believe that GCD was a feasible and desirable alternative during the current international period.[34] At the Eighty-one Party Conference in Moscow, a major debate apparently took place about the proper line on disarmament, with the Chinese accusing the Russians of having "absurd" ideas.[35] A number of West European delegates apparently criticized the Chinese position. The text of the conference document revealed a compromise between the Soviet and the Chinese position, with simply a mixing of sentences reflecting the views of the two countries. The major paragraph on disarmament read as follows:

> The meeting considers that the implementation of the programme for general and complete disarmament put forward by the Soviet Union would be of historic importance for the destinies of mankind. To realise this programme means to eliminate the very possibility of waging wars between countries. It is not easy to realise owing to the stubborn resistance of the imperialists. Hence it is essential to wage an active and determined struggle against the aggressive imperialist forces with the aim of carrying this programme into practice. It is necessary to wage this struggle on an increasing scale and to strive perseveringly to achieve tangible results—the banning of the testing and manufacture of nuclear weapons, the abolition of military blocs and war bases on foreign soil and a substantial reduction of armed forces and armaments, all of which should pave the way to general disarmament. Through an active, determined struggle by the socialist and other peace-loving countries, by the international working class and the broad masses in all countries, it is possible to isolate the aggressive circles, foil the arms race and war preparations, and force the imperialists into an agreement on general disarmament.[36]

---

[34] The evidence for this is summarized in Dallin, *Soviet Attitudes*, pp. 250-52.

[35] Edward Crankshaw in the *Observer*, February 12, 1961. Cited in Dallin, *Soviet Attitudes*, p. 252.

[36] Translation in Hudson *et al.* (eds.), *The Sino-Soviet Dispute*, pp. 191-92.

The official Chinese Communist Party resolution on the Moscow Conference took a significantly different line, one which stressed the need for an active anti-imperialist policy:

> ...Owing to the fundamental change in the international balance of class forces, a new world war can be prevented by the joint efforts of the powerful forces of our era–the socialist camp, the international working class, the national-liberation movement and all peace-loving countries and peoples. Peace can be effectively safeguarded provided there is reliance on the struggle of the masses of the people and provided a broad united front is established and expanded against the policies of aggression and war of the imperialists headed by the United States. Marxist-Leninists have never held that the way to socialist revolution necessarily lies through wars between states. The socialist countries have always persisted in the policy of peaceful co-existence and peaceful competition with the capitalist countries, advocated the settlement of international disputes through negotiation, advocated disarmament, the banning of nuclear weapons, the disbandment of military *blocs*, the dismantling of military bases in foreign territory, and the prevention of the revival of militarist forces in West Germany and Japan. The peace proposals put forward by the socialist countries, and first of all by the Soviet Union, have won warm endorsement and support from people the world over. The Communist Party and the people of China have always regarded the safeguarding of world peace, the realization of peaceful co-existence and the prevention of another world war as their most urgent tasks in the international struggle....
>
> The solidarity of the socialist camp and of the international communist movement is the most important guarantee for victory in the struggle of all peoples for world peace, national liberation, democracy and socialism.[37]

Here the crucial difference between the Russian and Chinese positions was laid down. Both parties agreed that world war could be prevented, but the Russians stressed the role of disarmament and international agreements in this connection while the Chinese stressed the role of the

---

[37]"CCP Resolution on Moscow Conference." Dated January 18, 1961; translation released by NCNA, January 20, 1961. Reprinted in Hudson *et al.* (eds.), *The Sino-Soviet Dispute*, pp. 222-23.

solidarity of the international Communist movement and the struggle against the imperialists.

Public polemics on the disarmament question subsided during most of 1961, but in December the Chinese returned to the attack in two *People's Daily* editorials and in a speech by the Chinese delegate at a World Peace Council meeting in Stockholm. The theme expressed in the two editorials was that the Kennedy administration had shown by its actions that it was determined to pursue an aggressive policy by building up positions of military strength and that therefore the socialist camp had to oppose this action by building up its own strength and opposing the forces of imperialism. The speech by delegate Liu Ning-I at the Stockholm World Peace Council constituted a full-scale public attack on the Soviet position. Liu Ning-I began his speech by noting that there were some who felt that peace could only be attained via the route of general and complete disarmament, that the national liberation movement should be subordinated to the search for GCD. He declared, however, that "bearing responsibility for the fate of hundreds of millions of people, the Chinese delegation must state that it decidedly cannot agree with this erroneous and totally harmful view." He asserted that in fact the struggle for national liberation was the most urgent task confronting the peoples of the world. "The view that striving for disarmament should become the central task of all countries and peoples is clearly not in accordance with the practical situation of the oppressed peoples and of states suffering aggression." The peace movement, the Chinese representative declared, must support the national-liberation movement because only in the success of the liberation movement could there be world peace. Liu Ning-I further emphasized that United States imperialism, far from seeking disarmament, was in fact building up its military forces. He concluded that the roadblocks in the way of general and complete disarmament should not be overlooked, and he argued that primary attention should be given to support for wars of national liberation.[38]

---

[38]The editorials were entitled "Holding Aloft the Marxist-Leninist Revolutionary Banner of the Moscow Statement," *People's Daily*, December 1, 1961, and "A Year-End Balance Sheet of the Kennedy Administration's Policy of Aggression," *Ta-kung Pao*, December 30, 1961. A text of the "Speech by Liu Ning-I at the World Peace Council, Stockholm, December 18, 1961," was given in *People's Daily*, December 21, 1961. Translations of all three documents appear in Alexander Dallin, *Diversity in International Communism* (New York: Columbia University Press, 1963), pp. 212-21, 229-37.

In the version of Liu Ning-I's speech printed in the *Peking Review* it was

During 1962, the Chinese not only concentrated on the position that one needed to support war of national liberation and give this precedence over general and complete disarmament, but they began to stress the position that disarmament should concentrate on the elimination of nuclear weapons, rather than seeking to eliminate all weapons including conventional arms.[39] According to the Chinese:

> In August 1962 the Soviet Government formally notified China that the Soviet Union would conclude an agreement with the United States on the prevention of nuclear proliferation. This was a joint Soviet-U.S. plot to monopolize nuclear weapons and an attempt to deprive China of the right to possess nuclear weapons to resist the U.S. nuclear threat. The Chinese Government launched repeated protests against this.[40]

In December, 1962 the Chinese released their article, "The Differences Between Comrade Togliatti and Us," the first of a series of polemics clearly directed at the Soviet Union. These publications, culminating in the *Proposal Concerning the General Line of the International Communist Movement*, released on June 14, 1963, continued to stress the Chinese opposition to GCD ahead of support for wars of national liberation, while reiterating Chinese support for limited agreements concerned with banning nuclear weapons. At the same time the Soviet line on GCD continued to come under attack:

> If one regards general and complete disarmament as the fundamental road to world peace, spreads the illusion that imperialism will automatically lay down its arms and tries to liquidate the revolutionary struggles of the oppressed peoples and nations on the pretext of disarmament, then this is

reported that Liu had said that "we always hold that the problem of universal disarmament is of great significance for the defence of peace. Therefore the Chinese Government supports the proposals for universal disarmament." *Peking Review*, IV, No. 52 (December 29, 1961). Quoted in Dallin, *Diversity in International Communism*, p. 230n.

[39] This aspect of Chinese arms control policy is considered below.

[40] The Origin and Development of the Differences Between the Leadership of the CPSU and Ourselves, p. 47.

deliberately to deceive the people of the world and help the imperialists in their policies of aggression and war.[41]

A few months later, the Soviet Union concluded the three-environment Test Ban Treaty with the United States, and the Sino-Soviet debate, as a whole and in particular in relation to disarmament, escalated into open polemics. During this period, as will be indicated below, the Chinese concentrated their attention on attacking the test ban and in proposing an alternative program for nuclear disarmament. At the same time, the Chinese continued their same line on GCD. They argued that GCD is not possible without the abolition of capitalism and that it should be subordinated as a tactical line to support for wars of national liberation. This continues to be the Chinese position, and in fact, as will be seen below, they now go further in stressing the undesirability of any attempts to limit conventional armaments.

## TEST BAN TREATY

According to the Chinese, the Russians informed them in the fall of 1962 that they were considering going ahead with an atmospheric test ban agreement and were not prepared to share nuclear weapons or nuclear weapons information with the Chinese in order to make it unnecessary for them to test. The Chinese state that in September and October of 1962 and again in June of 1963 they made clear to the Russians that they would not be willing to adhere to a test ban treaty and urged the Soviet government not to sign such an agreement. According to the Chinese:

> ...We solemnly stated that we would not tolerate the conclusion, in disregard of China's opposition, of any sort of treaty between the Soviet Government and the United States which aimed at depriving the Chinese people of their right to take steps to resist the nuclear threats of U.S. imperialism, and that we would issue statements to make opposition known.
>
> We hoped that after such earnest counsel from us, the Soviet leaders would rein in before reaching the precipice and would not render matters irretrievable. Unfortunately, they did not pay the slightest attention to our counsel. They

[41] *A Proposal Concerning the General Line of the International Communist Movement—The Letter of the Central Committee of the Communist Party of China in Reply to the Letter of the Central Committee of the Communist Party of the Soviet Union of March 30, 1963* (Peking: Foreign Languages Press, 1963), p. 30.

finally concluded the treaty on the partial halting of nuclear
tests with the United States and Britain, thereby attempting
to bring pressure to bear on China and force her into her
commitments.

The whole course of events amounts to this: First the
Soviet Government tried to subdue China and curry favour
with U.S. imperialism by discontinuing assistance to China.
Then it put forward all sorts of untenable arguments in an
attempt to induce China to abandon its solemn stand. Failing
in all this, it has brazenly ganged up with the imperialist
bandits in exerting pressure on China. [42]

With the opening of the Moscow talks between the United States, Great
Britain, and the Soviet Union which led to the initialing of the Test Ban
Treaty, the Chinese published in the *People's Daily* an editorial making
public their opposition to this move. The editorial declared that the Test
Ban Treaty was designed to prevent "Socialist countries other than the
Soviet Union from conducting nuclear tests and possessing nuclear
capability" and that "what is of more serious consequence is that to
cease nuclear test according to the U.S. proposal may give rise to a
false sense of security among the peoples and lull their vigilance in the
struggle to defend peace." The editorial concluded:

We consider it our duty to expose thoroughly the U.S. fraud
in connection with termination or partial termination of nuclear
tests. We hope that the Soviet Union will not fall into this
trap.

World peace is being seriously threatened by the U.S. imperialist policy of nuclear war preparations and nuclear blackmail. All peace-loving countries and peoples of the world are
pressing equally for a total ban on nuclear weapons and for
the prevention of nuclear war . . . . The outcome of this struggle
can only be the elimination of nuclear weapons by man and
not of man by nuclear weapons. [43]

After the Test Ban Treaty was signed, the Chinese launched a bitter
attack on the treaty and the motives which lay behind it on the part of
the Soviet Union and the United States. On July 31, the Chinese govern-

[42]"Statement by the Spokesman of the Chinese Government—A Comment on the
Soviet Government's Statement of August 3." Dated August 15, 1963; translation in *Peking Review*, VI, No. 33 (August 16, 1963), p. 15.

[43]Translation in *Peking Review* (July 26, 1963), pp. 47-49.

ment issued a statement calling for total nuclear disarmament and denouncing the treaty. This precipitated an exchange of statements between the Soviet government and the Chinese government in which the views of the two countries, not only on the test ban but on a variety of related issues, were aired.[44]

The Chinese put forth in these statements the view that the Test Ban Treaty is for the Soviets simply an excuse not to share their nuclear weapons with the Chinese. They argue that the treaty will create a false sense of security and is merely an expression of the dangerous and disturbing détente developing between the United States and the Soviet Union, designed to enable the two nuclear powers to dominate the world. They argue also that the treaty will permit the United States to proceed with underground tests and hence with its development of tactical nuclear weapons. And they state that the treaty, since it has been signed by the Chinese Nationalists, would provide a means of establishing a two-China situation if Peking adhered to it.

The Chinese refused to accept the Russian view that the treaty was a step on the road to nuclear disarmament. They pointed out to the Russians that the Soviet government had itself issued a number of statements condemning a three-environment test ban and pressing for a total ban. At the same time, however, the Chinese suggested that a total ban would be no more attractive to them, for it would still be a device aimed at preventing them from getting nuclear weapons. In light of the knowledge that they would, within a relatively short time, be conducting nuclear tests, the Chinese could not but be unhappy about Soviet willingness to enter an agreement banning such tests, thereby creating major political problems for China in relation to the underdeveloped world. The Chinese reacted bitterly to the Test Ban Treaty for still another reason: they took it as a sign of the determination of the Soviet Union to establish friendly relations with the United States at the expense of good relations with China and to establish a Soviet-American duopoly of power in the world.

In trying to counteract the effect of their refusal to sign the Test Ban Treaty, the Chinese began to make explicit their own approach to the problem of arms control and disarmament and to indicate the kinds of agreements that they might be willing to sign.

---

[44]These exchanges, except for the final statement by the Soviet government, have been published in a pamphlet *People of the World, Unite, for the Complete, Thorough, Total and Resolute Prohibition and Destruction of Nuclear Weapons* (Peking: Foreign Languages Press, 1963). The last Soviet statement, issued on September 21, 1963, is translated in *Current Digest of the Soviet Press*, XV, No. 38 (October 16, 1963), pp. 3-15.

## NUCLEAR ARMS CONTROL

As indicated above, during the early 1950's China supported the Soviet position in favor of the total elimination of nuclear weapons. The Chinese now claim that they were unhappy in 1956 when the Soviet Union indicated a willingness to accept limitations on nuclear weapons short of their total abolition. The Chinese say that they then had to evaluate the Soviet proposals on their merits:

> From 1946 to 1956, the Soviet government insisted on the complete prohibition of nuclear weapons. They were correct then and we firmly supported them. In their summary report to the Twentieth Congress of the Communist Party of the Soviet Union in 1956, the Soviet leaders divorced the cessation of nuclear tests from the question of disarmament. Subsequently, they were wrong on certain issues and correct on others and we supported them in all their correct views. But on July 25th, 1963, they were altogether wrong, and it is quite natural that we should resolutely criticize them.[45]

In their attacks on the Soviet GCD position, discussed above, the Chinese always made it clear that they were in favor of a prohibition on nuclear weapons and were prepared to support limited arms control steps in this direction. For example, in their *Proposal Concerning the General Line of the International Communist Movement*, the Chinese declared:

> The complete banning and destruction of nuclear weapons is an important task in the struggle to defend world peace. We must do our utmost to this end.
>
> ... The possibility of banning nuclear weapons does indeed exist. However, if the imperialists were to accept an agreement to ban nuclear weapons, it decidedly will not be because of their "love of humanity" but because of the pressure of all people of all countries for the sake of their own vital interests....
>
> It is necessary for the socialist countries to engage in negotiations of one kind or another with the imperialist countries. It is possible to reach certain agreements through

---

[45]Translation in *Peking Review* (August 16, 1963), p. 15.

negotiation by relying on the correct policies of the socialist countries and on the pressure of people of all countries....[46]

In a statement which they issued just before the signing of the Test Ban Treaty, the Chinese committed themselves to a step-by-step effort to obtain a complete ban on the use of nuclear weapons:

> At present the nuclear powers have acquired technical data necessary to them through a series of nuclear tests. They not only have stockpiled large numbers of nuclear weapons but are also continuing to manufacture them. In these circumstances the step that is of real practical significance is not to cease nuclear testing alone but first of all to make these countries undertake the obligation not to use and manufacture nuclear weapons.... The cessation of nuclear tests will have positive significance only when it forms a component part of the program for general disarmament and the total prohibition of nuclear weapons. If one undertakes to stop nuclear testing as a separate measure, it will be playing right into the hands of the United States, and running counter to the aspirations of the world's peoples for a total prohibition of nuclear weapons and the prevention of nuclear war.
>
> We are in favor of achieving a total prohibition of nuclear weapons stage by stage. This goal may be obtained by following the procedure mentioned above [i.e., the obligation not to use and manufacture nuclear weapons], or its attainment may be promoted by the establishment and expansion of nuclear-weapon free zones. Both methods hinge on the fact that the countries possessing nuclear weapons must undertake practical obligations.[47]

After the Test Ban Treaty was signed, the Chinese issued a statement attacking it. They went on to repeat their own argument on disarmament and proposed a conference of the heads of government of all countries of the world to "discuss the question of the complete prohibition and thorough destruction of nuclear weapons and the question of taking the above-mentioned four measures in order to realise step by step the complete prohibition and thorough destruction of nuclear weapons."[48] The limited steps proposed at this time by the Chinese were:

[46] Translation in pamphlet (Peking: Foreign Languages Press, 1963), pp. 33-35.

[47] Translation in *Peking Review* (July 26, 1963), p. 48.

[48] Translation in *Peking Review* (August 2, 1963), p. 8.

(a) Dismantle all military bases, including nuclear bases, on foreign soil, and withdraw from abroad all nuclear weapons and their means of delivery;

(b) Establish a nuclear weapon-free zone of the Asian and Pacific region, including the United States, the Soviet Union, China and Japan; a nuclear weapon-free zone of Central Europe; a nuclear weapon-free zone of Africa; and a nuclear weapon-free zone of Latin America. The countries possessing nuclear weapons shall undertake due obligations with regard to each of the nuclear weapon-free zones;

(c) Refrain from exporting and importing in any form nuclear weapons and technical data for their manufacture;

(d) Cease all nuclear tests, including underground nuclear tests.

On August 2, 1963, the Chinese government sent the statement to all heads of government.[49] North Vietnam, North Korea, and Albania came down explicitly on the Chinese side. The reaction of other countries, indicated some, if limited, support for the Chinese position. The only clear-cut support from a non-Communist regime came from Cambodia, which, in a statement issued on September 20, 1963, and released by NCNA, described the Test Ban Treaty as "an illusory promise to peace." This statement, issued under the name of the Cambodian head of state, Prince Sihanouk, declared that:

> We prefer to be with China alone than with the multitude of countries who in case of danger would leave us in the cold .... Our international policy is based on neutrality. But should we be obligated one day to choose between China and the others, we would, without hesitation, choose to be on the side of the People's Republic of China, for she alone would take the trouble to fight on our side in case of aggression from our neighbors.[50]

In December, 1963 and January, 1964, the Chinese Communist Premier, Chou En-lai, toured a number of African countries to discuss the forthcoming Afro-Asian conference and apparently also to explain China's stand on disarmament.[51] Chou visited a total of ten African countries

---

[49] Translation in *Peking Review* (August 9, 1963), p. 7.

[50] NCNA broadcast, September 21, 1963, at 1515 GMT; printed in BBC *Summary of World Broadcasts*, Far East/1362/C/1 (September 26, 1963).

[51] Robert A. Scalapino, "Sino-Soviet Competition in Africa," *Foreign Affairs*, XLII (July 1904), pp. 640-54, W. A. C. Adie, "Chou En-lai on Safari," *China Quarterly*, XVIII (April-June 1964), pp. 174-94.

and sought to explain the Chinese unwillingness to sign the Test Ban Treaty and to present in favorable light China's interest in nuclear disarmament. Although in many of the countries Chou was sharply questioned about China's unwillingness to sign the Test Ban Treaty, not only by newsmen in press conferences but also by government officials, in the end he was able to find acceptable common language for a paragraph on disarmament in each of the communiqués. Chou in each case was willing to endorse the proposal for an African nuclear-free zone which had been proposed at the Conference of African States and was willing to go so far as to express China's support for "general disarmament" in return for a clause calling for "the complete prohibition and thorough destruction of nuclear weapons." A typical formulation appeared in the communiqué with Guinea:

> Both parties reaffirm their determination to continue their efforts in combatting imperialism and defending world peace. They stand for general disarmament and the complete prohibition and thorough destruction of nuclear weapons. The Chinese side expressed support for the decision contained in the resolution on general disarmament adopted at the African Summer Conference (Addis Ababa, 1963) proclaiming Africa to be a zone free of nuclear weapons and demanding the removal of all foreign military bases from Africa.[52]

An indication of the kind of statement that Chou was probably pressing for but did not succeed in obtaining from any of the governments was indicated by his answer to a question at a press conference in Somali:

> The Chinese government has consistently stood for the complete prohibition and thorough destruction of nuclear weapons and proposed that a conference of heads of government of all countries be convened to discuss this problem. We are deeply convinced that so long as all peace-loving countries and peoples of the world unite and wage an unremitting struggle against imperialist policies of aggression and war, nuclear weapons can be prohibited and nuclear war can be prevented.[53]

[52]Translation in *Peking Review*, VII, No. 6 (February 7, 1964), p. 27. The ten countries that Chou visited are, in chronological order, the United Arab Republic, Algeria, Morocco, Tunisia, Ghana, Mali, Guinea, Sudan, Ethiopia and Somalia. The trip lasted from December 14 to February 4, 1964. The text of the communiqués are all printed in the *Peking Review*.

[53]Translation in *Peking Review*, VII, No. 7 (February 14, 1964), p. 16.

Another indication of the real Chinese view came when Chou also went to Albania in the midst of his trip to Africa. At the end of his stay, the joint Sino-Albanian communiqué reflected the Chinese position:

The two parties denounce the U.S.-British-U.S.S.R. partial nuclear test ban treaty as a big fraud to fool the people of the world. This treaty is designed to monopolize nuclear weapons. It can neither prevent U.S. imperialism from developing nuclear weapons nor stop it from supplying nuclear weapons to its allies. It can only weaken the defences of the socialist camp and help U.S. imperialism in unilaterally building up nuclear supremacy and in more unscrupulously carrying out nuclear blackmail. Since the conclusion of the tripartite treaty, the United States has repeatedly carried out underground nuclear tests, stepped up the manufacture and development of many types of nuclear arms, further strengthened the network of bases for guided missiles with nuclear warheads, intensified the deployment of nuclear submarines abroad and actively engineered the establishment of the multilateral nuclear force of the NATO bloc. The conclusion of the tripartite treaty has increased the threat of nuclear war. Facts have shown that making one concession after another to imperialism can only encourage the aggressive forces, increase the danger of war and jeopardize world peace.

The two parties hold that a new world war can be prevented, a nuclear war can be averted and world peace can be safeguarded so long as all peace-loving forces of the world, namely, the socialist camp, the national-liberation movement, the revolutionary movement of the peoples and all peace-loving countries and people unite and from the broadest possible united front to wage an unremitting struggle against the aggressive and war policies of imperialism headed by the United States.

The two parties reaffirm that the Governments of China and Albania always stand for *general disarmament* and for the complete prohibition and thorough destruction of nuclear weapons. The Albanian Government fully supports the proposal of the Chinese Government for the convocation of a conference of the government heads of all countries of the world to discuss the question of the complete prohibition and thorough destruction of nuclear weapons. Both parties maintain that it is necessary to strengthen constantly the defence capabilities of all countries in the socialist camp so long as

imperialism rejects general disarmament and the complete
prohibition of nuclear weapons.[54]

During late 1963 and early 1964 the Chinese Communists issued a
series of statements commenting on the "Open Letter of the Central
Committee of the Communist Party of the Soviet Union" which was issued
on July 14, 1963. In these statements, most notably in "Two Different
Lines on the Question of War and Peace," the Chinese made clear their
differences with the Russians on the possibility of avoiding local wars,
on the danger of nuclear war, and on the possibility of negotiated agreements with the United States.[55] They stressed in these statements the
importance of resolute struggle against imperialism and the need to stress
wars of national liberation. At the same time they indicated, without
stressing it, their support for some negotiations and for certain kinds of
nuclear arms control agreements.

During this period, the Chinese also refused to endorse several
measures taken by the Soviet Union in the disarmament field. They
described without comment the hot-line agreement and implied that it was
simply part of the détente effort which they deplored. They attacked the
agreement on limiting the production of fissionable material.[56] They also
deplored Khrushchev's proposal for an agreement outlawing the use of
force in semi-territorial and boundary problems.[57]

[54]Sino-Albanian Joint Statement. Dated January 8, 1964; text in *China and
Albania—Friends in a Common Struggle: A Collection of Speeches and Documents from the Visit of Chinese Leaders to Albania* (Peking: Foreign Languages Press, 1964), pp. 144-45. The Albanians were either not yet willing
to accept Chinese opposition to general and complete disarmament or else
had not yet fully understood the Chinese line. Hoxha, in a speech welcoming
Chou, declared that China "strives for the unconditional prohibition of all
nuclear tests, destruction of nuclear stockpiles, and *general and complete
disarmament*" (italics added). Speech by Enver Hoxha, First Secretary of the
Central Committee of the Party of Labour of Albania, at the Banquet of Welcome Given by the Albanian Party and Government. Dated January 7, 1964; in
*China and Albania*, p. 102.

[55]Translation in *Peking Review*, VI, No. 47 (November 22, 1963), pp. 6-16.

[56]NCNA, April 22, 1964. For a more recent and detailed criticism of the pro-
posal to ban production of fissionable material, see Tung Wei-jen, "U.S.
Monopoly Capital and the Nuclear War in History," *Peking Review*, VIII, No. 5
(January 29, 1965), pp. 13-16.

[57]NCNA, February 2, 1964.

## THE CHINESE NUCLEAR DETONATION AND AFTER

At the time of their first detonation of a nuclear device, in October, 1964, the Chinese began to stress their positive interest in certain kinds of nuclear disarmament leading ultimately to the destruction of all nuclear weapons. They also began to discuss in some detail their opposition to some measures in addition to the Test Ban Treaty and in general to articulate much more the Chinese position on disarmament and arms control questions.

The statement issued by the Chinese government at the time of the detonation, on October 16, 1964, reiterated the Chinese support for nuclear disarmament:

> The Chinese government hereby formally proposes to the governments of the world that a summit conference of all the countries of the world be convened to discuss the question of the complete prohibition and thorough destruction of all nuclear weapons, and that as a first step, the summit conference should reach an agreement to the effect that the nuclear powers and those countries which may soon become nuclear powers undertake not to use nuclear weapons, neither to use them against non-nuclear countries and nuclear-free zones, nor against each other.[58]

At this point, for the first time, the Chinese singled out a ban on the use of nuclear weapons as the most important and most desirable first step toward total nuclear disarmament. The same kind of statement formally committed the Chinese not to use nuclear weapons. "The Chinese Government hereby solemnly declares," the statement went, "that China will never at any time under any circumstances be the first to use nuclear weapons."[59]

While the Chinese waited until they could claim to be a nuclear power before making this commitment and before stressing a ban on the use of nuclear weapons, they had frequently listed such a ban as one of the desirable steps toward nuclear disarmament. They also indicated that they did not believe that socialist countries should see nuclear weapons first. As already indicated, the Chinese, just before the Test Ban Treaty was signed, suggested that either a ban on the use of nuclear weapons or

---

[58]Translation in *Peking Review*, VII, No. 42 (October 16, 1964), pp. ii-iv.

[59]*Ibid.*

a stress on nuclear-free zones could form the basis of the first steps which, the Chinese argued, would be necessary to obtain, eventually, complete nuclear disarmament.[60] In 1963, commenting on the Test Ban Treaty, the Chinese government declared:

> Nuclear weapons in the hands of socialist countries shall always be defensive weapons against the nuclear threats of the imperialists. In contrast to the imperialists, socialist countries have no need to use nuclear weapons for blackmail or gambling and must not do so.[61]

With the background of statements on the need for a ban on the use of nuclear weapons and the Chinese declaration in the detonation statement, Chou En-lai sent a second letter to the heads of government of all nations, calling again for a world-wide conference but this time with the emphasis on reaching agreement on a ban on the use of nuclear weapons. The full text of Chou's letter reads as follows:

> On October 16th, 1964, China exploded an atom bomb, thus successfully making its first nuclear test. On the same day the Chinese government issued a statement on this event, setting forth in detail China's position on the question of nuclear weapons. The Chinese government consistently stands for the complete prohibition and thorough destruction of nuclear weapons. China has been compelled to conduct nuclear tests and develop nuclear weapons. China's mastering of nuclear weapons is entirely for defense and for protecting the Chinese people from the U.S. nuclear threat. The Chinese Government solemnly declares that at no time and in no circumstances will China be the first to use nuclear weapons.
>
> The Chinese Government will continue to work for the complete prohibition and thorough destruction of nuclear weapons through international consultations and, for this purpose, has put forward in its statement the following paraposal:
>
> That a summit conference of all the countries of the world be convened to discuss the question of the complete prohibition and thorough destruction of nuclear weapons, and that, as a first step, the summit conference should reach an agreement to the effect that the nuclear powers and those countries

[60]See above, pp. 118-19.

[61]Translation in *Peking Review*, VI, No. 36 (September 6, 1963), p. 14.

which may soon become nuclear powers undertake not to use nuclear weapons, neither to use them against non-nuclear countries and nuclear-free zones, nor against each other.

It is the common aspiration of all peace-loving countries and people of the world to prevent a nuclear war and eliminate nuclear weapons. The Chinese government sincerely hopes that its proposal will be given favorable consideration and positive response by your government.

Please accept the assurances of my highest consideration.[62]

The Chinese apparently passed this proposal to the United States at the Warsaw talks, this being, according to press reports, the first such use of the Warsaw talks. The American government branded the proposal as a "smoke screen"; other nations were more responsive.[63] The reaction to this Chinese proposal was considerably greater and more favorable than was that to the similar Chou En-lai letter of a year before. The Soviet Union and the Communist countries of Eastern Europe, both China's Communist allies there and countries more closely aligned with Russia, endorsed the proposal for a conference of the heads of state.[64] At the same time, the Soviet government sought to make it clear that the proposal for a ban on the first use of nuclear weapons was in fact a long-standing Soviet position which the Chinese were now only lately giving strong support to. Soviet Foreign Minister Gromyko told the United Nations General Assembly on December 7, 1964, that:

> The proposal of the CPR to call a conference of the heads of world states to discuss the problem of a total ban on nuclear weapons and the total destruction of them and the problem of reaching an understanding, as a first step, and a repudiation by states of the application of these weapons deserves positive consideration. This is consistent with what the Soviet government has often proposed.[65]

[62]Text in *Peking Review*, VII, No. 43 (October 23, 1964), p. 6.

[63]*New York Times*, October 22, 1964, p. 3.

[64]*New York Times*, December 26, 1964, p. 14, and January 4, 1964, p. 5; *Peking Review*, VIII, No. 3 (January 15, 1965), p. 3.

[65]"Soviet Government Memorandum on Steps To Further Ease International Tension and To Limit the Arms Race." Text in *Current Digest of the Soviet Press*, XVI, No. 50 (January 6, 1965), pp. 9-11.

An article in the Soviet English-language propaganda journal *International Affairs* (Moscow) in January, 1965 discussed a "ban on nuclear weapons," stressing the long-standing Soviet commitment to this proposal and tracing the many times at which the Soviets had made such a proposal. Only in the midst of a paragraph discussing the increased support which the proposal had recently received from groups such as the Ecumenical Council and Asian, African, and Latin American countries was China mentioned, and then merely in passing. "Recently the Chinese People's Republic came out in favor of a nuclear arms ban."[66]

In addition to pressing the proposal for a conference of heads of state, Chinese propaganda media stressed the Chinese desire for limited steps leading to the abolition of nuclear weapons. On October 22, the *People's Daily* published an article entitled, "Break the Nuclear Monopoly, Eliminate Nuclear Weapons," which began to spell out the Chinese rationale for an argument not to use nuclear weapons and emphasized that the United States had refused to make a unilateral commitment such as the Chinese had done. The editorial noted:

> This concrete proposal by the Chinese government that agreement be reached first on not using nuclear weapons is practical, fair and reasonable, easily feasible and involves no question of control. If all the countries concerned are willing to make this commitment, then the danger of nuclear war will be immediately reduced. And this would mean a big initial step towards the ultimate goal of complete prohibition and thorough destruction of nuclear weapons. After that it would be possible to discuss the question of the halting of all kinds of nuclear tests, the prohibition of the export, import, proliferation, manufacture and stockpiling and destruction of nuclear weapons. Obviously, the U.S. government has no reason at all to reject this proposal if it has the slightest desire for peace.[67]

The editorial went on to attack the United States for avoiding any direct substantive comment on the Chinese proposal and for instead urging China to sign the Test Ban Treaty. The editorial charged that the United States was not in fact interested in preventing proliferation of nuclear weapons as it suggested but was engaged in sharing nuclear

---

[66] M. Lvov, "Ban Nuclear Weapons," *International Affairs* (January 1965), pp. 9-14.

[67] Translation in *Peking Review*, VII, No. 44 (October 30, 1964), pp. 6-7.

weapons with its European allies. The editorial also implied that China was not herself opposed to proliferation. This theme had appeared previously in the Chinese discussion during the period immediately following the test ban when Peking argued the need for as many socialist countries as possible to develop nuclear weapons. Here the Chinese did not appear to be limiting the argument to socialist countries:

> The United States cannot maintain its nuclear monopoly any longer. This is highly beneficial to the complete prohibition and thorough destruction of nuclear weapons. The hope of preventing nuclear war and prohibiting nuclear weapons does not lie in consolidating the U.S. nuclear monopoly but in breaking it. And the more thoroughly it is broken, the greater will be the possibility of completely prohibiting and thoroughly destroying nuclear weapons. Such is the dialectics of the development of things.[68]

China has put increasing emphasis on the importance of an agreement with the United States for a ban on the use of nuclear weapons. The chairman of the People's Republic of China, Liu Shao-chi, in one of his infrequent public statements, reiterated the Chinese desire for an agreement banning the use of nuclear weapons as a first step and declared that "it is a serious test for the U.S. government whether it accepts this proposal and undertakes this obligation."[69] In December, 1964, reacting to the sending of the American Polaris submarine "Daniel Boone" into the Pacific, the Chinese implied that they might well have made a concrete proposal to the United States for a bilateral agreement on this question:

> Shortly after its first nuclear test, China proposed to the United States that the governments of both countries should issue a formal statement pledging that neither of them would at any time or under any circumstances be the first to use nuclear weapons. If the United States had any sincere desire for peace, it would have been easy to reach an agreement. However, it has turned a deaf ear to our reasonable proposal, and, what is more, it is attempting to frighten us with Polaris missile submarines. This is both absurd and ludicrous.[70]

[68] Ibid.

[69] Translation in Peking Review, VII, No. 45 (November 6, 1964), p. 6.

[70] Peking Review, VIII, No. 1 (January 1, 1965), p. 20.

The Chinese seem to seek a world-wide agreement, and in particular agreement among the nuclear powers, for a treaty banning the use of nuclear weapons. In addition, China proposes, perhaps as an interim measure, parallel declarations by the United States and China in which each commits itself not to use nuclear weapons first.

In November of 1964, the Chinese published an editorial in the *People's Daily* which stated in detail the current Chinese position on questions of arms control and disarmament.[71] The editorial noted that China accepted the need for limited first steps, commenting that everyone agreed that in order to reach the goal of a complete abolition of nuclear weapons, "certain practical measures have to be taken." Since this is agreed, "the question is how the first step should be taken so as to facilitate the attainment of the goal rather than produce an adverse effect." The article then considered in turn the following first steps which have been proposed:

a) the three-environment Test Ban Treaty
b) complete test ban treaty
c) destruction of means of delivery
d) no-first-use agreement

Considering first the three-environment Test Ban Treaty, China repeated her objections to the treaty, concluding that it "not only puts off indefinitely the complete prohibition of nuclear weapons but also serves as a smoke screen for U.S. nuclear war preparations."

Turning to the possibility of a complete test ban treaty, the editorial noted correctly that there is renewed pressure for such a treaty but argued that in fact there is little difference from a partial ban. Such a treaty, the Chinese assert, would serve to perpetuate the superpower nuclear monopoly and "only set a false sense of security and weaken the struggle for all peace-loving people for the complete prohibition of nuclear weapons." The Chinese recognize that the signing of a complete Test Ban Treaty would further strengthen the hands of American and Soviet leaders who argue that this is the road to nuclear disarmament and that it would increase the pressure on China to accept the agreement.

Next the editorial considered the proposal made by the French and also in the first stage of the Soviet-proposed GCD treaty that "destruction of delivery vehicles with nuclear weapons can be taken as a primary measure for realizing the complete prohibition of nuclear weapons."

---

[71] "New Starting Point for Efforts to Ban Nuclear Weapons Completely." Translation in *Peking Review*, VII, No. 48 (November 27, 1964), pp. 12-14. The translation is reproduced here as Appendix A.

The editorial states that while this position as it stands seems attractive, it cannot be effective since "ordinary aircraft can carry nuclear weapons as well as strategic bombers." This is particularly true for the United States since it has small but powerful nuclear weapons. Not only that, but the proposal involves the linking of conventional with nuclear armaments reduction, greatly complicating the question, and, in addition, must involve the question of control, "which is a great obstacle to arms reduction delivery put up by the United States."

In the process of rejecting this proposal China was able to make it clear that nuclear weapons could be carried in conventional planes. That is to say, China may already have a nuclear delivery capability. At the same time, the statement was designed to answer General de Gaulle, who, in responding to Chou En-lai's letter proposing nuclear disarmament, reiterated the French proposal for destruction of delivery vehicles.[72] In a brief paragraph the Chinese pointed quite effectively to all the problems connected with this proposal.

Having rejected the alternative first steps, the editorial proceeded to discuss in more detail the Chinese proposal for a ban on the first use of nuclear weapons. It laid out several criteria for evaluating a first stage proposal:

> The first step must facilitate the taking of further steps and be conducive, not detrimental, to the attainment of the aim of the complete prohibition of nuclear weapons. This step must help check the nuclear arms race instead of serving as a smoke screen and help lessen the threat of nuclear war instead of increasing the threat. It must serve to promote the struggle of the peace-loving people of the world over for the complete prohibition of nuclear weapons, and not lower their vigilance and pull the wool over their eyes.

The consequence, according to the Chinese, of signing an agreement not to be the first to use nuclear weapons is that the nuclear powers would be able to cease the testing and production of nuclear weapons. The United States then also, according to the Chinese, would be unable to intimidate others with nuclear weapons or set up nuclear bases or spread nuclear weapons to other countries. The stockpiling of nuclear weapons would be unnecessary. This set of observations would presumably apply to the United States, the Soviet Union, France, and Great Britain. "Those countries not now possessing nuclear weapons would agree not to develop their own nor import them from other countries. . . .

[72]De Gaulle's letter to Chou En-lai was dated October 29, 1964, and released by Peking NCNA, International Service in English, on November 9, 1964.

Those which may soon possess them [China] will undertake not to use nuclear weapons, not to use them against non-nuclear countries." Hence while the agreement not to use nuclear weapons, according to the Chinese, is supposed to inhibit American nuclear deployment in a number of ways, it would prevent China only from using nuclear weapons against the United States or other nuclear powers. This section of the editorial concluded by noting that, since no control is necessary, the agreement would be easy to reach. The possibility of a bilateral agreement between the United States and Communist China was suggested.

The editorial went on to consider the proper setting for holding talks on disarmament questions. It noted that the United States had declared recently that it had no objection to China's participating in the Geneva Eighteen-Nation Disarmament Conference, but it pointed out that the Geneva talks are conducted within "the framework of the United Nations" and that China would have nothing to do with the United Nations until her rights as the sole legitimate representative of the Chinese people were restored. The Chinese charged that the Geneva Conference was

> under the manipulation and control of the United States and can in no way reflect the aspirations of the people. . . . It is more difficult for the Geneva Disarmament Conference to solve the question of complete prohibition of nuclear wea-pons than for a camel to pass through the needle's eye. We thank the U.S. Government for its generosity in not opposing China's participation in the Geneva Disarmament Conference but we must tell it frankly that it will not have the pleasure of our company.

The editorial then considered the proposal that the five nuclear pow-ers should hold negotiations to discuss questions of nuclear weapons. Without identifying United Nations Secretary-General U Thant as the author of this proposal, the Chinese made clear their disapproval. They argued that the question of nuclear weapons affects all the countries of the world and asked: "What right do the five countries possessing nu-clear weapons have to deprive more than a hundred countries of their say and make arbitrary decisions on such a major question affecting the destiny of mankind?" The Chinese indicated that they were not prepared to accept an invitation to five-power talks. The editorial concluded:

> The struggle for the complete prohibition and thorough destruction of nuclear weapons has been going on for many years. Now is the time to take practical and feasible steps to obtain this objective. The Chinese Government's pro-posal has opened up a new avenue for the complete pro-

hibition of nuclear weapons. It proposes to reach first of all an international agreement guaranteeing against the use of nuclear weapons, so as to provide a new starting point for their complete prohibition. It is our belief that no matter how U.S. imperialism may try to obstruct this, the Chinese Government proposal will win the ever increasing support of peace-loving countries and peoples. The Chinese people will fight together with them to push the struggle for the prohibition of nuclear weapons onto a new path.

This editorial is the most comprehensive statement of the current Chinese position. The Chinese argue that an effort should be made to control only nuclear weapons and not conventional forces and that the control of nuclear weapons should proceed on a step-by-step basis. They urge that the first step be a ban on the use of nuclear weapons, and they are prepared to endorse other preliminary steps, such as nuclear-free zones. The Chinese have opposed a number of other possible first steps, including the nuclear Test Ban Treaty and a total test ban treaty as well as a cutoff on production of fissionable materials or an effort to control strategic delivery systems. They appear to be interested in promoting their disarmament proposals either in the context of a world-wide conference or through bilateral negotiations with the United States.

Communist China's position on disarmament has apparently changed substantially since the early 1950's, when Peking was completely supporting the Soviet stand. Now the Chinese are not only actively opposing Soviet proposals but are also pressing proposals of their own. It should be noted, however, that major changes have occurred in the Soviet position and that the Chinese of 1964 stand very near where the Soviets of 1946 did. That is, priority should be given to elimination of the nuclear weapons that the enemy has.

Similar to the Soviet position in the late 1940's and early 1950's, the Chinese approach to disarmament and arms control is primarily political. They view the subject not as one which involves enhancing or threatening military security but rather as a means of promoting political objectives directly. [1] Arms control and disarmament have come, for the Chinese, to be equated with an effort by the United States and the Soviet Union to establish a duopoly of power in the world. The Chinese see arms control as an attempt to cut off the nuclear club at two members, who would then, presumably, divide and rule the world. To the Chinese, the attempt to get arms control agreements is simply part and parcel of the attempt to establish a détente. And to the Chinese, a détente means the selling out of Chinese interest by the Russians for the sake of their own European-oriented political objectives.

The Chinese also feel that arms control and disarmament, as defined by the two superpowers, tend to exclude support of wars of national liberation. The Soviet Union, as indicated above, has argued that such wars should be subordinated to the drive for world peace and general and complete disarmament. The United States has specified that it will not accept any comprehensive disarmament agreement unless the agreement is accompanied by a means to prevent support for wars of national liberation. The Chinese strongly oppose any agreement that explicitly or implicitly implies an obligation not to give aid to just wars of national liberation, i.e., those seeking the overthrow of bourgeois imperialist-supported regimes.

[1]Whether this is still the Soviet view or whether it has changed is beyond the scope of this enquiry. It would appear, however, that the Chinese are convinced that the Soviets are interested in securing general and complete disarmament.

Finally, the Chinese view is that emphasis on the need for general and complete disarmament, or, in fact, for any kind of disarmament agreement with the imperialist countries, is politically undesirable because it tends to lower the morale of the population of socialist and other anti-imperialist countries, thus reducing their will to oppose attempts of the United States (and perhaps the Soviet Union) to use nuclear blackmail to secure political objectives.

From the point of view of their military security, the Chinese would also find sufficient reasons to oppose any arms control or disarmament agreements limiting their own ability to improve their forces. The Chinese behave as an anti-*status quo* power in territorial and political as well as military terms. They are determined to develop the weapons of a modern superpower, particularly nuclear weapons and associated delivery systems, and are therefore most unwilling to accept any agreement that implies freezing of the military *status quo* by interfering with their attempts to get nuclear weapons and delivery systems and to modernize their own conventional forces. They would, of course, have no reason to object on narrow security grounds to agreements by which the superpowers restricted their own armaments.

In addition, the Chinese probably lack any positive military security incentive for negotiating arms control agreements. The Soviet leaders recognize that a direct nuclear exchange with the United States could mean destruction in a very short time, and they have, therefore, developed a security interest in measures such as the hot line that reduce the danger of an accidental nuclear war. The Chinese military leaders cannot see any similar advantage to them from any conceivable arms agreement with the United States.

All the foregoing might lead one to predict that the Chinese position is that arms control and disarmament are undesirable and that no proposals for disarmament could be taken seriously. However, as was made clear above, the Chinese have in fact put forward a proposal for complete nuclear disarmament and have suggested, as a first step, a pledge by the nuclear powers not to be the first to use nuclear weapons. They indicated a willingness to consider other proposals, such as nuclear-free zones. The major reason for this apparent inconsistency in Chinese policy is clearly the attempt to establish friendly relations with at least certain African, Asian, and Latin American states. The Chinese failure to sign the Test Ban Treaty hurt them in their relations with these countries and forced the Chinese to counterattack with their own proposal for more radical and comprehensive nuclear disarmament. Chou En-lai, on his African tour in 1964 and elsewhere, has been able to fall back on the

Chinese proposal as China's answer to the test ban and argue that, as soon as other nuclear powers are prepared to give up nuclear weapons, the Chinese will do likewise. There does not appear to be any reason at all to believe that the Chinese expect this proposal to be adopted or, in view of the inability to detect hidden stockpiles, that they would find it acceptable even if the West and the Soviet Union did. Nevertheless, their espousal of this position is probably a *sine qua non* for continuing friendly relations with various African, Asian, and Latin American states and enables the Chinese to provide some answer to their very unpopular rejection of the test ban. In addition, the Chinese have sought to appeal in countries such as Japan to various left-wing groups that tend to be pacifist. Here again the Chinese have needed to propose a counter to the Test Ban Treaty in the form of a more radical proposal. Such a proposal could form a rallying point for those leftists who are prepared to accept the Chinese position that the test ban was essentially discriminatory and therefore should be rejected in favor of the complete elimination of nuclear weapons by all countries.

The Chinese no doubt see a campaign against nuclear weapons as essentially a continuation of the Soviets' campaign in the early 1950's, which they supported and which was aimed primarily at preventing the possible use of nuclear weapons by the United States. The Chinese now confront the United States in a totally unequal encounter in which American nuclear power could quickly destroy any Chinese ability to wage war. Given this situation and given the fact that the United States now has an abundance of nuclear power, only political motivations and fear that the Soviet Union would be driven into the war could deter American use of nuclear weapons in a Chinese-American clash. This has led the Chinese to be cautious in a situation which might lead to American involvement and to seek to suggest that the Soviet Union would still come to the aid of the Chinese in the event of attack. They have also continued with political propaganda campaigns, including the proposal for a ban on the use of nuclear weapons, a move designed to reduce the likelihood of America's using nuclear weapons, reduce it by raising the political cost of taking such a step.

For the present, then, the primary Chinese incentives in the arms control and disarmament field concern political-propaganda problems. On the one hand, they oppose arms control as symbolic of the Soviet-American détente and as threatening support for wars of national liberation. On the other, they give lip service to at least certain forms of disarmament and arms control as part of their appeal to underdeveloped countries and also as part of their attempt to prevent the United States from using nuclear weapons—in part by generating support in Asian countries.

It appears extremely unlikely that this situation will change in the near future and that the Chinese will become interested in any limited or comprehensive arms control measures.[2] It seems clear, however, that given the current frame of mind of the Peking leadership and barring a major change in orientation following the removal of Mao from the scene, the Chinese will demand, at the very minimum, admission to the United Nations, removal of Taiwan from the United Nations, and perhaps United States recognition before they will be willing to enter into any formal arms control or disarmament negotiations. Even then they are unlikely to accept any agreements before they have developed substantial nuclear weapons and delivery capability and unless the agreements do not imply an abandonment of the Chinese commitment to support wars of national liberation.

It is very likely that the Chinese will also be wary of any arms control agreements as long as they continue to view them as a device of Soviet-American hegemony. This suggests that only a major improvement in Sino-Soviet relations or the development by the Chinese over the long run of a capability which they felt was in some way sufficient to match that of the United States and the Soviet Union would lead the Chinese to be willing to discuss measures for arms stabilization and perhaps arms reduction.

While it is important to state these probable preconditions and to stress that the Chinese are unlikely to sign significant arms control agreements or adopt an "arms control posture," one cannot exclude the possibility that the Chinese would be willing to enter into a limited number of specified formal agreements or accept various kinds of tacit arrangements, even without these conditions being met. As elaborated below, the Chinese have already accepted a number of tacit limitations, particularly in the form of wartime restraints. They might be willing to accept others even in peacetime. However, the current Chinese attitude toward arms control makes the possibilities of formal agreement appear extremely unlikely.

[2]The question of how to begin moving the Chinese along this path and where it might ultimately lead is discussed in Chapter XII.

## VARIETIES OF ARMS CONTROL

In discussing the current Chinese attitude toward various arms control measures in more detail the typology used by Dallin and others in a recent study of Soviet attitudes toward arms control is employed.[3] For this reason, some categories appear that are not directly relevant to the Chinese situation.

1. Preventive Measures

There would be little if any Chinese interest in measures designed to prevent the deployment of existing weapons systems or to forestall new deployments.

Efforts to control research and development have come up against difficult problems of definition as well as inspection in Soviet-American relations. For the Chinese, there is the additional difficult problem that they are unwilling to accept any kind of freezing of research and development that would prevent them from catching up to the United States and the Soviet Union. The willingness of the Russians to accept the freeze implicit in the Test Ban Treaty stems at least in part from the fact that they appeared to be very close to, if not on a par with the United States in development of various kinds of nuclear weapons. Part of the Chinese objection to the Test Ban Treaty was precisely that it permitted continued testing underground. It is in the area of low-yield tests which can be conducted underground, the Chinese noted, that improvements in the American nuclear arsenal were most likely. The Chinese have made it clear that they will not accept any limitation on their own testing, presumably at least until they come up to current Soviet (or United States) capabilities. Limitations on other weapons capabilities, including delivery systems, likewise will be unappealing to the Chinese until after they have developed sufficient delivery systems, including presumably both medium-range missiles and ICBM's.

A second measure, and one which has appeared promising in the Soviet-American context, is that of preventing the proliferation of nuclear weapons. However, we have already indicated that the Chinese have, up until now at least, not adopted the traditional position of a nuclear power, that of wishing to have proliferation end with their attainment of nuclear

---

[3]Alexander Dallin et al., The Soviet Union and Disarmament: An Appraisal of Soviet Attitudes and Intentions (New York: Praeger, 1965), pp. 127-41.

status. On the contrary, the Chinese argue that the more socialist countries—and, at least on a few occasions, the more countries in general—which have nuclear weapons, the better. The Chinese suggest that the spread of nuclear weapons will not only make it easier to resist American nuclear blackmail but also hasten the day when nuclear weapons will be totally eliminated.[4]

The Chinese do not appear to have publicly discussed the question of catalytic war. They probably recognize that their own nuclear force may some day be in a position to at least be able to threaten to trigger the Soviet nuclear force against the United States. Insofar as they have considered this problem, it has probably been in the context of a useful instrument of Chinese politics rather than a danger to be avoided by international agreement.

Preventive measures in the typology presented by Dallin also include efforts to reduce the risks of war. Measures of this kind have primarily focused on strategic interaction between nuclear delivery systems and on the problem of surprise attack in central Europe. Since the Chinese do not pose any direct military threat to American nuclear forces in the Pacific or in the United States, there has not been any problem of danger of war by reciprocal fear of surprise attack. The Chinese appear to be much more concerned about the possibility of a deliberate American strike than one rising out of technical or political accident.

When the Chinese develop a medium-range nuclear delivery system and, later, an intercontinental one, they will presumably still be relatively vulnerable to American attack. At the same time American land-based air and missile forces in the Pacific will presumably become vulnerable to Chinese missile attack. In this situation there may develop some interest on both sides in reducing the possibility of war by accident or miscalculation. However, as in the case of the Russians, this interest may express itself in the form of unilateral actions designed to reduce the vulnerability of nuclear forces.

## 2. War Control

The Chinese have joined the Russians in deriding such notions as "limited general war" as simply being a cover for American attempts to rationalize a first-strike strategy against socialist countries. The Chinese have even more reason than the Russians to deny the possibility of limiting a general war in ways that make more conceivable an American nuclear attack against China.

---

[4]The question of non proliferation agreements and their possible relevance to China is the subject of Chapter V.

The Chinese have, however, shown considerable interest in limitation of local wars and have, in fact, operated with considerable restraint in conventional military conflicts. [5]

### 3. Strategic Force Reductions

Certainly for a very long time to come, the Chinese will be seeking to build up their delivery forces and are very unlikely to be willing to accept any limitation on their own production in return for any conceivable concession from the West.

The Chinese would also be actively opposed to any Soviet-American agreement limiting the size of the strategic forces of the two superpowers, even though it would be to China's strategic advantage in that it might enable Peking to develop an effective deterrent force more easily. The Chinese would view such an agreement as part of the effort between the two to establish a deténte leading to their control of the world. They would also see such a move as similar to the test ban, that is, an effort to establish a limitation in the field in which the Chinese will be soon carrying on activity and which the superpowers have already made major advances and have large-scale forces in being.

### 4. Limited Stabilizing Measures

Under this category Dallin includes measures designed to increase the stability of the nuclear deterrent. As indicated above, the Chinese do not appear to have given any attention as yet to the problem of the stability of the strategic balance between the United States and China as it will begin to develop over the next five to ten years. In relation to Soviet-American agreement, the Chinese view would again be a political one, seeing such agreements as steps toward a detente and as symbolizing the mutual interest of the two superpowers against the rest of the world.

### 5. Confidence-Building and Symbolic Measures

The Soviet Union has in recent years placed particular stress on confidence-building measures designed to pave the way toward more substantial agreement and in particular toward general and complete disarmament. The Soviet interest in items such as the Antarctica Treaty, the test ban, and other limited steps which were being negotiated during 1963 has been interpreted at least in part in this light. [6]

[5]This subject is discussed in detail in Chapter VII. The possible role of arms control in dealing with insurgency is discussed in Chapter VIII.

[6]See, for example, Dallin's listing of such agreements, *Soviet Attitudes*, p. 133.

Here again the Chinese have shown little or no interest. The very notion of building confidence depends on the belief accepted by the Russians and rejected by the Chinese that there are at least some men of good will in the government of the United States. The Russian view seems to be that forces for peace must be encouraged by the signing of confidence measures. The Chinese view is that there are no men of good will in the American hierarchy and that such measures can only encourage American leaders to believe that the possibilities for nuclear blackmail and other offensive measures against the socialist camp have increased.

The Chinese have been interested in one measure which Dallin includes under confidence-building, that of a ban on the first use of nuclear weapons. As was indicated above, however, the Chinese interest in such an agreement does not seem at all to relate to improving relations with the United States. Rather it is aimed at improving Chinese relations with other countries and in seeking to develop political pressures that would inhibit the American use of nuclear weapons and the threat of American use of nuclear weapons.

## 6. Conventional Force Limitations

The Soviet Union is committed to conventional force limitation. Such limitation is included as part of its proposal for general and complete disarmament. The Chinese, on the other hand, reject not only GCD but also proposals for any less extreme limit on conventional forces.

Probably opposition to conventional force limitations stems from the Chinese desire, for political propaganda reasons, to keep attention focused on nuclear weapons. The main threat to the security of China comes from the nuclear capability of the United States. The Chinese emphasis is on curtailing the possibility of this force being used. In addition, the Chinese recognize that they have a large, powerful army, one whose capabilities tend to be overestimated in Asia, if not in the United States. To some extent, this army serves as a counterweight to American nuclear power in Asia, in somewhat the same way as the Soviet army did in Europe in the early postwar period. Hence the Chinese are unwilling to accept any limitations on this force which will eliminate its psychological role in Asia or which will actually reduce its capability to fight beyond its borders and to defend China in the event of an American attack. The large Chinese army also plays a major role within China, as indicated in Chapter IV.

## 7. International Organization

The Chinese are intensely hostile toward international controls and toward the possibility of an international control organization operating in a disarming or disarmed world. As indicated above, the Chinese charge that the United Nations itself is under the control of the imperialist powers. Hence they would reject any form of control institution set up within the United Nations context. Given their emphasis on the elimination of nuclear weapons, the Chinese can and presumably would argue that international control mechanisms are unnecessary since nations would maintain their own conventional military capability.[7]

## 8. Regional Measures

The Chinese attitude toward nuclear-free zones appears to be an ambiguous one. On the one hand, they are in favor in principle of nuclear-free zone arrangements and continue to stress their support for such arrangements outside the Far East. In the Far East, on the other hand, their approach has been colored by the recognition that the Soviet interest in an Asian free-zone arrangements was designed at least in part to try to prevent China from becoming a nuclear power.[8] The Chinese position is that a nuclear-free zone would have to include the United States and the Soviet Union.

China might be interested in a nuclear-free zone agreement which saw the removal of American and Soviet nuclear weapons from the Asian and Pacific region in return for a Chinese promise not to station their nuclear weapons within a specified number of miles of their own border. The Chinese interest in such an arrangement would presumably be based on a belief that America would be less likely to use nuclear weapons if there were no forces which could be used almost instantaneously in the event of crisis. In addition, the removal of American nuclear power from Asia might be symbolic, suggesting to the countries of the area withdrawal of an American commitment to defend them against a Chinese attack.

[7]These issues are discussed at greater length in Chapter XI.

[8]See pp. 99-102.

Should Communist China accept a formal arms control agreement, she would be subject to a body of international law applying to such questions as the conclusion, interpretation, and abrogation of such agreements. Some forms of arms control agreement would also raise questions of treaty enforcement, including inspection of Chinese territory. It is important, therefore, to examine Communist China's attitudes toward international law, the role of United Nations peace-keeping operations, and inspection to see what implications her attitudes may have for the negotiation of arms control agreements in which she was to be included. Here we are concerned with her attitudes rather than specific reactions to particular arms control agreements, since the latter is the subject of Chapter XII.

In simple terms, the United States places national interest first but includes in her interpretation of national interest a belief that the rule of law in the international arena serves long-run national interests, her own and that of others, at least under usual circumstances. This does not mean that the United States is never prepared to break treaties or that it allows the United Nations or the International Court of Justice to determine its foreign policy. It does mean, however, that the United States may sacrifice some of its immediate short-run interests, provided it is not a major sacrifice, if such a move will enhance international law or the role of the United Nations and hence the long-term interests of the United States. Thus the United States, for example, abides by some United Nations resolutions which it has voted against.

Communist China's attitude toward international law, not surprisingly, is substantially different from that adopted by the United States. This chapter will start with an appraisal of China's attitude toward international law and treaties, followed by a discussion of Peking's position with regard to U.N. peace-keeping operations, both those that have involved China and those that have not. The final section will be an attempt to ascertain Communist China's attitude toward secrecy and the extent to which international inspection is likely to be a stumbling block to possible future arms control agreements.

## ATTITUDES TOWARD INTERNATIONAL LAW

Although China's attitude toward international law is very different from that of the United States, it doesn't follow that the Communist

Chinese totally reject international law.[1] Evidence that Communist China recognizes that international law has a role to play is indicated by China's "invoking of principles of international law in the text of international agreements, by the justification of controversial foreign policy gambits in terms of international law; by criticism of the foreign policies of their opponents, especially the United States, as being in violation of international law; and by the teaching of international law in mainland law schools."[2]

Basically, however, international laws and treaties, in Peking's eyes, are tools of foreign policy in a much narrower sense than is the case for the United States. All countries, of course, comply with laws and treaties, in many cases whether or not this suits their convenience, and the need for reciprocity or the threat of sanctions and embarrassing propaganda can often make compliance appear necessary. The question, therefore, is whether Chinese concern with international law and treaties in any way goes beyond necessity and just what in Chinese eyes constitutes necessity. How embarrassing to them, for example, are accusations of treaty non-compliance? To answer this question, one must look first at Peking's view of the role of international law, then at the consistency or lack of it with which China invokes international law in particular instances, and finally at the record of Chinese compliance with treaties actually drawn up and signed by the Communists themselves (i.e., treaties reached after 1949).

Communist China's spokesmen quite explicitly maintain that international law is no more nor less than a tool of foreign policy which, like government itself, serves the class interests of those who rule, i.e., those who own the means of production. Peking, therefore, distinguishes between "bourgeois international law" and "socialist international law." Relations between capitalist and socialist countries are not based on laws which reflect their mutual interest but, instead, are the result of the existing balance of power under conditions of total conflict. There is some ambivalence among Chinese jurists as to whether this means that

---

[1]This discussion of China's attitude toward international law and agreements is based largely on a paper by R. Randle Edwards and Hungdah Ch'iu, "Communist China's Attitude toward International Agreements and International Organizations," prepared for the Airlie House Conference (hereafter cited as "Agreements and Organizations"). Some of the analysis is little more than a paraphrasing of that paper, but its authors should not be held responsible for any mistakes or erroneous conclusions drawn in this chapter.

[2]*Ibid.*, pp. 3-4.

all present international law possesses this duality or that the presence of the Soviet Union and other socialist nations has somehow modified existing law, so that it is neither bourgeois nor socialist but instead reflects the transition from capitalism to socialism. The weight of opinion in China, at present at least, still appears to view the two kinds of law as separate and in conflict, with the obvious implications that, since most international law was made by bourgeois states, it is thereby invalid.

When it comes to the invocation of international law in specific contexts, Communist China has been quite willing to use "rules of bourgeois international law" in support of its position, thereby presumably transforming them into "rules of socialist international law." The ways in which this has been done, however, imply that not only is all international law a tool of foreign policy but that no great care need be exercised in invoking it in a consistent fashion. In most, if not all cases, therefore, the Chinese regard international law as little more than a propaganda tool.

For example, the Chinese Communists maintain that international organizations have no sovereignty of their own. All sovereignty is possessed by nations and nations only. It follows, therefore, that international bodies have no right to interfere in the internal affairs of individual countries and that moves in that direction are simply a new form of bourgeois imperialism. This principle, among others, was invoked against United Nations action in the Congo. When the Soviet Union sent troops to Hungary in 1956, however, China argued that this was an exception to the rule because the Warsaw Pact included a provision for such action.

Another basic tenet of China's interpretation of international law is that a semi-autonomous region (vassal states, protected states, etc.) does not have the authority to conclude binding international agreements. This argument is part of the Chinese position that the Tibetan authorities could not bind China when they signed a border settlement with the British, hence the Sino-Indian border has never been fixed by treaty. On the other hand, Peking apparently agrees, in public at least, that Outer Mongolia, which was a part of China from 1689 until 1945, had the authority to conclude treaties. Since there has never been an official Chinese Communist declaration on the subject, Chinese legal writers appear to assume that the Outer Mongolian-Soviet "Mutual Assistance Pact" of 1936 is valid.

Treaties in the broadest sense include such things as agreements, acts, conventions, protocols, exchanges of notes, and declarations. Except for declarations, it is generally accepted that there is no significant difference between these forms of commitments in international law.

There is some question whether declarations are legally binding commitments. In at least some cases, there is no question as far as Peking is concerned. The Cairo Declaration and the Potsdam Proclamation are considered by the Chinese Communists to be legally binding, since it was in these declarations that Taiwan was to be returned to China. China's position on these declarations illustrates another aspect of international law as the Chinese see it. Peking maintained that the United States proposal on the peace settlement with Japan was improper because it was inconsistent with obligations undertaken by the United States in various declarations, including those at Cairo and Potsdam. In contrast, China supported the Soviet Union's proposal to change the status of Berlin as prescribed in the Yalta and Potsdam agreements on the grounds that the United States, United Kingdom, and France violated the agreements.

This does not mean that Peking doesn't try to maintain a semblance of international legality. In international relations, however, one party can often find some technical loophole which satisfies the form, if not the substance, of legality. Chinese use of legal terminology to justify their actions, therefore, does not appear to constitute any genuine concern for international law except for its propaganda value. The Communist Chinese have used the concept of "unequal treaties" almost as an all-purpose excuse or justification for avoiding compliance with or denouncing treaties distasteful to them. "Unequal treaties" are those concluded between parties where one party is weaker or subject to coercion, that is, not fully equal to the other. Although the concept is not accepted by the West, it is not without considerable moral and political validity and nationalistic appeal in areas subject in the past to Western imperialism. It is hard to see, for example, why China now should be required by international law to carry out treaties forced on the Manchus at gun point. Peking, however, doesn't confine use of the concept to such obvious cases, nor does she always apply the rule where it would seem reasonable to do so. She did not demand that the Soviet Union surrender the fruits of Czarist and Soviet imperialism in Manchuria and Sinkiang. Instead, new treaties were worked out.[3] To the south, the British and Portuguese are

---

[3]This statement refers to Russian positions in various joint stock companies operating in China, Port Arthur, etc. in the early 1950's. Recently the Chinese appear to be taking a somewhat different attitude toward Soviet occupation of what they consider to be Chinese territory.

still permitted to retain Hong Kong and Macao. On the other hand, "the United States-Kuomintang Treaty of Friendship, Commerce and Navigation, signed on November 4, 1946, is cited as a prime example of an unequal treaty whose provisions appear, on the surface, to grant equal rights to each party. It is charged that, in actuality, however, the treaty acted as a cover for the United States' exploitation of China." [4] Even the Test Ban Treaty is labeled unequal because it places the United States, the Soviet Union, and the United Kingdom in a special position where they can continue to test underground, but others cannot test at all, because testing aboveground is necessary, the Chinese argue (incorrectly), to the development of first-stage nuclear weapons. In contrast, no Chinese writer has ever maintained that the provision in the UN charter giving the Big Five veto power in the Security Council and on the question of charter amendment constitutes an unequal treaty. Nor have they argued that this provision violates state sovereignty.

As already suggested, Communist China is not alone in taking a casual attitude toward particular aspects of international law. Numerous examples of inconsistencies and the use of equally transparent loopholes can be found for most nations that have existed long enough to make agreements that they wanted to break. The main point is that China has shown no real interest in developing a meaningful system of international law. Law, after all, tends to maintain the *status quo* or at least encourages change by evolution rather than revolution. Peking's reasons for opposing the *status quo* were elaborated at length in Chapter I and need not be repeated here.

What then is the Chinese Communist attitude toward treaties and similar agreements which they themselves negotiated? Does their attitude toward these differ from their attitude toward the examples discussed above, none of which actually involved the Chinese Communists as a signatory? [5] Two hypotheses have been argued: one that Peking obeys the letter but not the spirit of any formal agreement she enters into, and another that bilateral agreements with China are more likely to be workable than multilateral treaties. Neither hypothesis is testable without further research. The assumption behind these hypotheses is that the Chinese are over-meticulous about the shades of meaning of any

[4]Edwards and Ch'iu, "Agreements and Organizations," pp. 43-44.

[5]Airlie House Conference participants generally agreed that much additional work was needed before any firm conclusions on Chinese Communist behavior could be reached in this regard.

formal obligations they assume. Since the Chinese Communists in effect
reserve the right to interpret the provisions of a treaty themselves or in
negotiation (i.e., argument) with other signatories and because they are
likely to be unreasonable (from the Western point of view) in the positions
they take in such negotiations, the "best" treaties are those which involve minimum room for further interpretation by any signatory. The vaguer
the provisions of an agreement are, or the more complex the agreement is
because of the need to take several parties' interests into account, the
greater the need for further negotiation and hence the probability that
the agreement will prove unworkable.

Conspicuous Chinese treaty behavior, however, does not seem to
support the above hypotheses; rather it seems to confirm the view that
Chinese compliance with treaties to which they are signatories, as with
international law in general, is determined by what Peking conceives to
be in the interests of its general foreign policy actions of the moment.
Chinese Communist compliance with the letter and usually the spirit of
bilateral trade agreements, particularly those with the West, is not conditioned by the fact that they are bilateral. Any other behavior by Peking
would jeopardize China's already very weak position in international
trade. Any businessman who wants to stay in business for any length of
time, particularly a small businessman, knows he must either play by the
accepted rules of the game or at least not get caught breaking them. Communist China is in the position of the small businessman, with the prospects for circumventing the rules without getting caught virtually
non-existent. There are too many people waiting to publicize such a cir-
cumvention, even at times when none has occurred.

Peking's compliance with border agreements signed since 1949 can
be looked at in the same light. It would make no sense to violate border
treaties with Burma or Nepal at a time when China is trying to get India
to the conference table in order to ratify China's possession of the Aksai
Chin area of Ladakh. India's bargaining position would be considerably
enhanced if it could argue that border agreements to which China is a
signatory are meaningless; therefore, China must demonstrate its sincerity by some act, such as withdrawal from the disputed areas before
negotiation.

When compliance with agreements proves inconvenient, however, there
is no evidence which suggests that Communist China is reluctant to break
or ignore those agreements. The Korean armistice agreement, for example, included a provision limiting the kinds of equipment which could
be introduced into either North or South Korea after the armistice, but
this was broken apparently as soon as the Chinese and North Koreans

decided there was some advantage in having certain weapons in the North. The fact of violation was given considerable publicity by the United States, but this had no noticeable deterrent effect. The Neutral Nations Supervisory Commission, set up to oversee the agreement officially, was paralyzed, presumably at the instigation and under the guidance of the Chinese, by the veto power of its two Communist members (Poland and Czechoslovakia).

The agreements concerning Laos have met with a similar fate. True, it is North Vietnamese and not Chinese troops which are violating the accord by being in Laos, but, as argued in Chapter I, North Vietnamese actions in Laos appear to have complete or nearly complete Chinese support and thus also reflect the Chinese attitude toward international accords. It is worth pointing out, however, that, although Western publicity regarding Communist violations has had little effect, the Communists have not been eager to admit those violations publicly themselves. Thus, when American aircraft first attacked Pathet Lao positions on the Plaine des Jarres in June, 1964, the Communists found themselves in an awkward position, because the anti-aircraft positions attacked weren't supposed to be there in the first place. Fortunately, from the Chinese and North Vietnamese point of view, the problem of how to publicize the attacks was solved when a headquarters unit was attacked and several Chinese killed.

Although Peking does not find it advantageous to defy or openly violate international agreements to which it is a signatory, she is not highly sensitive to Western reactions and public opinion. The regime is concerned, on occasion, with reactions in the underdeveloped world where it is trying to win support, but much of the underdeveloped world, for obvious reasons, is not very responsive to Western propaganda regarding Chinese behavior.

Chinese Communist treaty behavior and attitude toward international law in general is not a very encouraging sign as to how China is likely to act if it ever does sign an arms control agreement, unless that agreement is clearly in Chinese interests. Any agreement forced on China by the pressure of circumstances is likely to be abrogated as soon as those circumstances change.

## ATTITUDES TOWARD INTERNATIONAL ORGANIZATION

It remains to be seen whether Peking's attitude toward the UN and UN peace-keeping operations in any way modifies the above statements Communist China has always proclaimed its complete agreement with, and endorsement of, the formally stated purposes of the United Nations organization. Its position in this regard was clearly stated as early as 1945 by Mao Tse-tung:

> In regard to the establishment of an institution to preserve international peace and security, the Chinese Communist Party completely approves of the proposals made at the Dumbarton Oaks Conference and the decisions concerning this question made at the Crimea (Yalta) Conference. The Chinese Communist Party welcomes the San Francisco Conference of United Nations representatives. The Chinese Communist Party has already sent its own representative (Tung Pi-wu) to join the Chinese delegation at the San Francisco Conference in order to express the will of the Chinese people.[6]

Not to support the United Nations, in principle at least, would tend to brand Communist China in the eyes of much of the world, including most of the Afro-Asian underdeveloped world, as a force opposed to peace in general, not just the *status quo* or "imperialism" in particular. Furthermore, Peking probably genuinely wants to occupy the Chinese seat in the UN because the UN would provide China with a forum for exercising its growing power and influence, although there would also be disadvantages in having to take formal stands on many issues. Even if Peking does not want to participate actively in the United Nations, it still is in her interest to want membership, provided that membership is offered her in a proper manner (i.e., by the replacement of Taiwan with the "legitimate" representatives of China).

A more precise index of Peking's attitude toward international bodies and the use of international action to resolve problems is in her reactions to the role of the UN in specific situations to maintain peace.[7] The nature of the Chinese response to some situations becomes particularly clear when compared with that of the Soviet Union. Essentially "the Soviet response has increasingly tended to permit international political cooperation in the maintenance of peace in the belief that the Communist

---

[6]Edwards and Ch'iu, "Agreements and Organizations," p. 66.

[7]Most of this discussion of Chinese attitudes toward the peace-keeping functions of the UN is based on a paper prepared for the Airlie House Conference by Mervyn W. Adams, "Communist China's View on the UN Role in Maintaining Peace and Security" (cited hereafter as "China's View on UN Peace Role").

system will eventually conquer 'imperialism' by economic means, whereas the Chinese have seen that a nuclear stalemate does not preclude opportunities to gain political victories through the graduated use of violence short of world war."[8] The general Chinese attitude toward the UN, then, is reflection and application of the basic Chinese foreign policy position which divides her from the U.S.S.R.

The Chinese Communist position on UN peace-keeping action reveals additional aspects of Chinese attitudes about the international arena. In the first place, the Chinese position on specific UN activities is partly conditioned by the fact that Peking is excluded from participation in these activities. More important, Communist China was on the receiving end of the largest of all such actions, the UN "police action" in Korea. On February 1, 1951, the General Assembly of the United Nations declared Communist China guilty of aggression, and on May 18 the Assembly recommended the application of an embargo by member states against China. The UN action in Korea appeared in Peking's eyes to be even worse because it was connected with the question of hostilities in the Taiwan Straits. It is worth noting, nevertheless, that although the Chinese Communists argued that the United Nations was no more than a tool of U.S. imperialism in Korea and was acting illegally because it excluded a permanent member of the Security Council from its proceedings, they never called for the abolition of the UN itself. In fact, even though they considered all United Nations' resolutions illegal, Wu Hsiu-ch'uan, at the Security Council in November, 1950 (on invitation from the Council) proposed that the UN condemn U.S. aggression against Taiwan and Korea and that it call for withdrawal of the United States from Taiwan and withdrawal of all non-Korean forces from Korea.

Ever since the experience in Korea, Communist China has looked with a jaundiced eye on all UN peace-keeping operations, even those which have helped China's "friends." For example, during the British-French invasion of Egypt in November, 1956, UN resolutions on November 4 and 5 authorized establishment of a UN command for a United Nations emergency force. The Soviet Union was content to abstain on the vote, but China expressed suspicion of the resolution because she felt it might allow U.S. "neo-colonialism" to supersede British and French "colonialism." It is not certain, however, whether China, had she had the opportunity, would have voted against the establishment of an emergency force, a move which would not have gained her any popularity in the underdeveloped world.

[8]*Ibid.*, p. 1.

The strength of China's dislike of UN peace-keeping operations is more clearly brought out by a comparison of Chinese and Soviet attitudes toward specific operations since 1958, i.e., from what we now know were the beginnings of the Sino-Soviet dispute. The two cases available for study are the Lebanon-Jordan crisis in the middle of 1958 and the Congo crisis which began in mid-1960.

On May 22, 1958, Lebanon asked the Security Council to meet and discuss alleged United Arab Republic intervention in its internal affairs.

> On June 11, the Security Council adopted, with the Soviet Union abstaining, a Swedish resolution providing for the despatch of a UN Observation Group to Lebanon (UNOGIL) to insure against any illegal infiltration of arms or personnel into the country. In explaining his vote, the U.S.S.R. representative reiterated that the Lebanese complaint was unfounded, noted the resolution said nothing about the substance of the complaint, and pointed out that neither the U.A.R. nor Lebanon had opposed the resolution. [9]

China, in a *People's Daily* commentary on June 18, in contrast, "suggested that the mission was merely an 'instrument of U.S.-British intervention' since it was doing nothing to halt the importation of Western arms and personnel into Lebanon." [10] Both China and the Soviet Union opposed the sending of British and American troops to Jordan and Lebanon in July, but this was an action taken outside of the United Nations, partly because of the ineffectiveness of the UN, and hence reflects little on Chinese and Russian conceptions of the proper role of UN operations.

The Congo crisis erupted in early July, 1960. On July 14, the Security Council adopted a Tunisian resolution, with Soviet concurrence, "calling on the Belgian Government to withdraw its troops and authorizing the Secretary-General to provide military assistance to the Congolese Government until Congolese forces could maintain order." [11] On July 22, the Soviet Union voted for a second resolution much like the one of July 14. Communist China, however, suggested throughout July and August that "U.S. imperialism" was operating "under the UN flag." A *People's Daily* editorial of July 20 stated:

[9]*Ibid.*, pp. 15-16.

[10]*Ibid.*, p. 16.

[11]*Ibid.*, p. 21.

> In "supporting" the Tunisian resolution, the U.S. does not want the UN to check the Belgian aggression. On the contrary, it has an ulterior motive. The U.S. propaganda machine is advocating the establishment of a permanent UN police force to "assist" the Congolese Government" in restoring order" .... The Congo looks forward to "military assistance" from the UN not for the purpose of "restoring internal order" but to halt aggression by Belgian troops. [12]

By the middle of August, Belgium had not withdrawn, and the UN's inability to enter secessionist Katanga led to progressive Soviet disillusionment with the operation; but instead of calling for the United Nations to leave the Congo, Russia voted for a resolution (on August 9) authorizing the UN to enter Katanga. Peking, in a *People's Daily* article on August 22, came out firmly against the whole UN operation in the Congo (ONUC):

> UN intervention in the Congo is formally based on the resolution adopted by the Security Council on July 13. Impartial public opinion pointed out at the time that this Security Council resolution would open a convenient door to U.S. imperialist intervention in the Congo and establish an evil precedent of encroachment upon the sovereignty of new independent nations in the name of the U.N. Numerous historical facts over the past 15 years have repeatedly testified to the fact U.S. imperialism uses the UN as its instrument of aggression. [13]

After the series of events which culminated in the murder of Patrice Lumumba in late January, 1961, Soviet action was directed at removal of Dag Hammarskjöld as Secretary-General. On February 21 a three-nation resolution adopted by the Security Council, with the U.S.S.R., only, abstaining, "urged the UN to prevent civil war, arrange cease-fires, and halt military operations, using force as a last resort; called for the evacuation of foreign military personnel from the Congo; and reaffirmed earlier Assembly and Council resolutions." China, in contrast, stressed

---

[12]"Peking Press Supports Congolese Struggle," NCNA, July 20, 1960; translation in SCMP, 2304 (July 26, 1960), p. 15.

[13]"What Has the United Nations Brought to the Congo?" *People's Daily*, August 22, 1960; translation in *Current Background*, No. 634, pp. 62-64.

its "support for the Gizenga Government, called for sanctions against the Belgian aggressors, for the arrest of Tshombe and Mobutu and the dis-armament of their troops, and the withdrawal of ONUC." [14]

This accumulation of evidence suggests that Communist China is, if anything, even less interested in upholding the peace-keeping authority of the United Nations than in international law in general or in adhering to its own treaties in particular.

Chinese pronouncements in connection with Indonesian withdrawal from the United Nations on January 7, 1965, contained an even stronger anti-UN element than the statements on the Congo. In brief, the Chinese have argued that as long as the UN is primarily only a United States tool for support of "reactionary," "imperialist" groups around the world, and Malaysia in particular, Indonesia is right to withdraw. In fact, Peking argues that, unless the United Nations is drastically reorganized so as to eliminate United States control, consideration should "be given to the setting up of another United Nations, a revolutionary one, so that rival dramas may be staged in competition with the existing U.S.-manipulated United Nations for people to make the comparison." [15]

Suspicion of American intentions and American influence within the United Nations would bias Peking against any UN role in an arms control agreement. The chances that this position would change much if Communist China attained UN membership are not encouraging. If it were a member, Peking might have to couch its opposition to a UN role in any substantive operation in somewhat different and more subtle terms, but it is doubtful that the basic opposition itself would be altered.

## SECRECY AND INSPECTION

It does not follow from the discussion in this chapter that no formal arms control agreements are possible because the Chinese don't con-sistently support rules of international law, standard treaty behavior, or the United Nations. Any nation will comply with a treaty if it is in its interest to do so, and sanctions for breaking a treaty are one means of establishing that interest. To apply sanctions, however, one must know for certain a violation has occurred. Under many circumstances such knowledge can only be acquired by some form of on-site inspection.

---

[14]Adams, "China's View on UN Peace Role," p. 23.

[15]"Vice-Premier Chen Yi Declares China Backs Indonesia," *Peking Review*, Vol. VIII, No. 5 (January 29, 1965), p. 7.

Certainly Chinese behavior in obstructing the bodies set up to super-
vise the agreements dealing with the Korean War and Laos-Vietnam does
not lead one to believe that China would enthusiastically embrace the
idea of inspection. Inspection by any national or international body would
violate Peking's highly defensive sense of national sovereignty. It would
also tend to accentuate the extent to which any agreement between China
and the West would appear to be a sellout of revolutionary ideals.

On the other hand, there are grounds for arguing that Communist China
might prove to be more willing to consider allowing inspection on Chinese
territory than has the Soviet Union. The reasons for holding this position
are based, not on an obscure analysis of differences between Russian
and Chinese psychology, but on an appraisal of differences in the two
countries' basic interests.

First of all, the intelligence advantages are nowhere near as lopsided
in favor of the United States as they would be in a Soviet-American inspection agreement. Aerial surveillance by American-built Nationalist
Chinese planes, among other things, probably has made it possible for
the United States to stay abreast of military operations within China in a
way that was never possible with the Soviet Union. In addition, Peking's
ability to collect intelligence on the United States is much more limited
than is that of the Soviet Union.

Secondly, roving inspectors within China might be less politically
disruptive and, conversely, less politically informative than would be a
similar group operating with the Soviet Union. [16] Thoroughgoing control,
it might be argued, has enabled the regime so to shape the individual
Chinese's view of the outside world that casual contacts with outsiders
would not affect the attitudes of the people or enable outsiders to learn
enough to change the outside world's view of China. Peking would not
be able to exercise the same degree of selectivity over inspection teams
as it does in the granting of tourist visas, nor would it necessarily be
able to control the inspection team's itinerary within China. Nevertheless,
the regime would have little to fear politically. The system of mutual
surveillance would operate just as effectively against foreign inspectors
as against foreign tourists. Street committee chairmen would be no less
vigilant, and the population as a whole would be no more frank. Inspectors would not be attending school or working in a factory or engaged
in some other situation where this system might break down. The Soviet
NKVD might have been able to perform a similar screening function for

---

[16] This point was made by one of the conferees and concurred in by several
others, although some skepticism was expressed.

Stalin, although the gaps probably would have been much greater. In any case, Soviet police surveillance today is not remotely up to the standards of Chinese mutual surveillance.

It doesn't follow from this discussion that Communist China would welcome inspection, only that inspection might prove less of a stumbling block to an arms control agreement than it has been for the Soviet Union, if China wanted that agreement for other reasons. There would still be considerable reluctance to accept inspection for reasons of national sovereignty and revolutionary momentum, if no other.

The fact that the question of inspection may not of itself present an insuperable obstacle for the Chinese does not lend much encouragement to the hope that Peking might be induced to conclude a workable arms control agreement, even if China saw some advantage in making such an agreement. China's respect for the established methods of resolving such things as different interpretations of a particular treaty provision is slight. If the agreements were at all complex or allowed for much interpretation, the process of resolving differences might disrupt the treaty even though the agreements reached were still basically in the interests of both parties. Once Peking felt the settlement was working against Chinese interests, no compunctions about weakening the fabric of international law would deter the regime from breaking the agreement. Even with inspection, Chinese sensitivity to foreign propaganda directed against China is not very great. A formal agreement, therefore, would probably have to include, along with inspection, some very clear sanctions, of more substance than a propaganda barrage.

A major assumption in this study is that it is extremely unlikely that the Chinese Communist regime will sign any formal arms control agreements within the next five or ten years.[1] This conclusion is based mainly on the belief that the Chinese are interested in building up their military capability and are therefore unlikely to be interested in agreements that stabilize the military balance. Many such agreements would, in the Chinese view, also have undesirable political effects, particularly those involving implications of a détente between China and the West.[2] One should ask, too, whether there are any arms control agreements that the United States would be interested in having the Chinese Communist regime sign.

The situation with reference to Peking is in marked contrast to that now existing vis-à-vis the Soviet Union. The United States government has proposed at the Geneva Eighteen-Nation Disarmament Conference a series of collateral measures that it would be prepared to negotiate and sign with the Soviet Union at any time the Soviets were interested. If and when it became clear that the Soviets were interested in these and a whole series of other arms control measures, the American list could probably be very substantially increased in a relatively short time. Certainly various government agencies and to a larger extent a number of private analysts would have many additional suggestions to propose. At least for the moment, then, we are not short of agreements that appear to the American government and to private analysts in the United States to be of interest both to the United States as well as to the Soviet Union.

The case of the Chinese is, however, very different. The United States, of course, desires to have the Chinese sign the Test Ban Treaty. It also would presumably be interested in having the Chinese adhere to a treaty for general and complete disarmament (GCD), although apparently the American draft treaty outline has been designed so that the Chinese could be excluded from at least the first stage.

With reference to the test ban, it is very difficult to make a case that the signing of the treaty would be in Peking's interest. The Chinese are

[1]This was also an assumption at the Airlie House Conference. In fact many participants considered this so obvious as not to be worth discussing.

[2]As noted above, however, the Chinese do engage in various kinds of tacit negotiations with the United States on wartime and peacetime military deployment and use of military force and also participate in various armistice negotiations and agreements.

determined to become a nuclear power for reasons which certainly make sense to them and are at least understandable to American analysts. Probably for political reasons the United States will find it advantageous to keep pressing the Peking regime to sign the Test Ban Treaty and pointing out to the rest of the world that the Chinese are unwilling to do so. But it seems clear that the United States government does not have and should not have any great expectation that China will in the near future adhere to the Test Ban Treaty without a comprehensive agreement on major political issues.

We have, then, a situation in which the measures that the United States is interested in signing with the Soviet Union appear to be relatively numerous, while measures that the United States might sign with the Communist Chinese regime are few or non-existent. Why is this so?

There are several obvious reasons. The first of these is that the Soviet Union now poses and will continue to pose for the indefinite future the most serious threat to American security and the only threat which could in a very short time lead to direct destruction of American territory. There is, therefore, a major American interest in seeing that this power is not used either deliberately or by accident. This has led to extensive concentration on developing effective unilateral military postures and on proposing arms control measures to reduce the likelihood of a war between the United States and the Soviet Union. The United States also has much more direct contact with the Soviet Union, both in the sense of political and diplomatic interchanges of various kinds and in the sense that the military forces of the two countries interact and confront each other in a variety of ways. Soviet and American ground forces directly face each other in Central Europe. The Soviet Union and the United States compete in the development of advanced weapons systems such as missiles and space satellites of various kinds. Both countries now recognize that the size of their budget and the specific development programs of the two countries clearly interact with each other, and each is affected by what the other does.

The same is clearly not true of the Chinese Communists. They have no weapons systems comparable to American systems. The interaction between the size of the American defense budget and the Chinese defense budget is very slight, if it exists at all. And the military forces of the two countries confront each other only perhaps in the Taiwan Straits. Thus, for a variety of political and military reasons, much greater attention has been focused on possible agreements with the Soviet Union, and there has been much greater progress, in the sense of the development of apparently interesting proposals.

One of the most important reasons for the asymmetry in U.S. understanding of the problem of arms control relations with the Chinese as distinct from the Russians is probably an intellectual one. There is not any consensus in the United States, either within the government, judging by what emerges in public statements from various agencies and officials, or in the academic community concerned with arms control as to what it means even in very general terms to be arms control minded. This problem is even greater in relation to China. In official U.S. government terminology, "arms control" and "disarmament" are often taken as synonymous. Another view is in fact to take the two as being the same thing but to look upon an interest in arms control as simply an interest in GCD and a belief that GCD can be obtained in the reasonable future, either by a single negotiation leading to a treaty or following a series of limited arms control steps. This approach would view limited steps toward arms control arrangements which included China as being important insofar as they politically and militarily pave the way for general and complete disarmament.

A closely related approach would be to say that becoming arms control minded is not desirable for the Chinese, as distinguished from becoming disarmament minded. It would view an interest by China in arms control as a possible deterrent to her interest in substantial or possibly limited reductions in forces and would suggest that the only suitable policy is to seek as quickly as possible to arrive at comprehensive disarmament.

The third approach is essentially political, viewing arms control and disarmament measures mainly in terms of their effect on international political relationships—for example, their effect on the level of tension in the world or the possibility for détente. This approach would suggest that the details of an agreement, particularly the military security implications, are not very important as long as the agreement does not damage national security interests. In this sense, to become arms control minded is to be willing to enter into arms control agreements for the same motivations and with the same expectations with which one would enter various kinds of political agreements.

Finally, there is the approach to arms control and disarmament which views arms control as one aspect of military policy designed to increase the military security of a country as well as that of its potential enemy. Or, as one of the authors has put it:

> We mean to include [in the term arms control] all the forms
> of military cooperation between potential enemies in the in-
> terest of reducing the likelihood of war, its scope and violence

if it occurs, and the political and economic costs of being prepared for it. The essential feature of arms control is the recognition of the common interest, of the possibility of reciprocation and cooperation between potential enemies with respect to their military establishments.[3]

In the United States, this approach to the study of arms control evolved under the impetus of the growing Soviet threat and with the image, carried over from strategic studies in general, of a bipolar world. The fundamental assumptions on which arms control theory have been based include that of bipolarity, some kind of compatibility if not parity in strategic weapons systems, and direct threats posed by the major military powers against each other. The basic assumption of arms control thinking has been that even given real political differences and clashes between the two countries, agreement might be possible. Weapons systems themselves somehow increase the danger and likelihood of nuclear war. Therefore, adjustments in weapons systems can reduce the likelihood of war, or the destruction if war occurs, even if they do not change the political situation.

According to this approach, a country becomes arms control minded when it begins to ask itself what cooperative elements, as well as competitive elements, there are or should be in its military relations to potential enemies and how these can be embodied in formal agreements or tacit understandings. It is in this sense that the question of how China can be made arms control minded is dealt with here. In order to get some feeling for the procedures and the kind of change which is involved, it is instructive and useful to consider the process whereby the Soviet Union has become increasingly arms control minded over the last several years.[4] At first, the Soviet Union was intensely hostile to notions of arms control as they were put forward in the American academic community in the early 1960's. The Soviets tended to view arms control as being a substitute for the proposals for GCD which they were advocating. While the Soviets continue to view some American arms control writing (and American arms controls) as designed to manipulate the strategic balance in the interest of the United States and as being opposed to efforts to secure an agreement leading to GCD, they have nevertheless

---

[3]Thomas C. Schelling and Morton H. Halperin, *Strategy and Arms Control* (New York: Twentieth Century Fund, 1961), p. 2.

[4]Alexander Dallin *et al.*, *The Soviet Union and Disarmament: An Appraisal of Soviet Attitudes and Intentions* (New York: Praeger, 1965).

come to adopt at least some of the ways of thinking and attitudes toward military force which can be identified with arms control.

On one level the Soviets have begun to be interested in what have now come to be called collateral measures. They signed and ratified the Test Ban Treaty, they accepted the General Assembly resolution banning weapons of mass destruction in outer space, they agreed to parallel pronouncements by the governments of the United States, Great Britain, and the Soviet Union of decisions to cut back on production of fissionable materials, and they agreed to establish the hot-line between the United States and the Soviet Union. They have tabled a series of additional collateral measure proposals at the Geneva Eighteen-Nation Disarmament Conference and in general have accepted the validity and usefulness of limited steps. The kinds of steps and the timing of the steps accepted by the Soviet Union thus far suggest that the Soviets view limited arms control measures as having two essentially different kinds of purposes. One, exemplified by the hot-line agreement, might be called the more narrowly strategic arms control purpose of making accidental war less likely. The second purpose, exemplified by the Test Ban Treaty and the Soviet Union's desire to have additional agreements apparently largely for the purpose of creating the impression of détente and the image of progress in the arms control field, seems primarily to be politically motivated and to be associated both with the current line of Soviet strategy vis-à-vis the West and vis-à-vis Communist China. That is to say, for the Russians, arms control has to some extent become a way of distinguishing themselves from the Chinese, of proving that coexistence can work, and of attempting to improve their relations with the West.

At the same time, the Soviets continue to press for GCD and to urge that it is the primary task facing the world. They insist that collateral measures must be compatible with GCD and must be conceived in a context of looking forward to the ratification of a GCD agreement.

At the level of unilateral military policy the Soviets also seem to have become more aware of the cooperative elements in their military strategy.[5] They have begun to take a variety of steps in the instruction in and employment of control of their strategic forces which would seem to reduce the likelihood of accidental war.

All this is not to suggest that the problem of getting the Soviets interested in arms control has been solved in that the Soviets have become

[5]See Thomas Wolfe, *Soviet Strategy at the Crossroads* (Cambridge: Harvard University Press, 1964).

completely arms control minded. Nevertheless, substantial progress has
been made in dealing with the Soviet Union, and this progress should be
analyzed in considering the Chinese problem, both to understand the
differences and to see where techniques of communication and education
which appear to have been at least partly successful with the Soviets
might be applicable to Peking.

If one examines the Sino-American military confrontation through the
eyes of an arms control specialist, it is very difficult to discover the
functions an arms control agreement might be designed to serve in terms
of those enumerated above.[6] It is hard, if not impossible, for one to find
instabilities in the Sino-American military relationship itself which might
be ameliorated either by unilateral steps or by tacit understandings or
formal agreements. The danger of war in the Pacific would appear to
arise from conflicting political objectives and the Chinese attempt, by
proxy or otherwise, to increase the area under their control. The character-
istics and deployment of weapons systems on the two sides do not appear
in any significant way to increase the possibility of war. There would
thus appear to be very little scope for arms control agreements based on
the intellectual assumptions and analytical categories which have been
developed to deal with the Soviet-American military relationship. This
suggests that if the United States is to think seriously about the possibility of arms control negotiations with the Peking regime, it needs to
rethink the notions of arms control and perhaps develop a whole new set
of concepts and assumptions based on a very different kind of military
confrontation than exists with the Soviet Union. This effort would be
complicated, not only by the fact that there is no consensus in the United
States on the proper arms control approach even to the Soviets, but also
by the very substantial political complications which would accompany
any effort to discuss and analyze agreements of any kind with the Peking
regime. Alternatively, the United States might adopt a political attitude
toward arms control with China and seek agreements for political reasons which did not damage but also did not improve the American security position.[7]

[6]This leaves aside the agreements or tacit understandings related to war limitation or war termination, which were discussed in Chapter X. For a listing of
possible security functions relating to arms control and developed with the
Soviet Union in mind, as well as an elaboration of the arms control approach
discussed here, see Schelling and Halperin, *Strategy and Arms Control*,
pp. 9-39.

[7]If we start, as was done in the case of the Soviets, with the basic notion that
the purpose of arms control agreements is to try to embody in formal or tacit

In considering, then, the problem of making China arms control minded, it is necessary to distinguish between a general philosophy and the substance of specific agreements. The first problem is to decide what approach one would like the Chinese to adopt in viewing their military forces and making decisions about procurement, placement, and utilization of these forces. Second, one must consider the substance of the agreements, whether tacit or formal, which one would like to see the Chinese begin to think about. In terms of general philosophy, it is possible to distinguish two necessary but not sufficient elements. The first involves the question of viewing the use of military force as a political instrument, one which can and should be controlled by political means—that is to say, an acceptance of the belief that the kinds of forces one has, the way they are used in wartime and in peacetime, should be determined by political considerations, taking into account the probable reaction of the enemy to one's moves and with a willingness to limit the use of force at hand for various purposes. As has been indicated above, this element of the philosophy of arms control is one the Chinese leadership undoubtedly finds and probably will continue to find completely congenial. The fact that the Party must be in control of the military has been a basic tenet of Maoist doctrine.

A second element of the philosophy of arms control is the one that the Chinese are likely to find uncongenial. This is the notion that there is a cooperative as well as a competitive element in the nature of the military forces of potential enemies. The Chinese tend to view the struggle with a political opponent as a fight to the finish and as good in itself. They accept the Leninist principle that the essential question in politics

understandings a common interest associated with the procurement, deployment, or use of military forces, it should be possible, even taking into account the fact that at least low-level incidents of violence between the United States and Communist China are much more likely than major violence between the United States and the Soviet Union, to develop a structure of insights and recommendations based on the perceived common interest in avoiding accidental war.

However, any such effort would have to take into account the fact that in certain situations the United States may want to threaten or actually engage in large-scale destruction on the Chinese mainland and the fact that the United States does not appear willing to formally recognize the permanence of the Peking regime.

All of those present at the Conference who had been involved with the development of arms control measures notions in relation to the Soviet Union were agreed that these appeared to be at least inadequate and possibly irrelevant to the Chinese Communists. There was a general feeling that there was a need for a kind of rethinking of assumptions and concepts of the same kind which occurred in the intellectual community in relation to the Soviet Union and arms control in the early 1960's.

is "who-whom?"—who will defeat whom?[8] Both at the political and at
the military level they have tended to assume that struggle must be all-
out and end in the total defeat of one party or the other. Nevertheless,
they have recognized the need for political compromises of a tactical
nature, for temporary truces, and for being willing to settle for less than
total victory at a particular time. But what they have probably not at all
thought about, at least explicitly, is possible cooperative aspects in the
actual procurement, deployment, and use of military forces. They have
not at all begun to think about changes in the military strategies on one
side or the other that might be of benefit to both sides. It is this line of
thinking which will need to be developed if the Peking regime is to become arms control minded.

As was indicated above, the current Chinese attitude toward arms
control is to view it entirely in political terms and at two levels. The
Chinese see the agreements now being negotiated by the United States
and the Soviet Union as aimed at stabilizing the political and military
balance between the two superpowers and as operating to make the capitalist camp stronger than the socialist camp. They either are not aware
of, or pretend not to notice, the serious military effects of the agreements which have been negotiated so far and which are under discussion.
Rather they have looked upon the agreements—as perhaps the Soviets do—
as having an essentially political purpose.[9] What, then, can the United
States do now or in the future to try to make China more arms control
minded?

As noted earlier, there is no communication as yet between the United
States and Communist China in the field of arms control, even at the most
non-political and technical levels. Making China arms control minded
requires, first, more and better channels of communications between the
United States and the Peking regime. Of great importance will be the
political decisions taken by the United States in terms of its future relations with Peking. As a number of participants at the conference put it,
the question of how the United States can make China arms control minded really should be reformulated to ask what price the United States is
prepared to pay in order to make China arms control minded. The price
which these participants had in mind was a political one.

---

[8]Cf. Chapter I.

[9]No one at the Conference was aware of signs that the Chinese are familiar
with or in any way sympathetic toward the basic notions of arms control and
the possible utility of tacit understanding and formal agreements, as these
notions are discussed in the United States.

Specifically within the realm of arms control, the United States needs both to formulate much more clearly what it wants the Chinese to believe and then to decide what channels of communication it is willing to use and which are likely to be effective in getting the message across to Peking.

In view of the different interpretations and approaches toward arms control, sketched earlier, there does not appear to be, nor is there likely to be, a consensus as to what the United States would want the Chinese to believe about arms control or the attitude that the U.S. would like them to take toward long-range management of military forces and international conflict. If it is the official position of the American government that GCD is an obtainable goal, then the United States would seek to negotiate actively during the coming years with an expectation that a plan for general and complete disarmament could be put into effect, say within the decade. If this is the working premise, then the U.S. probably should seek to convey to the Chinese a sincere wish for general and complete disarmament. The American government should be working to counteract what appears to be the current Chinese belief—that GCD is impossible as long as there exist states with conflicting interests based on different class structures. The Chinese view is that GCD is impossible until capitalism disappears and that it is not even desirable to talk about the subject because it reduces the will of the people to fight against imperialism. To change their public position would probably require a demonstration to the Chinese that the political propaganda disadvantages of adhering to this line in face of American and Soviet espousal of GCD is unprofitable. To really change Chinese attitude, to lead them to believe that in fact GCD is a goal worth seeking, would require a number of fundamental changes in the American political approach to China and the countries on the Chinese periphery. For one thing, the United States would have to make clear its willingness to begin negotiations with the Chinese on the terms of a GCD agreement. Then under this assumption, the United States must seek ways to convey to the Chinese how it believes such ticklish questions as internal wars in Southeast Asia or the size of Chinese forces should be dealt with. If GCD is to be taken seriously in the near future, it is not enough to say that stage one, which is perhaps the first three years of the plan, may be accomplished without the adherence of the Chinese. It is clear that one would not want to sign an agreement that was designed to be of main value if it proceeded to substantial disarmament, unless one had some indication that the Chinese were willing at least to consider and negotiate on the basis of terms acceptable to the United States.

So far it seems that the United States has not regarded the likelihood of complete and general disarmament within a decade seriously

enough to worry about how to get the Chinese committed to it and ultimately involved in negotiations. There remains the question, however, as
to whether the United States should prefer to have the Chinese continue
considering GCD as utopian and thinking about arms control measures
either in terms of the contribution they make to military security in an
armed world or in terms of their political implications, without taking
into consideration, as both the United States and the Soviet Union seem
to do, the implications of such measures for GCD.[10]

In considering the substance of what the United States would like the
Chinese Communists to be interested in, the problem becomes more difficult. No one at the Conference was aware of any specific arms control
measures, either tacit or formal, except the Test Ban Treaty and, presumably, the treaty for general and complete disarmament as proposed by
the United States in Geneva, that the United States was interested in
having the Chinese Communists adhere to. In contrast to the situation
vis-à-vis the Soviet Union, to whom the United States has proposed a
large number of collateral measures that it would be interested in negotiating and with regard to which a very large number of other proposals have
been made by private individuals, there appears to be a lack of concrete
suggestions for specific arms control agreements between the United
States and China. Here it need only be noticed that the process of beginning to communicate with the Chinese about arms control possibilities
would be substantially enhanced if the United States were able to accompany its general discussion of the subject with some specific examples
of the kinds of agreements that it was interested in negotiating. The very
act of indicating an interest in negotiating a particular agreement has
very important political implications relating to possible recognition of
the Chinese Communist regime.[11] To develop the substance of agree-

---

[10]One participant at the Conference suggested that the major American motiva-
tion for espousal of GCD was that the Soviets had put forward proposals in
this area and that therefore it was necessary for political-psychological reasons
to counter this with an American GCD proposal. A second participant respond-
ed that, if this was in fact so, it might be logical and desirable to let sleeping
dogs lie in the case of the Chinese and not try to encourage them into a public
commitment or a real belief in the possibility of GCD. A third participant suggested that, whatever the Soviet belief in earlier years, the Sino-Soviet conflict made it virtually certain that the Soviets no longer took the possibility
of GCD seriously.

[11]The United States has signed several political agreements to which the
Chinese Communists have also been a party, including the Laos Agreement
of 1962.

ments which the United States might be interested in signing with the Chinese also requires decisions by the United States as to whether or not it wants to be in a position to threaten or to actually undertake military operations designed to overthrow the Chinese Communists. There would be very small scope for formal negotiated arms control arrangements if the United States is committed to overthrowing the Chinese Communist regime, forcefully if necessary. However, should the United States believe that military action, given any foreseeable Chinese provocation, is highly unlikely against the Chinese mainland, the scope for agreement may be substantial, provided serious and detailed thought is given to the question of the mutual interests which the United States and China may have which might be embodied in various kinds of arms arrangements. However, unless this is done, the prospects for beginning an arms control dialogue with the Chinese even at the unofficial level are likely to be very small.

Even if all these obstacles—which are essentially problems of internal American policy and politics—are overcome, there will remain the question of how to begin a dialogue with the Chinese which would have as its end making the Chinese arms control minded and lead to negotiation and signing of formal agreements and the development of tacit arrangements.

One possible channel of communication is, of course, the Geneva Conference. The Chinese have stated that they will not attend the Geneva Eighteen-Nation Disarmament Conference until they are admitted to the United Nations. However, in terms of beginning an arms control dialogue with the Chinese, it is not at all clear that inviting them to Geneva would be helpful even if they were to be willing at some time to attend. For one thing, a large part of the Geneva negotiations are taken up with the discussion of GCD. As suggested previously, it might well not be in the interests of the United States to force the Chinese to take an explicit stand on this issue and to begin negotiations about this question. In addition, the Soviets are at the Geneva Conference, and their presence would probably mean that the Chinese would view the negotiations as more important in terms of their conflict with the Soviet Union than of any relationship, particularly in the arms control field, with the United States. The stands the Chinese took, the speeches they made, would be directed at and influenced by the knowledge that the Russians were there, and their actions would become part of the evolving Sino-Soviet rift. Finally, Geneva is at least one of the places in which the United States carries on negotiations with the Soviet Union about arms control agreements, which, whether correctly or incorrectly, are viewed by the Chinese as being detrimental to their own interest. The presence of the Chinese at these negotiations is unlikely to make it easy for the United

States and the Soviet Union to reach whatever agreements may be possible for them.[12]

Arms control discussions between the United States and China should, if possible, be kept separate from Soviet-American and Sino-Soviet dialogues. It would be helpful to find a channel of communication and discussion separate from the Geneva talks. One possibility is obviously the Warsaw talks carried on between the American and Chinese ambassadors to Poland. In these discussions the United States might, in a variety of ways, try to prompt the Chinese into beginning to think about arms control questions. One possible method is to begin to question the Chinese about the implications of the disarmament proposals that they themselves have made. If the Chinese proposal for the total elimination of nuclear weapons has substantial implications for various aspects of arms control, including inspection and verification, the problem of residual possibility of hidden stockpiles, etc., simply asking questions pointedly to the Chinese about their own proposals may force them to think about how seriously they really take their own proposals, what the possible implications are, and what other measures might complement or better fulfill their objectives. In addition, the United States might use the Warsaw talks to present to the Chinese any arms control proposals which this government develops and which it felt might be of interest to both countries. Such proposals might be presented not only with a possible view to their acceptance and implementation but also with a view toward furthering the dialogue by forcing Chinese consideration of American proposals. But generally, American officials can communicate with the Chinese by public statements. The Chinese are close readers of Western speeches and Western press comment and hence can be reached by this method, provided the messages are sufficiently important to be brought to the attention of the top-level policy makers.

However, as was emphasized above, the content of any communications by the United States implying or stating the kinds of arms control agreements which might be in the mutual interests of the United States and Communist China would necessitate prior American political decisions, first, to begin such negotiations and, second, to be actually willing to sign agreements with the Peking regime.

These political preconditions, however, need not be met in order to broaden the areas of contact between China and the United States in a general way, not related directly to arms control. One potentially fruit-

[12]At least some participants at the Conference expressed a view that the Chinese should be invited to Geneva because this is where formal arms control negotiations were taking place. It should be noted that this view tended to look upon possible agreements as being world-wide in scope.

ful way in which China might be made arms control minded at the level
of specialists is through individual discussion between technicians and
academicians in fields related to arms control. Such discussions might
well come about as a result of expanding contacts between Chinese and
foreign individuals in a wide variety of areas. Before this can happen,
however, there must be more opportunities which can be exploited. One
field for further exploration by private and semi-governmental groups in
the United States is that of finding or creating forums at which intellectual contact between Americans and Chinese delegations or individuals
can be fostered, contacts that would avoid the issue of Chinese membership in the United Nations, American recognition or withdrawal from
Taiwan, etc. This is bound to be a slow process at best. It may never
lead to anything fruitful in the arms control field, either because contacts
in this particular area will be discouraged or because those with whom
contact is made will not have access to policy makers.

The most important way in which the United States can communicate
to the Chinese about military affairs and is likely to do so in the future
will remain, therefore, in the deployment and use of its military force,
not in direct person-to-person contact on either an official or a private
level. The United States has now come clearly to recognize that the decisions it makes on the deployment of its forces and on its military budget and how it explains these actions have an important effect on Soviet
decision making. The same is probably true of the Chinese, although
possibly to a somewhat lesser extent, since the Chinese scope for decision making about defense is more limited. Nevertheless, this is an
important, perhaps the most important, communication which currently
exists and is likely to continue to exist. The United States should recognize that what it says about the role that nuclear weapons might play in
its policy, what it says about support which it might give or might not
give the Chinese Nationalists in the effort they might make to return to
the mainland—all could affect Chinese decisions on their military budget
and the disposition of their military forces. The United States has in
fact used the disposition of its military forces to convey a number of
messages to the Chinese Communists, but none of these have concerned
possible attempts to influence the Chinese military forces in a way that
would be to mutual advantage on both sides. Such form of communication
is likely to be for some time the most important way of making the Chinese arms control minded and having them implement a reciprocal policy.

# XIII  THE IMPACT OF ARMS CONTROL ON CHINA

Although neither the United States nor the Communist Chinese regime believes it at all likely that China will sign any arms control agreements in the foreseeable future, this does not mean that the relationship between China and arms control is an unimportant one or that the Chinese have not been affected by discussions about arms control and specific arms control agreements. The Chinese find they must take a stand on disarmament questions and present and defend their own arms control proposals. Their position on arms control and disarmament has become extremely important for the Chinese and has substantially affected their diplomatic posture in other fields, their relations with allies, friends, and enemies, their propaganda efforts throughout the world.

To observe that China is unlikely to sign any agreements is not to dismiss the importance of considering the relationship between arms control discussions and agreements and Chinese policy. It is rather to suggest that the focus should be on the impact of these discussions and agreements on unilateral Chinese policy. This impact is a very substantial one and one that has been overlooked, not only in general consideration of the subject, but also in relation to particular agreements.

The experience of negotiating and implementing the Test Ban Treaty demonstrates not only the extent to which the affect of arms control on Chinese policy can be overlooked but also its great significance. Most discussions in the United States and attempts to evaluate the test ban focused on its effect on the Soviet-American military balance and on the likelihood of its helping to prevent the spread of nuclear weapons. Correctly, various analysts noted that the Chinese were unlikely to sign such an agreement, and hence the test ban was seen in some sense to be irrelevant to China and certainly not to affect the Chinese nuclear program. At the same time, in seeking to evaluate changing Soviet motivations in signing the Test Ban Treaty, the interrelation between the test ban discussions and Sino-Soviet relations has probably been underestimated.[1] In retrospect, it would appear that a major effect of the nuclear test ban was its impact on Chinese policy and the efficacy of various Chinese political and propaganda strategies.

Ever since they began to discuss with the West a separate agreement banning nuclear weapons tests, the Russians have undoubtedly been concerned with the effect this would have on their relations with the

---

[1]This is not meant to imply that the Sino-Soviet issue has been dominant in Moscow's thinking about the test ban. Certainly other issues, such as relations with the West and the military pressures to test or not to test, have been of importance.

Chinese and whether or not they would be able to bring the Chinese into the agreement. During 1957 and 1958, the Russians apparently anticipated that they could bring the Chinese in by promising them additional such assistance with their nuclear weapons program as would make testing unnecessary. After 1959, the Soviets were forced to recognize that if they did make a decision to go ahead with a test ban, it would have very serious consequences for their relations with the Chinese. One possible explanation for the apparent lack of Soviet interest in a nuclear Test Ban Treaty during the early 1960's may be their recognition of the very direct adverse effect it would have on Sino-Soviet relations.

When the Soviets did finally decide in the spring of 1963 that they would sign the Test Ban Treaty, they did so in a way which accentuated its interaction with Sino-Soviet relations and the fact that it was clearly recognized by them to be an anti-Chinese move. The Harriman mission, which came to Moscow to negotiate the treaty, arrived at the time that the Chinese delegation, which was seeking at least to patch up the Sino-Soviet conflict and end the public debate, was still in Moscow. The Soviets clearly gave more attention to the test ban group, with Khrushchev participating in the discussions, and no doubt intended this as a deliberate slap at the Chinese and a deliberate effort to emphasize that they were opting for a policy of détente with the West, even if it would be at the expense of a further disintegration in Sino-Soviet relations.

In signing the treaty, therefore, the Russians were aware that they were precipitating a major crisis in the International Communist movement. It is impossible and, for the purposes of this discussion, unnecessary to try to determine whether the Soviets signed the treaty deliberately to precipitate a crisis in Sino-Soviet and international Communist relations or whether they recognized this as an undesirable but inevitable by-product. The results of the Russians' signing could clearly be anticipated, and they followed rapidly.

The Chinese quickly indicated that they would not sign the Test Ban Treaty. The West, however, had probably not anticipated the degree of the vehemence of their denunciation or the repercussions that it would have. The actual signing of the treaty and the Soviet admonition in public to the Chinese to sign it marked a turning point in the Sino-Soviet public dialogue in which the Russians and the Chinese were advocating very different positions on a major international issue. The Soviets took an almost irrevocable step in signing the Test Ban Treaty and thereby eliminating even the possibility of a *pro forma* harmony in Sino-Soviet policies on important international questions.

At the same time, the Soviet action may have increased the anxiety in Communist China that the Russians or the Americans, or the two acting jointly, might make some move to destroy Chinese nuclear facilities.

The Chinese interpreted the treaty as symbolizing the Russian determination to seek coexistence with the United States at any price.

The Test Ban Treaty not only further deepened the public and private Sino-Soviet disputes, but it also further split the International Communist movement. Before the treaty was signed, a number of Communist Parties, notably the Vietnamese, but also the Japanese, the Indonesians, and others, had tried to remain relatively neutral in the Sino-Soviet dispute and to urge the two major Communist Parties to reconcile their differences. But the Test Ban Treaty forced all of these smaller parties to take sides in the dispute, to come down solidly in either the Soviet or the Chinese camp. The North Vietnamese and the Japanese, for example, sided with the Chinese in this issue and, in general, in the dispute. This increased the probability of a formal split of the International Communist movement into two camps, one headed by the Russians and one by the Chinese. It also virtually eliminated the valuable middle men who might have been used when and if both regimes decided that they would like to reconcile their differences.

The consequences of this decision by national Communist Parties to side with the Russians or the Chinese over the test ban may be very significant. For example, the Vietnamese, having chosen the Chinese side on this issue, may now expect greater aid from the Chinese for their operations in South Vietnam and Laos than they were previously getting. The Chinese may have had to make some specific guarantees and offers of increased aid to the Vietnamese in order to force their support in the test ban issue. And they may also have had to promise economic assistance to make up for an expected cut in Soviet aid.

For the Japanese Communist Party, the decision to side with the Chinese was particularly difficult because the test ban was very popular in Japan and the Japanese people have an intense anti-nuclear feeling. This may mean a very substantial setback for the Japanese Communist Party in its efforts to increase its influence in Japan and to promote support for China and eventual diplomatic recognition of the Peking regime by the Japanese government.

The Test Ban Treaty may then turn out to be a landmark in the evolution of the International Communist movement. If this is true, it emphasizes the great significance of arms control for the Chinese.

The signing of the treaty by most of the countries of the world not only had an important impact on the International Communist movement but also affected Communist China's relations with other states in Asia. China's efforts to present itself as a peaceful nation with no desires to expand its control over other Asian states were set back by its refusal to sign a treaty which was signed by every non-Communist Asian nation but Cambodia. The isolation of China from the basic norms and desires of the general world community was highlighted, as was the possibility that she had foreign policy objectives which required her to abstain from the Test Ban Treaty.

The Test Ban Treaty issue has also forced a split in most of the united-front groups established by the Russians and the Chinese in order to promote Communist influence in the underdeveloped areas. In each one of these groups, a struggle has taken place between the forces supporting the Chinese position, and hence opposed to the test ban, and those supporting the Russian position. This has set back probably both the Russian and Chinese effort to win support among leftist groups. On the diplomatic level as well, the Chinese have been forced to discuss the test ban and to explain their reasons for not signing the treaty. As was indicated above, [Chou En-lai, during his trip to Africa in the winter of 1963-1964 had to spend a good deal of his time defending the Chinese position.]

It is not clear how persuasive the Chinese arguments against the treaty have been with the leaders of uncommitted countries in Asia, Africa, or elsewhere in the world. It would appear, however, that most of these countries would prefer that the Chinese sign the treaty, that China's efforts to win influence in these countries and to appear as their champion has been set back by her refusal to go along with the will of virtually every nation of the world.

If, then, the general question of the Chinese attitudes toward disarmament and toward specific issues, such as the test ban and a nuclear-free zone in the Pacific, has important implications for Chinese policy, what is the consequence of this for American policy?

First and most obviously, the United States might give more consideration than it has to the likely impact on China of any proposal it makes. Chinese relations, not only with the United States but also with the Soviet Union, the rest of the Communist bloc, and the underdeveloped countries of Asia, Africa, and Latin America can be affected by nominally unrelated American actions. As was clear in the case of the test ban, it is very easy for the United States to get caught up in what seems the more immediate and important questions of the Soviet-American military relationship and American political objectives and overlook what could in fact be more important, the impact on China of any arms control measures or proposals. The test ban may have had more of an impact on China than any future measure will, but any arms control negotiations which the United States conducts with the Soviet Union will affect the Chinese in a similar way, if not degree.

In its propaganda and diplomatic offensives in the underdeveloped areas, the United States might well seek to exploit the weaknesses in the Chinese position created by the stand China has been forced to take in the Sino-Soviet polemics. The Chinese disdain of the possibility of disarmament, the Chinese failure to sign the Test Ban Treaty, the Chinese assertion of the need to create additional nuclear powers, these are all positions which are unpopular with most of the countries of the world. Laying stress on these issues, rather than on the false issue of the Chinese desire for nuclear war, might make extremely effective propaganda. It might also serve to highlight the threat which China poses to any evolving international political community.

It would seem that the Chinese share the belief prevalent in the West that there are not likely to be any formal arms control agreements signed between the United States and Communist China nor indeed by Communist China with any other country. At the same time, the Chinese are undoubtedly aware of the political and diplomatic importance of the stand they take on the general subject of disarmament and on specific arms control agreements. They are beginning to think about arms control and to state their own positions more clearly. The United States, therefore, should pay more attention to the interaction between its arms control position and the foreign policy of Communist China.

### NEW STARTING POINT FOR EFFORTS TO
### BAN NUCLEAR WEAPONS COMPLETELY

More than a month ago, the Chinese Government, simultaneous with its announcement of the explosion of China's first atom bomb, solemnly declared to the whole world that China will never at any time and under any circumstances be the first to use nuclear weapons. The Chinese Government also formally proposed to the world's governments that a summit conference of all countries be convened to discuss the question of the complete prohibition and thorough destruction of nuclear weapons, and that, as the first step, the conference should reach an agreement to the effect that the nuclear powers and those countries which may soon become nuclear powers undertake not to use nuclear weapons, neither to use them against non-nuclear powers and nuclear-free zones, nor against each other.

This proposal expresses the common aspirations of all peace-loving peoples of the world and has received the support of government heads in many countries. World public opinion has acclaimed it and considered it to be an important contribution to the complete prohibition and thorough destruction of nuclear weapons and to the cause of preservation of world peace.

It is true that the complete prohibition and thorough destruction of nuclear weapons can be realized only through hard and bitter struggles. Certain practicable measures have to be taken in order to attain this goal. This is agreed by all. Now the question is how the first step should be taken so as to facilitate the attainment of the goal rather than produce an adverse effect.

### TRIPARTITE TREATY: A COVER FOR
### U.S. NUCLEAR WAR PREPARATIONS

Some people say that the tripartite treaty for the partial suspension of nuclear testing is the first step towards the complete prohibition of nuclear weapons.

This claim has been utterly refuted by what has happened in the last year and more. As everybody knows, the tripartite treaty was signed when the United States had already acquired enough technical data on atmospheric nuclear testing. This treaty in no way hampers the United States from continuing to use, manufacture and stockpile nuclear weapons, nor from conducting underground nuclear testing to develop tactical nuclear

[1]This translation of the November 22, 1964, *People's Daily* editorial is reproduced in its entirety as it appeared in the *Peking Review*, Vol. VII, No. 48 (November 27, 1964), pp. 12-14.

weapons, still less proliferating nuclear weapons under the smokescreen of the so-called multilateral nuclear force. On the contrary, the United States is using the tripartite treaty to pinion other countries, including those possessing nuclear weapons, so as to obtain nuclear superiority for continuing its policy of nuclear blackmail and threats. The United States is also using this treaty to hoodwink the peace-loving people of the world and weaken their struggle for the complete prohibition of nuclear weapons. The tripartite treaty, therefore, not only puts off indefinitely the complete prohibition of nuclear weapons but also serves as a smokescreen for U.S. nuclear war preparations.

## A COMPLETE TEST BAN NOW ONLY STRENGTHENS U.S. NUCLEAR MONOPOLY

Some people say that the complete prohibition of nuclear weapons can begin with the complete banning of nuclear testing.

On the face of it, such a ban sounds slightly better than a partial ban. In actual fact, there is little difference. The United States has carried out hundreds of nuclear tests of various kinds and possesses a huge nuclear arsenal. Under such circumstances, even a complete ban on nuclear testing will still leave this U.S. nuclear overlord intact. It will have no positive significance whatsoever if it is not accompanied by the prohibition of the use, production, stockpiling, import, export and proliferation of nuclear weapons. It can only serve to consolidate U.S. nuclear monopoly, deprive other countries of their legitimate right to develop nuclear weapons to resist the U.S. nuclear threat. It can only spread a false sense of security and weaken the struggle of all peace-loving peoples in the world for the complete prohibition of nuclear weapons. Far from enjoying peace and security as a result of a complete ban on nuclear testing, the world, on the contrary, will be subjected to even more serious nuclear threats by the U.S. nuclear overlord. It is just because of this that even a man like Dean Rusk is talking zealously about the need to conclude a so-called complete nuclear test ban treaty in the hope of using it to substitute the increasingly discredited tripartite treaty and further deceive the world's peace-loving peoples. Isn't it clear as daylight whom a complete ban on nuclear testing will benefit?

## PROPOSAL TO DESTROY DELIVERY MEANS COMPLICATES ISSUE

Some people say that destruction of the delivery vehicles of nuclear weapons can be taken as a primary measure for realizing the complete prohibition of nuclear weapons.

At first glance, such opinion seems to be not entirely senseless. But after a careful study, it is not difficult to see that this suggestion has a serious weakness. Devils are devils, whether they have long or short legs. Conventional weapons can launch nuclear bombs as well as the intercontinental ballistic missile. And ordinary aircraft can carry nuclear weapons as well as strategic bombers. The means of delivery is no longer as important a problem as it used to be, particularly since the United States is working hard to develop small but powerful nuclear weapons. The proposal to first of all destroy the means of delivery in effect confuses the question of complete prohibition of nuclear weapons with the question of reduction of conventional arms and thus greatly complicates the issue. Moreover, this proposal will inevitably involve the question of control which is the great obstacle to arms reduction deliberately put up by the United States during the disarmament talks. That is why although people at the disarmament negotiations have worn their lips thin and many years have been wasted, U.S. arms expansion has continued year by year. If the complete prohibition of nuclear weapons should begin with the destruction of the means of delivery only heaven knows when this goal will ever be attained.

## NOT TO USE NUCLEAR WEAPONS: THE EFFECTIVE STEP TOWARDS COMPLETE PROHIBITION

As the first step towards the complete prohibition of nuclear weapons, it is necessary to get at the real key question and not be bogged down by some minor and side issues. This first step must facilitate the taking of further steps and be conducive, not detrimental, to the gradual attainment of the aim of the complete prohibition of nuclear weapons. This step must help check the nuclear arms race instead of serving as a smokescreen and help lessen the threat of nuclear war instead of increasing the threat. It must serve to promote the struggle of the peace-loving people the world over for the complete prohibition of nuclear weapons, and not lower their vigilance and pull the wool over their eyes.

It is precisely in the light of these principles that the Chinese Government has proposed that the various countries should agree to undertake not to use nuclear weapons, as the first step towards the complete prohibition of nuclear weapons. The Chinese government proposal is reasonable and practicable.

It is very easy for the countries possessing nuclear weapons to do this provided they harbour no aggressive intentions. After they have undertaken not to use nuclear weapons, it will no longer be necessary for them to continue nuclear testing and the production of nuclear weapons. The United States will then be unable always to intimidate others with nuclear weapons nor set up nuclear bases and spread nuclear weapons in other countries under this or that pretext. Then, the stockpiling of nuclear weapons will become unnecessary.

As for those countries which do not possess nuclear weapons, they will have no need to develop their own or import them from other countries, since the countries possessing nuclear weapons and those which may soon possess them will undertake not to use nuclear weapons, not to use them against non-nuclear countries.

Many countries at present are keenly interested in the establishment of nuclear-free zones. However, to really free the nuclear-free zones from the threat of nuclear war it is first necessary for the nuclear powers to undertake not to use nuclear weapons. Otherwise, the establishment of nuclear-free zones would be impossible and even if they be set up in name, all it means is that the non-nuclear countries would be deprived of their legitimate right to develop nuclear weapons to resist the nuclear menace and be bound hand and foot, while the nuclear powers would in no way be affected in their continued production, stockpiling and even use of nuclear weapons. Consequently, the sole result would be: the larger the nuclear-free zone, the graver the U.S. imperialist nuclear threat to the non-nuclear countries.

No question of control is involved in undertaking first of all not to use nuclear weapons. So long as the countries concerned have peaceful intentions, agreement can be reached quickly. Therefore this is simple and can be easily carried out.

For 20 years the peace-loving peoples of the world have resolutely opposed the U.S. imperialist policy of nuclear blackmail and threats and have demanded the complete prohibition of nuclear weapons. There will be hope for the realization of this aim if the pledge is first of all taken not to use these weapons. This will be a major victory for the people of the world who cherish peace. It will inevitably inspire them with ever greater confidence in the struggle for the complete prohibition and thorough destruction of nuclear weapons, and the development of this struggle will provide greater possibility of an early realization of this noble objective.

To undertake first of all not to use nuclear weapons is the only realistic and effective step towards complete prohibition. The Chinese Government has taken the lead in declaring that at no time and under no circumstances will it be the first to use nuclear weapons, and it is willing to reach an international agreement guaranteeing against their use. The question now is whether the U.S. Government is willing to make the same commitment. The U.S. Government claims to be "peace-loving" while at the same time obstinately opposing the Chinese proposal for a world summit conference. We would like to ask the U.S. Government: if your peace babble is worth anything at all, are you willing to reach agreement with China, pending the convening of a world summit conference, on the question of guaranteeing not to use nuclear weapons?

## CHINA WILL NOT TAKE PART IN
## GENEVA DISARMAMENT TALKS

It seems that the U.S. authorities have no desire either to hold a world summit conference or to reach a bilateral agreement with China against the use of nuclear weapons. They have been declaring, evidently with an ulterior motive, that they have no objection to China's participation in the Geneva disarmament talks, thus trying to substitute the 18-nation disarmament talks for a summit conference of all countries.

We would like to point out that the Geneva disarmament talks are conducted within the framework of the United Nations. Over the past 15 years, the United States has deprived China of its legitimate rights in the United Nations by various sinister and despicable means. Now that China has nuclear weapons, the United States wants to drag her into the affairs of the United Nations. What is behind all this? Frankly speaking, China will have nothing to do with the United Nations as long as the latter fails to restore to the representative of the People's Republic of China the legitimate rights as the representative of the sole legal government of the Chinese people and as long as the illegal status of the representative of the Chiang Kai-shek clique is not nullified. This stand of ours is absolutely unalterable.

Furthermore, under the manipulation of the United States, the United Nations had proved itself completely incapable of handling the disarmament question. For 18 years since the adoption of the resolution on "principles concerning the general adjustment and reduction of arms" at the first U.N. General Assembly in December 1946, the assembly has discussed the disarmament question every year but has failed to make any headway because of U.S. obstruction. On the contrary, the thicker the disarmament talks smokescreen, the more frantically the United States has carried out arms expansion and war preparations. U.S. military expenditure rose from 12,900 million dollars in 1949 to 60,000 million dollars in 1964. U.S. expenditure on the making of nuclear weapons increased from 200 million dollars in 1947 to 3,000 million in 1963. This is the greatest mockery of the U.N.-sponsored disarmament talks.

The Geneva 18-nation disarmament conference is in fact still under the manipulation and control of the United States and can in no way reflect the aspirations of the peoples. The conference has been in session for two and a half years, and a pile of proposals of all kinds have been put forward but not a single question of substance has been solved. Even though some peace-loving countries are participating in the talks, this can in no way make the United States less peremptory. Thus, the Geneva disarmament conference has likewise served as a smokescreen for U.S. imperialist armament expansion and war preparations. It is more difficult for the Geneva disarmament conference to solve the question of complete prohibition of nuclear weapons than for a camel to pass through the needle's eye. We thank the U.S. Government for its generosity in not opposing China's participation in the Geneva disarmament conference, but we must tell it frankly that it will not have the pleasure of our company.

## ALL COUNTRIES MUST HAVE THEIR SAY

There is also the suggestion that the five countries possessing nuclear weapons should hold negotiations to discuss questions concerning nuclear weapons. We do not approve of this proposal either.

The reason is that the question at present is primarily one of a certain nuclear power posing a threat to all non-nuclear countries. It is a question which has a vital bearing on peace and security in the world. On this question, the more than 100 sovereign countries of the world, big or small, with or without nuclear weapons, should have the same say. What right do the five countries possessing nuclear weapons have to deprive more than 100 countries of their say and make arbitrary decisions on such a major question affecting the destiny of mankind?

China has consistently stood for discussion by all countries of the question of banning nuclear weapons. This was our stand when we did not have nuclear weapons. Now that we have them we still adhere to this stand. We have only one objective, namely, to make joint efforts with all peace-loving countries and people throughout the world to strive for the realization of complete prohibition and thorough destruction of nuclear weapons, and by no means to use nuclear weapons to raise our own prestige and manipulate international affairs. So-called talks among the five countries possessing nuclear weapons would in fact be a nuclear club in disguise. We will not join such a club even if an invitation is sent us together with a sedan chair.

The struggle for the complete prohibition and thorough destruction of nuclear weapons has been going on for many years. Now is the time to take practical and feasible steps to attain this objective. The Chinese Government's proposal has opened up a new avenue for the complete prohibition of nuclear weapons. It proposes to reach first of all an international agreement guaranteeing against the use of nuclear weapons, so as to provide a new starting point for their complete prohibition. It is our belief that no matter how U.S. imperialism may try to obstruct this, the Chinese Government proposal will win the ever increasing support of peace-loving countries and peoples. The Chinese people will fight together with them to push the struggle for the prohibition of nuclear weapons on to a new path.

## PARTICIPANTS in the CHINA ARMS CONTROL CONFERENCES

China Arms Control Conference
July 9-19, 1964

Airlie House
Warrenton, Virginia

*Participants:*

Professor Davis B. Bobrow
Department of Politics
Princeton University

Mr. Hedley Bull
The London School of Economics
   and Political Science

Professor Alexander Dallin
Russian Institute
Columbia University

Professor Alexander Eckstein
Department of Economics
University of Michigan

Professor Morton H. Halperin
Center for International Affairs
Harvard University

Mrs. Alice Langley Hsieh
The RAND Corporation
Santa Monica, California

Mr. Thomas C. Irvin
U.S. Arms Control and Disarmament
   Agency

Professor Tadao Ishikawa
Department of Political Science
Keio University
Tokyo, Japan

Dr. John M. H. Lindbeck
East Asian Research Center
Harvard University

Mr. William P. Maddox
U.S. Arms Control and
   Disarmament Agency

Mr. Robert E. Matteson
U.S. Arms Control and
   Disarmament Agency

Dr. Richard Moorsteen
The RAND Corporation
Santa Monica, California

Professor Robert North
Department of Political Science
Stanford University

Colonel Kent K. Parrot
U.S. Arms Control and
   Disarmament Agency

Professor Dwight Perkins
East Asian Research Center
Harvard University

Professor Thomas C. Schelling
Center for International Affairs
Harvard University

Professor H. Franz Schurmann
Center of Chinese Studies
University of California
Berkeley

Hon. Michael N. F. Stewart
Imperial Defence College
Seaford House
London

Professor George E. Taylor
Far Eastern and Russian Institute
University of Washington

Professor Donald Zagoria
Institute for Communist Studies
Columbia University

Dr. Allen S. Whiting
Office of Research and
    Analysis for the Far East
Department of State

*Rapporteurs:*

Ellis Joffe
East Asian Research Center
Harvard University

Michael R. Gordon
Graduate School of Public
    Administration
Harvard University

*Executive Secretary:*

Lois Driscoll
East Asian Research Center
Harvard University

China Arms Control Conference
December 18-19, 1964

Sheraton-Commander Hotel
Cambridge, Massachusetts

*Participants:*

Professor Robert R. Bowie
Center for International Affairs
Harvard University

Professor Fred C. Iklé
Center for International Studies
M.I.T.

Professor Jerome A. Cohen
Harvard Law School

Mr. Thomas C. Irvin
U.S. Arms Control and
    Disarmament Agency

Professor Morton H. Halperin
Center for International Affairs
Harvard University

Dr. John M. H. Lindbeck
East Asian Research Center
Harvard University

Mr. George Modelski
Woodrow Wilson School of Public
    and International Affairs
Princeton University

Colonel Kent K. Parrot
U.S. Arms Control and
    Disarmament Agency

Professor Dwight Perkins
East Asian Research Center
Harvard University

Professor Lucian W. Pye
Center for International Studies
M.I.T.

Professor Thomas C. Schelling
Center for International Affairs
Harvard University

Professor Benjamin I. Schwartz
East Asian Research Center
Harvard University

Dr. Allen S. Whiting
Office of Research and Analysis
    for the Far East
Department of State

# INDEX

Accidental War, 137, 159
Adams, Mervyn W., 148n, 152n
Adie, W. A. C., 119n
Africa, 41, 44, 91, 119-20, 121, 171
Afro-Asian Conference, 179
Agreements, formal, 161, 162n, 164, 165
Agreements, tacit, 161, 162n, 164, 165
Agricultural Crisis, 1959-1961, 30
Aid, purpose of Chinese, 45
Air Force, Chinese, 4, 36-37
Albania, 6, 45, 119, 121
Algeria, 58, 120n
Antarctica Treaty, 138
Arms Control, Chinese attitudes toward, 1, 28, 19, 40-41, 59, 132-40, 155-67
Arms Control, Chinese proposals for, 98-131
Arms Control, impact on China, 168-72
Arms Control Negotiations, China, 27, 102-104, 109, 127, 131
Arms Control, see disarmament, non-proliferation agreement, nuclear-free zone, nuclear weapons, Sino-Soviet dispute, Test Ban Treaty
Arms Purchases, 30-31
Army, Chinese, 4, 36, 76
Atlas Missile, 34
Atomic Weapons, see nuclear weapons
Australia, 68-69, 70

Barnett, A. Doak, 98n
Bandung Conference, 20, 21
Berlin, 144
Bipolarity, 157-58
Brazil, 8
Brennan, Donald G., 98n
Bucharest Conference, 1960, 109
Buddhism, 25
Burma, 9n, 11, 41, 43, 45, 77, 146

Cairo Declaration, 144
Cambodia, 11-12, 43, 43n, 44, 45, 77, 119, 170
Cameroons, 9n

Canada, 70
Castro, Fidel, 44
Catalytic War, 137
Ceylon, 45
Chen Yi, 105
Ch'en Yun, 23
Chiang Kai-shek, 13
Ch'iu, Hungdah, 142n, 145n, 148n
Chou En-lai, 54, 66, 99, 100, 100n, 103, 119-20, 121, 122n, 124, 125, 129,
    129n, 133-34, 171
Civil War, (Chinese), 2-3, 75, 79, 80
Collateral Measures, 159, 164
Communes, 17, 20, 21, 22, 24, 32
Communication, wartime, 86-87
Communication, by U.S. to China, 162, 165-67
Conference of African States, 120
Conference on Chinese Attitudes toward Arms Control, 3n, 5n, 6n, 7n,
    8n, 10n, 13n, 17n, 21n, 23n, 28n, 31n, 33n, 35n, 36n, 69n, 70n, 73n,
    91n, 142n, 145n, 148n, 153n, 155n, 161n, 162, 162n, 164n, 166n,
Congo Crisis (1960), 143, 150-52
Conventional Capability, Chinese, 29, 36, 38
Conventional War, 75-82
Conventional Weapons, advanced, 37-38
Counter-insurgency, 95-97
Crankshaw, Edward, 109n, 110n
Cuba, 28, 43, 44, 45, 46, 59n, 96
Czechoslovakia, 43n, 147

Dallin, Alexander, 98n, 103n, 105n, 110n, 112n, 113n, 135n, 136, 137,
    138, 138n, 139, 158n
Daniel Boone, (submarine), 127
Declaration of War, 84
De Gaulle, Charles, 70, 129, 129n
Delivery Capability, Chinese, 29, 34, 35, 40, 129, 136, 137
Détente, 19, 132, 134, 135, 138
Diem, Ngo Dinh, 70
Dienbienphu, 88, 89
Diplomatic Negotiations, 4-5, 87-89
Disarmament, general and complete, 99, 105-14, 155, 157, 158, 163, 164,
    164n, 165
Disarmament, See Arms Control
Domestic Policy, Chinese, 20-27, 32-33

Dulles, J. F., 78
Dumbarton Oaks Conference, 148

Economy, China, 1, 4, 28-47
Edwards, R. Randle, 142n, 145n, 148n
Eighteen-Nation Disarmament Conference, 130, 155, 159, 165
Eisenhower, Dwight D., 6, 78, 80, 106
Escalation, Chinese doubts on, 59-60
Escalation, 59-60, 96n
Ethiopia, 120n

"Five-Anti" Movement, 20
Five Year Plan, first, 21
Force de Frappe, Chinese, 35
Force de Frappe, French, 34, 69, 70
Foreign Policy, Chinese, 20-28
Foreign Policy, Chinese, economics of, 28-47
Foreign Policy, Chinese, goals, 1-14
Foreign Policy, Chinese, role of ideology, 1-2, 4-18, 26, 33
Foreign Policy, Chinese, role of Military force, 76-78, 161
France, 5, 34, 65, 67, 68, 69, 70, 101, 128, 129, 144
Fukien Province, 77, 80
Futrell, Robert Frank, 87

GATT, 42
GCD, see Arms Control
GNP, Chinese, 30
Geneva Conference (1954), 20, 78, 79, 88, 89
Germany, 30, 31, 111
Ghana, 45, 120n
Goldhamer, Herbert, 50n
Gizenga Government, 152
Great Britain, 65, 69, 101, 115, 129, 159
"Great Leap Forward", 7, 17, 20, 21, 22, 23, 24, 31, 32, 38n
Griffith, William E., 52n, 53n, 54n, 59n, 60n, 63n, 64n, 105n
Gromyko, Andrei, 125
Guerrilla Forces, indigenous, 29
Guerrilla War, see Wars of National Liberation
Guinea, 3, 45, 120, 120n

Halperin, Morton H., 48n, 89n, 158n, 160n
Halpern, A. M., 62n

Hammerskjöld, Dag, 151
Harriman, Mission to Moscow, 1963, 169
Heavy Industry, Chinese, 30
Hinton, Harold, 104n
Hong Kong, 41, 145
Hot-line, 122, 159
Hoxha, Enver, 122n
Hsieh, Alice Langley, 48n, 51n, 98n, 99n, 100, 100n
*Hsüeh-hsi* Sessions, 25, 26
Hudson, G. F., 53n, 57n, 105n, 107n, 109n, 110n, 111n
"Hundred Flowers" Campaign, 20, 22
Hungary, 20, 45, 143


ICBM, 21, 34, 40
India, 2, 21, 33, 36, 39, 43, 68, 68n, 69, 70, 72
Indo-China, 20, 81, 83, 84, 87, 88, 89, 91; see also Laos, Vietnam
Indonesia, 3, 11-12, 33, 42, 44, 45, 68n, 72, 96, 152, 170
Inspection, 95, 152, 153-54, 166
Institute for Strategic Studies, 37n
International Law, Chinese attitude toward, 141-47
International Law, U.S. Attitude toward, 141-42
International Organization, Chinese attitudes toward, 147-52
Israel, 70


Japan, 2, 14-15, 30, 31, 33, 39, 41, 42, 50, 68-69, 69n, 70, 93, 100, 111


Java, 96
Joffe, E., 36n
John, Dr., 31n
Johnson, Lyndon B., 73, 91-92


Kahn, Herman, 90
Kang Sheng, 106
Kennedy, John F., 63, 80, 112
Khrushchev, Nikita, 6, 19, 48, 57, 57n, 99, 99n, 103, 103n, 106, 122, 169
Kishi, Nobusuke, 14-15
Kuo Mo-jo, 99
Kuomintang, see Nationalists, Chinese
Korea, 11, 39, 44, 45, 46, 77, 81, 119, 149
Korean Armistice Agreement, 89, 146
Korean War, 3, 5, 20, 24, 26, 29, 30, 37, 45, 50-51, 77, 78, 81, 83, 84, 85-86, 87-88, 149, 153

Land Reform, Chinese, 20
Laos, 11, 12, 13, 14, 46, 82, 83, 84, 86, 147, 153, 170
Laos Agreement, 1962, 164n
Latin America, 41, 43, 91, 119, 171
Leadership, Chinese, 16-17, 76
"Lean to One Side" Policy, 3
Lebanon-Jordan Crisis, 1958, 150
Limited Force, use of, 79-82
Limited War, 7, 83-93
Liu Chang-sheng, 108-109
Liu Ning I, 112, 112n-113n
Liu Shao-chi, 127
Local Wars, 57-60, 137-38
Lumumba, Patrice, 151
Lowenthal, Richard, 53n, 105n
Lvov, M., 126n

Macao, 145
MacFarquhar, Roderick, 53n, 105n
McNamara, Robert, 91-92
Mao Tse-tung, 1, 3, 23, 49, 50, 51, 52, 53n, 56, 57, 61, 75, 101, 135, 148
Massive Retaliation, 78
Malaysia, 42, 152
Mali, 120n
Manchuria, 4, 85-86
Mendes-France, Pierre, 89
Military Capability, Chinese, 28-29, 33-40
Mobutu, 152
Mongolia, 45
Morocco, 45, 120n
Moscow Conference, 1957, 61
Moscow Conference, 1960, 110-11

National People's Congress, 23, 100
Nationalists, Chinese, 2-3, 4, 5, 13, 39, 76-77, 78, 79, 80, 81, 116, 145, 167
Navy, Chinese, 4, 37
Nehru, Jawaharlal, 99
Nepal, 45, 146
Neutral Nations Supervisory Commission, 147
Non-proliferation Agreement, 1, 67, 71, 74, 113, 137n

Nuclear Blackmail, 4, 55-56, 65, 91, 133, 137, 139
Nuclear Capability, Chinese, 4, 6-7, 29, 63-66, 69-70
Nuclear Detonation, Chinese, 67, 69n, 73, 102, 103n, 123
Nuclear-free Zone, 98, 99-102, 119, 120, 123, 124, 125, 131, 133, 140, 171
Nuclear Strategy, Chinese, 35, 48-66
Nuclear Weapons, ban on use of: 102, 123-24, 127-28, 129, 130, 131, 133,
    134, 139; see arms control

Outer Mongolia, 4, 143

PLA, 75, 76-82
Pakistan, 68n, 72
Panikkar, K. M., 50n
"Paper Tiger", 85
"Peaceful Coexistence", 18, 20, 21, 59, 63, 111
P'eng Teh-huai, 23
Peng Chen, 57, 109
Perkins, Dwight H., 28n, 134n
Plutonium, 34
Poland, 20, 147
Potsdam Proclamation, 144
Press, Chinese, 25-26
Proliferation: 67-74, 126-27, 136-37; see also Non-proliferation Agreement

Quemoy Crises, 1958, 21, 79, 81, 90

Racism, 10
Rosecrance, R. N., 48n
Rusk, Dean, 13

SEATO, 79
Sanctuaries, 86
Scalapino, Robert A., 119n
Schelling, Thomas, C., 158n, 160n
"Serious Warnings", 79
Seventh Fleet, 3
Sihanouk, Norodom, 119
Sinkiang, 4
Sino-Indian Border Dispute, 8, 77, 78, 79n, 80, 86, 88-89, 143
Sino-Soviet Border Dispute, 4, 82
Sino-Soviet Crisis Relations, 65-66, 80, 87
Sino-Soviet Dispute, Chinese objectives, 5-10, 64, 114, 122

Sino-Soviet Dispute, Chinese Strategy in, 24, 26, 44n, 45, 150
Sino-Soviet Dispute, differences on arms control, 49, 53, 62, 63, 98-100, 105-108, 110, 113-18, 122, 132, 164n, 165, 169-71
Sino-Soviet Dispute, effect on Chinese military capability, 31
Sino-Soviet Dispute, on nuclear war, 54-55, 57-60
Sino-Soviet Dispute, on nuclear weapons, 64
Sino-Soviet Dispute, role of strategic balance in, 21
Sino-Soviet Dispute, role of Test Ban Treaty, 13
Sino-Soviet Dispute, Soviet Strategy in, 49
Somalia, 45, 120, 120n
South Africa, 70
Southeast Asia, 4, 11-14, 28, 41, 43
Soviet Aid to China, 37-38, 41
Soviet Military Aid, 81
Soviet H-bomb Test, 61
Soviet Troop Cuts, 107
Soviet Union, Foreign Policy, role of ideology, 1
Spirit of Bandung, 18
Sputnik, 6, 61
Stalin, Josef, 9, 9n, 11, 23, 154
Strategic balance, role of, 60-63, 138
Strong, Anna Louise, 50, 50n
Sudan, 120n
Sukarno, 72, 96
Summit Conference, 124
Surprise Attack, reciprocal fear of, 137
Syria, 45

Taiwan: 3, 36, 61, 73, 76, 79, 80, 81, 101, 135, 144, 148, 167; see also Nationalist China
Taiwan Straits, 78, 79n, 83, 84, 87, 88, 89-90
Tanganyika, 45
Ten-Power Disarmament Committee, 104
Test Ban Treaty, 11, 13, 134, 164
Test Ban Treaty, Chinese opposition to, 47, 48, 53, 62, 65, 68, 100-101, 110, 114-16, 118-21, 123-24, 126, 128, 131, 133, 136, 145, 155-56
Test Ban Treaty, complete, 128, 131, 134
Test Ban Treaty, impact on China, 168-71
Test Ban Treaty, Soviet interest in, 19, 63, 159, 169
Test Ban Treaty, see Arms Control, Sino-Soviet Dispute
Thailand, 2
"Three-anti" movement, 20

Tibet, 4, 80
Titan Missile, 34
Trade Embargo, effect of on China, 46-47
Trade, purpose of Chinese, 45
Treaties, Chinese compliance with, 143, 145, 147
Troop Reductions, 104
Truman, Harry S., 3
Tshombe, Moise, 152
Tung Pi-wu, 148
Tung Wei-j'en, 122n
Tunisia 120n
Twentieth Congress, CPSU, 1956, 117
Twenty-First Congress, CPSU, 1957, 99
Two-Chinas, 105

U Thant, 130
"Unequal Treaties", 144-45
United Kingdom, 41, 42, 144, 145
United Arab Republic, 5, 43, 45, 70, 72, 120n, 149, 150
United Nations, 3, 104, 107, 125, 140, 141, 143, 145, 147-52
UN, Chinese admission to, 103, 130, 135, 152, 167
U.S. Attack, Chinese fear of, 78
U.S., China's image of, 15
U.S., recognition of China, 135
Uranium 235, 34

Vietnam, Chinese goals in, 13-14
Vietnam, effect on Chinese policy of, 18, 39
Vietnam, North, 119, 147
Vietnam, North, Chinese aid to, 44, 45, 147, 170
Vietnam, North, relations with China, 11, 12-13, 44, 45, 77, 170
Vietnam, possibility of Chinese intervention, 82, 86
Vietnam, U.S. bombing of, 82, 83, 84, 91
Vietnam, U.S. role in, 28, 94, 96

WFTU, 108-109
War Termination Agreements, 89-90
Wars of National Liberation, 7, 8, 18, 19, 57-60, 75, 93-97, 105, 108n,
    112, 113, 114, 122, 132, 132n, 134, 135, 138
Warsaw Pact, 143
Warsaw Talks, 87, 88, 125, 166
Warsaw Treaty Organization, 103, 106

Western Europe, Chinese trade with, 41
Whiting, Allen, 35n
World Peace Council, 112
Wolfe, Thomas, 159n
Wolfers, Arnold, 104n
World War II, 17-18
Wu Hsiu-ch'uan, 149

Yalta Conference, 144, 148
Yemen, 44, 45
Yugoslavia, 6
Zanzibar, 45

*In Search of France,* by Stanley Hoffmann, Charles P. Kindleberger, Laurence Wylie, Jesse R. Pitts, Jean-Baptiste Duroselle, and François Goguel, 1963. Harvard University Press.

*Somali Nationalism,* by Saadia Touval, 1963. Harvard University Press.

*The Dilemma of Mexico's Development,* by Raymond Vernon, 1963, Harvard University Press.

*Limited War in the Nuclear Age,* by Morton H. Halperin, 1963. John Wiley & Sons.

*The Arms Debate,* by Robert A. Levine, 1963. Harvard University Press.

*Africans on the Land,* by Montague Yudelman, 1964. Harvard University Press.

*Counterinsurgency Warfare,* by David Galula, 1964. Frederick A. Praeger, Inc.

*People and Policy in the Middle East,* by Max Weston Thornburg, 1964. W. W. Norton & Co.

*Shaping the Future,* by Robert R. Bowie, 1964. Columbia University Press.

*Foreign Aid and Foreign Policy,* by Edward S. Mason (jointly with the Council on Foreign Relations), 1964. Harper & Row.

*Public Policy and Private Enterprise in Mexico,* by M. S. Wionczek, D. H. Shelton, C. P. Blair, and R. Izquierdo, ed. Raymond Vernon, 1964. Harvard University Press.

*How Nations Negotiate,* by Fred Iklé, 1964. Harper & Row.

*China and the Bomb,* by Morton H. Halperin (jointly with the East Asian Research Center), 1965. Frederick A. Praeger, Inc.

*Democracy in Germany,* by Fritz Erler (Jodidi Lectures), 1965. Harvard University Press.

*The Troubled Partnership,* by Henry A. Kissinger (jointly with the Council on Foreign Relations), 1905. McGraw-Hill Book Co.

*The Rise of Nationalism in Central Africa,* by Robert I. Rotberg, 1965. Harvard University Press.

*Pan-Africanism and East African Integration,* by Joseph S. Nye, Jr., 1965. Harvard University Press.

*Communist China and Arms Control,* by Morton H. Halperin and Dwight H. Perkins (jointly with the East Asian Research Center), 1965. Frederick A. Praeger, Inc.


Occasional Papers, Published by the Center for International Affairs

1. *A Plan for Planning: The Need for a Better Method of Assisting Underdeveloped Countries on Their Economic Policies,* by Gustav F. Papanek, 1961.

2. *The Flow of Resources from Rich to Poor,* by Alan D. Neale, 1961.

3. *Limited War: An Essay on the Development of the Theory and an Annotated Bibliography,* by Morton H. Halperin, 1962.

4. *Reflections on the Failure of the First West Indian Federation,* by Hugh W. Springer, 1962.

5. *On the Interaction of Opposing Forces under Possible Arms Agreements,* by Glenn A. Kent, 1963.

6. *Europe's Northern Cap and the Soviet Union,* by Nils Örvik, 1963.

7. *Civil Administration in the Punjab: An Analysis of a State Government in India,* by E. N. Mangat Rai, 1963.

8. *On the Appropriate Size of a Development Program,* by Edward S. Mason, 1964.

9. *Self-Determination Revisited in the Era of Decolonization,* by Rupert Emerson, 1964.

10. *The Planning and Execution of Economic Development in Southeast Asia,* by Clair Wilcox, 1965.

Publications Written under the Auspices of the

East Asian Research Center

Harvard University

(Published by Harvard University Press)

1. *China's Early Industrialization: Sheng Hsuan-huai (1844-1916) and Mandarin Enterprise,* by Albert Feuerwerker, 1959.

2. *Intellectual Trends in the Ch'ing Period,* by Liang Ch'i-ch'ao, translated by Immanuel C. Y. Hsü, 1959.

3. *Reform in Sung China: Wang An-shih (1021-1086) and His New Policies,* by James T. C. Liu, 1959.

4. *Studies on the Population of China, 1368-1953,* by Ping-ti Ho, 1959.

5. *China's Entrance into the Family of Nations: The Diplomatic Phase, 1858-1880,* by Immanuel C. Y. Hsü, 1960.

6. *The May Fourth Movement: Intellectual Revolution in Modern China,* by Chow Tse-tsung, 1960.

7. *Ch'ing Administrative Terms: A Translation of "The Terminology of the Six Boards with Explanatory Notes,"* translated and edited by E-tu Zen Sun, 1961.

8. *Anglo-American Steamship Rivalry in China, 1862-1876,* by Kwang-Ching Liu, 1962.

9. *Local Government in China under the Ch'ing,* by T'ung-tsu Ch'ü, 1962.

10. *Communist China 1955-1959: Policy Documents with Analysis,* with a Foreword by Robert R. Bowie and John K. Fairbank (jointly with the Center for International Affairs), 1962.

11. *China and Christianity: The Missionary Movement and the Growth of Chinese Antiforeignism, 1860-1870,* by Paul A. Cohen, 1963.

12. *China and the Helping Hand, 1938-1945,* by Arthur N. Young, 1963.

13. *Research Guide to the May Fourth Movement: Intellectual Revolution in Modern China, 1915-1924,* by Chow Tse-tsung, 1963.

14. *The United States and the Far Eastern Crisis of 1933-1938 (from the Manchurian Incident through the Initial Stage of the Undeclared Sino-Japanese War)* , by Dorothy Borg, 1964.

15. *China and the West, 1858-1861: The Origins of the Tsungli Yamen,* by Masataka Banno, 1964.

16. *In Search of Wealth and Power: Yen Fu and the West,* by Benjamin Schwartz, 1964.

17. *The Origins of Entrepreneurship in Meiji Japan,* by Johannes Hirschmeier (S.V.D.), 1964.

18. *Commissioner Lin and the Opium War,* by Chang Hsin-pao, 1964.

19 *Money and Monetary Policy in China, 1845-1895,* by Frank H. H. King, 1965.

DATE DUE